Lexical Phrases and Language Teaching

Lexical Phrases and Language Teaching

James R. Nattinger
Jeanette S. DeCarrico

Oxford University Press 1992

Oxford University Press
Walton Street, Oxford OX2 6DP

Oxford New York Toronto
Delhi Bombay Calcutta Madras Karachi
Petaling Jaya Singapore Hong Kong Tokyo
Nairobi Dar es Salaam Cape Town
Melbourne Auckland

and associated companies in
Berlin Ibadan

Oxford and *Oxford English* are trade marks of Oxford University Press

ISBN 0 19 437 164 6

Typeset in 11 on 12 pt Sabon by Wyvern Typesetting Ltd, Bristol
Printed in Hong Kong

To our parents

Contents

Acknowledgements   xii

Preface   xiii

PART ONE
Lexical phrases in language description

1   The nature and description of lexical phrases   1

1.1 Introduction   1

1.2 Competence, performance, and pragmatics   2
      1.2.1 Pragmatics as competence versus pragmatics as
             performance   3
      1.2.2 The nature of competence   6
      1.2.3 Pragmatic competence   6
      1.2.4 Pragmatic competence and form/function
             composites   11
      1.2.5 Conventions of lexical phrase selection   17
      1.2.6 Processing effort   19

1.3 Computer analysis of text   19
      1.3.1 Collocations in computer analysis   20
      1.3.2 Collocations in natural language processing   22

1.4 Prefabricated language and language acquisition   24
      1.4.1 Invariable routines and variable patterns   24
      1.4.2 The role of prefabricated language   25

2   Formal aspects of lexical phrases   31

2.1 Introduction   31

2.2 Prefabricated language and psychological processing   31
      2.2.1 Idioms and clichés   32
      2.2.2 Non-canonical phrases   33

2.2.3 Variability as points on a continuum   34
2.2.4 From less variable to more variable   35

2.3 Lexical phrases as variable units   36
    2.3.1 Lexical phrases, collocations, and syntax   36
    2.3.2 Categories of lexical phrase   37

2.4 Issues of form and flexibility   47
    2.4.1 Indirect speech acts as lexical phrase sentence
          builders   47
    2.4.2 Non-conventional indirect speech acts   48
    2.4.3 Conventional indirect speech acts   49
    2.4.4 Conventionalized sets and basic lexical phrase
          frames   49
    2.4.5 Distinctions in variability and lexical phrase types 54

3   Functional aspects of lexical phrases   59

3.1 Introduction   59

3.2 Functions of lexical phrases   59
    3.2.1 Social interactions   60
    3.2.2 Necessary topics   63
    3.2.3 Discourse devices   64
    3.2.4 Forms of lexical phrases in functional groups   65
    3.2.5 Lexical phrases in other languages   66

3.3 Lexical phrases in conversational discourse   71
    3.3.1 Patterns in conversation   71
    3.3.2 Interconnected functions   72

3.4 Lexical phrases in transactional discourse   74
    3.4.1 Interactional versus transactional discourse   75
    3.4.2 The role of discourse devices   75

3.5 Transactional spoken discourse   76
    3.5.1 Characteristics of discourse devices in spoken
          transactional discourse   77
    3.5.2 Spoken versus written discourse devices   78

3.6 Transactional written discourse   81
    3.6.1 Patterns in writing   82
    3.6.2 Characteristics of discourse devices in written
          discourse   82
    3.6.3 Integration   84
    3.6.4 Detachment   85

4   The organizing function of lexical phrases   90

4.1 Introduction   90

4.2 Macro-organizers   90
     4.2.1 The signaling function of macro-organizers in
            transactional discourse   91
     4.2.2 Double markers   93

4.3 Levels of discourse: co-ordination and subordination
     macro-organizers   94
     4.3.1 Levels and patterns: macro-organizers versus
            interactional discourse markers   97
     4.3.2 Category divisions   102
     4.3.3 Processing strategies: top-down and bottom-up   103
     4.3.4 Textbook models   104

4.4 Micro-organizers   104
     4.4.1 Macro/micro distinctions   105
     4.4.2 Macro/micro forms and functions   106
     4.4.3 Phrase length   107
     4.4.4 Dual functions   108

PART TWO
Applications for language teaching

5   Teaching spoken discourse: conversation   113

5.1 Introduction   113

5.2 Advantages of teaching lexical phrases   114

5.3 Teaching conversation with lexical phrases   116
     5.3.1 How learners learn a language   116
     5.3.2 Why learners learn a language   118
     5.3.3 Teaching activities   118

5.4 Indirect speech acts   121
     5.4.1 Universal functions and language-specific forms   124
     5.4.2 Teaching indirect speech acts   127

6   Teaching spoken discourse: listening comprehension   131

6.1 Introduction   131

6.2 Lexical phrases in academic lectures   132
     6.2.1 Macro-organizer functions in academic lectures   132

6.2.2 The recognition problem   133

6.3 Styles of academic lectures   134
    6.3.1 Lecture styles and macro-organizer characteristics   135
    6.3.2 Style switching   140

6.4 The function of macro-organizers in comprehending
    lectures   142
    6.4.1 Range of functions in lecture discourse: a
          comprehension problem   143
    6.4.2 Patterns of frequency in lecture discourse   150

6.5 Teaching lexical phrases for the comprehension of
    lectures   150
    6.5.1 Reading and vocabulary class   151
    6.5.2 Listening comprehension class   152

7   **Teaching written discourse: reading and writing**   157

7.1 Introduction   157

7.2 Theoretical stances   157
    7.2.1 Written discourse as both process and product   157
    7.2.2 Writers and readers as active participants   159

7.3 Teaching written discourse   160
    7.3.1 Knowledge of discourse forms   161
    7.3.2 Sentence-based perspective   161
    7.3.3 Process-centered discourse perspective   163

7.4 The structure of three kinds of written discourse   164
    7.4.1 Structure of a formal essay   164
    7.4.2 Structure of an informal letter   167
    7.4.3 Structure of a business letter   168

7.5 Teaching written discourse with lexical phrases   169

8   **Conclusions and prospects**   174

8.1 Introduction   174

8.2 The need for further empirical research   174

8.3 The theoretical nature of lexical phrases: further inquiry   176
    8.3.1 Criteria for defining language patterns   176
    8.3.2 Criteria for defining categories of lexical phrases   178
    8.3.3 Discourse analysis   180
    8.3.4 Lexicography   181

8.4 Language acquisition   183
8.5 Teaching   185

Appendix   190
Bibliography   205
Index   213

Acknowledgements

We are indebted to the many persons who provided us with information, advice, criticism, and encouragement. We wish to thank Zhou Minglang, Galina Misjura, Sandra Rosengrant, and Ana Wyatt for providing us with data from Chinese, Russian, and Spanish. We are especially grateful to Roni Lebauer for her generous sharing of data from academic lectures, and to Tony Dudley-Evans for material on the structure of academic lectures.

The book has also benefitted from comments on portions of the text by Thomas Dieterich and Susan Foster. We also wish to thank Kimberley Brown, Mel DeCarrico, Megan Esler, Diane Fox, John Longres, Beatrice Oshika, Helen Schley, and Marjorie Terdal for general comments, suggestions, and support.

Our greatest debt, however, is to Henry Widdowson, whose critical comments and sound advice guided our revisions of the manuscript and helped us clarify our vision of the final shape that the book was to take.

Preface

For many years, it was commonplace for teachers to turn to linguistic theory for grammars of what to teach in their language classes. But these grammars are not in themselves adequate as the only source of ideas for practical application in the classroom. Conventional grammars fall into three general, somewhat overlapping, categories and present language as either: (1) definitions of terms and lists of structures; (2) social prescriptions about appropriate language form; or (3) descriptions of the abstract language system, which linguists term 'competence', stated in highly general and parsimonious terms. None of these really provides a satisfactory description of language for the classroom. The first two kinds of grammar have already lost much of their formal appeal, for, ever since the waning of audio-lingualism and prescriptivism, teachers no longer feel it effective to teach language as simply an arrangement of 'meaningless' parts, nor do they feel it serves their purpose to teach only to external measures of correctness. The third sort of grammar, though, remains a powerful influence and continues to help shape classroom activity. Many still feel that the focus of language teaching should indeed be this abstract language 'competence', and they look to theoretical grammars of linguistic competence for ideas about what to teach. However, while grammatical rules cannot be ignored, the goal of language teaching is not just to teach abstract rules of competence, but also to get students to utilize these rules in comprehending and producing language successfully in appropriate contexts; and just teaching the underlying system of a language is no guarantee that students will learn to do that. Therefore, teachers need to focus equal attention on theories of language use, on descriptions of language production as well as those of language competence, for more immediately relevant ideas about how best to present language in a classroom. While it is helpful to understand how language structure can be efficiently described, it is equally helpful to understand how language is actually used. Indeed, in recent years many teachers have begun to look more to theories of language use for guidance in the classroom.

Theories of language use

Finding an appropriate theoretical framework of language use, however, presents its own difficulties. Consider performance grammars, for instance. Most theoretical grammars, with their focus on competence, have little that is useful to tell teachers about language performance. In these theories, performance consists mainly of the residue that has not been amenable to linguistic investigation of competence, and thus becomes a category invoked mainly to be dismissed. One must turn to psycholinguistics to find more positively wrought performance grammars. Even here, though, many grammars do not treat performance autonomously, but explore it only as it correlates with competence. For example, these grammars concern very general, abstract rules of psychological processing, based on underlying phonological and syntactic representations of competence, that operate, as competence does, independently of any context. They also describe universals of psychological processing to parallel the search for universals of competence, and thus fail to describe cross-linguistic differences in performance. Both characteristics lessen the relevance of these grammars for teaching. What teachers need are theories of language use that describe how people actually act upon their linguistic knowledge to achieve meaning in context.

One description of language use that has gained considerable influence is that of communicative competence, originally formulated by Hymes (1972), which focuses on rules of appropriate use rather than rules of grammar. However, as Widdowson (1989) observes, there are pitfalls here as well. For just as approaches that rely too heavily on achievement of rules of grammar often lead to dissociation from any consideration of appropriateness, so approaches that rely too heavily on an ability to use language appropriately can lead to a lack of necessary grammatical knowledge and of the ability to compose or decompose sentences with reference to it. There is, he says, 'evidence that excessive zeal for communicative language teaching can lead to just such a state of affairs' (Widdowson 1989: 131). His conclusion then, is that, 'the structural approach accounts for one aspect of competence by concentrating on analysis but does so at the expense of access, whereas the communicative approach concentrates on access to the relative neglect of analysis' (ibid.: 132). Given this state of affairs, what is needed, it seems, is an approach that provides some sort of middle ground in that it neglects neither.

Recent studies of language acquisition suggest an answer. For some time, teachers have reviewed language acquisition materials for ideas about what they might expect of their students in the class-room. The greater part of this research, following prevailing theory, has been designed to test notions of linguistic competence by establishing the extent to which a student's current performance is a correct or incorrect reflection of native-speaker competence. More recently, however, studies in language acquisition have begun to place more emphasis on how language develops for use in social interaction. In paying more attention to *how* rules are learnt, this research examines the path, rather than the goal, of language acquisi-tion (Bickerton 1981). Following that path can be illuminating for language teachers, for along the way we find common patterns among all types of language acquirers. This new direction in language acquisition research offers help for language teachers that competence models alone cannot, we believe; for it not only des-cribes the ways people actually use language, but it also suggests ways that first, second, *and* foreign language learning can be seen, and taught, as similar processes.

One common pattern in language acquisition is that learners pass through a stage in which they use a large number of unanalyzed chunks of language in certain predictable social contexts. They use, in other words, a great deal of 'prefabricated' language. Many early researchers thought these prefabricated chunks were distinct and somewhat peripheral to the main body of language, but more recent research puts this formulaic speech at the very center of language acquisition and sees it as basic to the creative rule-forming processes which follow. For example, first language learners begin with a few basic, unvarying phrases, which they later, on analogy with similar phrases, learn to analyze as smaller, increasingly variable patterns. They then learn to break apart these smaller patterns into individual words and, in so doing, find their own way to the regular rules of syntax.

In this book, we present a language teaching program that draws from this research. Using a unit called the *lexical phrase*, we discuss lessons that lead students to use prefabricated language in much the same way as first language learners do in order to learn how to produce, comprehend, and analyze the new language, and we show how this unit serves as an effective basis for both second language and foreign language teaching. This approach, we believe, avoids the shortcomings of relying too heavily on either theories of linguistic competence on the one hand, or theories of communicative com-petence on the other. Though the focus is on appropriate language use, the analysis of regular rules of syntax is not neglected.

The book is in two parts. Part One is a descriptive account of the lexical phrase and its role in language; Part Two addresses applications for pedagogy. In Part One, the first chapter develops the notion of 'lexical phrase', and examines its nature and role in an overall description of language, in computer analyzed texts and in language acquisition. Chapter 2 examines the structural differences among the various types of lexical phrases, and Chapter 3 describes their essential function in discourse, both spoken and written. Chapter 4 looks in more detail at functions in discourse, focusing especially on the role of lexical phrases in organizing overall patterns of the informational content in discourse. In Part Two, Chapter 5 looks as how phrases can be utilized as practical instruments for language pedagogy, and shows how these phrases can be used to teach conversation in both ESL and in foreign language classrooms. Chapter 6 deals with application of the lexical phrase approach in teaching comprehension, in particular, the comprehension of academic lectures, since current research shows this to be an especially difficult problem for many language learners. Chapter 7 outlines further applications of a lexical phrase approach, specifically to teaching reading and writing, with a focus on the three kinds of written discourse that most students become familiar with. In these chapters of Part Two, we illustrate how a lexical phrase approach offers efficient solutions to difficult pedagogical problems in the language classroom. Finally, Chapter 8 examines areas that seem important ones for further research, and suggests implications of a lexical phrase approach for researching various problems in applied linguistics.

The research on which this book is based includes a broad corpus of spoken discourse collected by the authors (and colleagues) from recorded academic lectures, student/teacher conferences, committee meetings, and a faculty senate meeting. It also includes data from written discourse collected from a variety of textbooks for ESL, textbooks for academic courses, letters to the editor of various news publications, and personal correspondence.

James R. Nattinger
Jeanette S. DeCarrico
Portland, July 1990

PART ONE

Lexical phrases in language description

1 The nature and description of lexical phrases

1.1 Introduction

The focus of this book is a lexico-grammatical unit, the *lexical phrase* (Nattinger 1980, 1986, 1988; DeCarrico and Nattinger 1988; Nattinger and DeCarrico 1989), which we believe offers a promising new direction for language teaching. As a preliminary definition, we might describe lexical phrases as 'chunks' of language of varying length, phrases like *as it were, on the other hand, as X would have us believe*, and so on. As such, they are multi-word lexical phenomena that exist somewhere between the traditional poles of lexicon and syntax, conventionalized form/function composites that occur more frequently and have more idiomatically determined meaning than language that is put together each time. These phrases include short, relatively fixed phrases such as *a _____ ago*, or longer phrases or clauses such as *if I X, then I Y,   the _____er X, the _____er Y*, each with a fixed, basic frame, with slots for various fillers (*a year ago, a month ago,   the higher X, the higher Y,   the longer you wait, the sleepier you get*). Each is associated with a particular discourse function, such as expressing time, *a month ago*, or relationships among ideas, *the higher X, the higher Y*.

Current research in computational studies of texts and in language acquisition, converges in a way that reveals the lexical phrase as an ideal unit which can be exploited for language teaching. One object of these studies has been the pervasive role that ritualization plays in language behavior. Just as we are creatures of habit in other aspects of our behavior, so apparently are we in the ways we come to use language. In the present chapter, we will show that routinized formulas and other sorts of prefabricated language chunks, which are products of this ritualization, seem to play a large part in both acquiring and performing language. We will examine the nature and role of these ritualized bits of language, first in an overall description of language, and then in computer analyzed texts and in language acquisition.

The theoretical issues to be examined include the question of whether lexical phrases, as form/function composites, should be viewed as belonging to a theory of competence, of performance, of pragmatics, or possibly as some combination of these. In particular, we will attempt to sort out ways in which principles governing lexical phrases interact with other components of grammar and pragmatics. We will then look at how lexical phrases are related to, yet different from, collocations, drawing on insights from studies in computational linguistics. Finally, we will consider findings from language acquisition research as further confirmation of the central role of lexical phrases in language learning.

1.2   Competence, performance, and pragmatics

In the Chomskyan model, linguistic competence is defined by an autonomous syntactic component capable of generating all the grammatical sentences of a language. This syntactic component is neutral as to speaker and hearer, and operates independently of phonological, semantic, and pragmatic considerations to generate grammatical strings of word classes. Linguistic performance in the Chomskyan model, on the other hand, accounts for language in use, subject to all of the limitations which can befall performance, such as interruptions, false starts, memory limitations, throat clearings, and so on; it is, therefore, an incomplete realization of the syntactic competence which underlies it.

Certainly, described in these terms, such ideal competence should indeed be the center of linguistic investigation, rather than a fractured, intractable performance which is only its messy realization. In many ways, however, these terms describe a dichotomy which is unnecessarily severe and exclusive. Between an autonomous syntactic competence and erratically performed speech, there is a large area of linguistic ability which is also orderly and subject to general rule. Indeed, it is this area of ability that has, in recent years, become the focus of study for many applied linguists whose main interest is language in use, either from a psychological, sociological, or pedagogical perspective. Quite understandably, then, one thing that has troubled these researchers, especially those concerned with language pedagogy, is the lack of description of pragmatic knowledge with respect to competence and performance in the Chomskyan model. This unhappy circumstance led many applied linguists and teachers to turn to a description of 'communicative competence', which includes the notion that the concept of linguistic competence must somehow be stretched to include the knowledge speakers have of how to use sentences to achieve meaning in context.

1.2.1   Pragmatics as competence versus pragmatics as performance

One of the earliest leading proponents of this communicative competence approach has been H. G. Widdowson. In Widdowson (1979:5), he states that 'there is a good deal of argument in favour of extending the concept of competence to cover the ability to use language to communicative effect'. Noting that conceptual features such as sociological setting of utterances, attitudes, and beliefs of the speaker and hearer, perceptual and memory limitations, noise level, etc., are all bundled together under performance, he nevertheless believes that,

> It is clear that some of the features listed under performance are also systematic and form a part of the speaker's knowledge of his language, and should therefore be considered as part of his competence ... It is part of the speaker's competence to be able to use sentences to form continuous discourse ... [and] to perform what Searle calls speech acts ... In brief, knowledge of a language does not mean only knowledge of rules which will generate an infinite number of sentences, but a knowledge of the rules which regulate the use of sentences for making appropriate utterances.
> (Widdowson 1979:12)

He refers to these pragmatic rules as 'rules of use', in which he includes rules such as Searle's appropriateness conditions on speech acts. For example, the appropriateness conditions for making a promise are that the speaker intends to carry out the promise, believes he or she is able to carry out the promise, believes the hearer wants it carried out, etc. Included also is Grice's principle of co-operation, by which speaker and hearer each assume the other is co-operating to make the communication successful, based on the maxims that the speaker says neither more nor less than necessary, speaks the truth, is being relevant, is being clear, and so on.

These rules, he says, 'account for the language user's knowledge of speech acts and can be said to constitute his basic communicative source of reference. The kind of inquiry conducted in Austin (1962) and Searle (1969), for example, is directed towards a formulation of rules and use' (ibid.:143).

In effect, then, Widdowson appears to maintain the essential dichotomy between competence and performance. Conceptual features such as memory limitations, noise level of the setting, and the like, remain as part of performance, but he extracts those systematic features of communication regulated by pragmatic rules of use, and in some sense shifts them out of performance, to be included as part of overall competence.

Many other researchers also seem to regard competence and performance as quite distinct matters, but they would disagree that pragmatic rules of use are a part of any type of competence. Instead, they maintain that it is strictly a matter of performance. A particularly clear statement of the view that equates pragmatics with performance is found in Katz (1977). Grammars, he states,

> are theories about the structure of sentence types ... Pragmatic theories, in contrast, do nothing to explicate the structure of linguistic constructions or grammatical properties and relations ... They explicate the reasoning of speakers and hearers in working out the correlation in a context of a sentence token with a proposition ... In this respect, a pragmatic theory is part of performance. (Katz 1977:19)

In this view, pragmatics is concerned solely with performance principles of language use, and not at all with the description of linguistic competence. Other proponents of this position include Kempson (1975, 1977); Wilson (1975); and Smith and Wilson (1979).

More recent studies, however, tend to be more in agreement with Widdowson's view of pragmatics as part of competence. Levinson (1983), for example, presents various arguments against equating pragmatics with performance factors. Rather, pragmatics is seen as a separate component within the overall theory, and further, as a component that interacts with both semantics and syntax. Levinson concedes that insofar as pragmatics is concerned with context, it can be claimed that by definition pragmatics is not part of competence. One problem, however, is that aspects of linguistic structure sometimes directly encode features of the context. For example, he notes, with pairs of lexical items such as *rabbit/bunny* and *dog/doggie*, the kind of appropriate speaker or hearer (a child) is encoded by the terms *bunny, doggie*. Further, if it is assumed that adequate grammatical descriptions must include specifications of the meaning of every word in a language,

> then we find words whose meaning-specifications can only be given by reference to contexts of usage. For example, the meanings

of words like 'well', 'oh', and 'anyway' . . . cannot be explicated simply by statements of context-independent content; rather one has to refer to pragmatic concepts like relevance, implicature, or discourse structure. So either grammars must make reference to pragmatic information, or they cannot include full lexical descriptions of a language.
(Levinson 1983:33)

Levinson concludes his discussion with the argument that pragmatics must be seen as a component in the overall theory, presumably as a part of competence, but one which interacts with the lexicon, semantics, and syntax. With respect to the lexicon, in addition to the examples cited above, he illustrates the existence of pragmatic dimensions of meaning in most deictic words, and in pairs such as *vous* versus *tu* in French, in which the former pragmatically encodes the socially superior or distant position of the hearer to the speaker. The reason, he claims, is that these aspects of deixis make no difference to the truth conditions of the sentences in which they appear, and thus lie outside of the scope of truth conditional semantics.

On semantics, Levinson cites Gazdar (1979), who provides evidence that truth conditions must be assigned to utterances, not sentences, that is, that contextual specifications are a necessary input to a semantic component. Therefore, pragmatics is prior to semantics (for detailed discussion, see Gazdar 1979:164–8). Levinson concludes that 'if pragmatics is, on occasion, logically prior to semantics, a general linguistic theory simply must incorporate pragmatics as a component or level in the overall integrated theory' (Levinson 1983:35).

With respect to syntax, he gives various data showing that in order to explain the distribution of certain expressions, we need to refer to pragmatic meaning. The distribution of *please* in pre-verbal position, for instance, is limited not by the sentence type, but by the pragmatic class of expressions having the illocutionary force of a request. Thus, for requests we have both statements and questions of the form *please shut the door, I want you to please shut the door*, and *can you please shut the door?*. However, these same sentence types are anomalous if they do not have the force of a request, as in *?the sun please rises in the west, ?can the sun please rise in the west?*.

In sum, linguists such as Levinson argue against defining rules or principles of pragmatics in communication as part of performance. While apparently seen as part of a speaker's competence, pragmatics is also seen as a component in its own right, and one that interacts in essential ways with other components of the grammar. On the other hand, although Levinson's arguments imply that we need a more comprehensive theory that goes beyond truth-conditional semantics, exactly how this theory is to incorporate various aspects of pragmatics has yet to be worked out.

1.2.2   The nature of competence

One possible objection to including pragmatic principles as 'a part of competence' is that while pragmatics together with the syntax, semantics, phonology, and the lexicon are in some sense all part of a speaker's overall knowledge of language, they are not the same *kind* of competence. For one thing, the 'rules' of use are less rigid and less amenable to formalization than are the rules of say, syntax or semantics. As one example, Grice's maxims are not 'rules' at all in this sense, but are simply guiding principles of co-operation in conversation. And, whereas rules of syntax cannot be disregarded without resulting in ungrammaticality, the maxims of conversation are often deliberately disregarded, or 'flouted', resulting in implicatures.[1]

Further, it is well known that conversational implicatures rely on context, whereas rules of sentence grammar do not (or at least not beyond certain choices of rules as appropriate in given contexts, as will be discussed below). So, for example, if speaker A asks *does Mary walk to school?*, and if speaker B replies, *she lives in Junction City*, the implicature that Mary lives too far away from school to walk will only go through if both speaker and hearer know that the school is in a city, or place, which is not within walking distance of Junction City. Another well known difference found in pragmatic competence is that conversational implicatures can be cancelled, but semantic entailments cannot. In a sentence such as *John has two children*, canceling the entailment that *John is a father* results in the contradictory *John has two children, but in fact he is not a father*. However, in a sentence such as *some of my friends are here*, canceling the implicature *not all* does not result in a contradiction at all, but instead seems more like an afterthought: *some of my friends are here — in fact they all are*.

1.2.3   Pragmatic competence

In order to avoid the confusion that arises in equating pragmatic principles of use to grammatical competence, we propose a distinction that neither transgresses the notion of competence in the strict sense of Chomsky's theory, nor banishes pragmatics strictly to performance factors. Rather, it simply builds on the theoretical notion of competence to account for this language ability. In order to stress that, though it is a related notion, this competence is not the same thing as linguistic competence in the strict sense, we might think of it as 'pragmalinguistic competence' (from Leech 1983), indicating that although it is not unrelated to the notion of grammatical competence, it is different in kind. It is in this sense that we use the term 'pragmatic competence' to refer to this ability.

In short, we believe that it is important to maintain a clear distinction between linguistic competence and performance on the one hand, and pragmatic competence on the other. Certainly Chomsky's insistence on the competence/performance distinction is valid, as his emphasis on linguistic competence has contributed greatly to our knowledge in the last three decades. And while we would agree with Widdowson (1979) that this narrowing of focus 'has excluded many features of language which must somehow be accounted for in a total description' (1979: 11), we hope to demonstrate that distinguishing between linguistic competence and pragmalinguistic competence helps to clarify the ways in which pragmatics interacts with other components of the grammar. In particular, we will argue that the areas of language use related to lexical phrases, as form/function composites, provide certain insights into how these components interact. Our claim will be that as forms in the lexicon, they are, of course, a part of grammatical competence, but that the relationship these forms have to particular functions in context is a matter of pragmatic competence.

A particularly illuminating discussion of pragmatic competence and grammatical competence is found in Widdowson's recent work. In Widdowson (1989) he argues against Hymes' original formulation of competence as some indistinct combination of both knowledge (of rules) and ability (for use). Instead, he maintains that the two must be distinguished as separate components of competence. That is, he says that

> competence has two components: knowledge and ability, and that these in principle relate to all four of Hymes' parameters (possibility, feasibility, appropriateness, performance) which in turn can be reformulated as grammatical competence (the parameter of possibility) on the one hand, and pragmatic competence (all the other parameters) on the other.
> (Widdowson 1989: 132)

Thus, his distinction is essentially compatible with the one we propose here, for his description includes the implicit assumption that grammatical competence (knowledge) and pragmatic competence (ability) are indeed different in kind.[2]

In what follows, we differ from Widdowson mainly in positing pragmatic competence not as a component parallel to (and in some sense on a par with) grammatical competence, but rather as a component which is positioned on a continuum somewhere between strict grammatical competence on the one hand, and performance factors such as processing, memory limitations, false starts, etc. on the other. It is a somewhat narrower description in that it does not assume that all parts of pragmatic competence are equally governed by the parameters of feasibility, appropriateness, or performance. Rather, it allows for finer distinctions to be made between, say, the principles governing certain aspects of the use of lexical phrases, as opposed to the more general principles of communicative use such as Searle's appropriateness conditions or Grice's Co-operative Principle. Thus, the principles governing the pragmatic aspects of lexical phrases would be positioned closer to principles of grammar than would appropriateness principles.

The reason for assuming a continuum model, then, is that because lexical phrases are lexico-grammatical units, that part of pragmatic competence governing their use appears to have closer links to grammatical competence than does the part governing appropriateness conditions or co-operative principles. For example, lexical phrases are subject to differing degrees of syntactic modification. Some, such as *for the most part*, are fixed phrases that allow no modification; others, such as *it's only in X that Y*, readily allow certain limited modification. The Y slot admits only full sentences, but the X slot can be filled with either an ordinary noun phrase or a gerund phrase, as in *it's only in <u>Venice</u> that <u>you find gondolas</u>, it's only in <u>running uphill</u> that <u>I have trouble breathing</u>.*

Further, while lexical phrases are prefabricated lexical chunks that are readily accessible as completely or partially assembled units, they are also for the most part analyzable by regular rules of grammar. So, for instance, the phrase *for the most part*, is readily analyzable as a prepositional phrase. With respect to this analyzability, however, Widdowson observes that it is just these 'linguistic environments of a lexical kind which have conditioning effects on the application of syntactic rules, and that knowing this is an essential part of knowing a language', and thus, 'an ignorance of the limits of analysability, of the variable application of grammatical rules, constitutes incompetence' (Widdowson 1989: 133–4). So, for instance, an ordinary time clause generated from scratch, can occur either before or after the matrix clause. Thus, both *close the door before you leave* and *before you leave, close the door* are grammatical and linguistically well formed. In contrast, though, this variant as applied to a lexical unit such as *look before you leap* yields what Widdowson calls 'the linguistically ill-formed' though 'syntactically grammatical' sentence, *before you leap, look* (ibid.: 133). This crucial point, it seems to us, not only supports our argument that principles governing the use of lexical phrases are closer in kind to the rules of grammar than are principles of appropriateness or co-operative principles, it also illustrates how this particular part of pragmatic competence can be seen as interacting with grammatical competence.

In order to make these points clearer, it may be useful to look at the approach to competence and pragmatics in Leech (1983). Leech defines pragmatics as the study of how utterances have meanings in situations, but he takes a 'complementarist' view of pragmatics, meaning that he views the principles of language use as a communicative system that is distinct from, but complementary to, the language itself seen as a formal system. Grammar, he maintains, must be separated from pragmatics. His claim is that 'grammar (the abstract formal system of language) and pragmatics (the principles of language use) are complementary domains within linguistics', and that 'we cannot understand the nature of language without studying both these domains, and the interaction between them' (Leech 1983: 4). At the same time, it is an approach which aims to relate the three levels of description—syntax, semantics, and pragmatics—to each other.

Among his major postulates for this formal–functional paradigm, is that 'the rules of grammar are fundamentally conventional; the principles of general pragmatics are fundamentally non-conventional, that is, motivated in terms of conversational goals' (ibid.: 5). For Leech, 'communicative grammar' refers to a linguistic description which relates grammatical forms to their various pragmatic utilizations.

From our point of view, one of the most important distinctions made by Leech is that of 'general pragmatics' and 'socio-pragmatics' versus 'pragmalinguistics', a term we find helpful in attempting to clarify our particular focus. General pragmatics is defined as the study of general conditions of the communicative use of language, whereas socio-pragmatics is the study of more 'local', culture-specific conditions on language use. More interesting for our purposes, pragmalinguistics, on the other hand, 'can be applied to the more *linguistic end of pragmatics—where we consider the particular resources which a given language provides for conveying particular illocutions'* (ibid.: 11, our italics).

Leech's illustration (Figure 1.2, ibid.: 11) is given below as Figure 1.

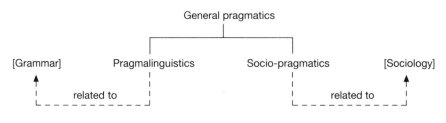

Figure 1

If Leech's diagram is thought of as the type of continuum we describe above, with the 'looser' performance factors added at the far right, the pragmatic competence governing lexical phrases would be positioned with pragmalinguistics, closer to grammar, and principles of appropriateness and co-operation would be positioned with general pragmatics or socio-pragmatics, closer to performance, depending on whether they are general conditions or culture-specific conditions on language use.

Other than the tantalizing suggestion that pragmalinguistics is somehow more intricately related to the 'more linguistic end' of pragmatics, Leech has little more to say about this notion. In this book he focuses on general pragmatics, though he does acknowledge the need for 'detailed pragmalinguistic studies which are language-specific' (ibid.).

Note that in Leech's terms, pragmalinguistics is still to be separate from the grammar itself, even though it is more closely related to the grammar than general pragmatics or socio-pragmatics. We depart from his model in that we extend the notion of pragmalinguistics to include pragmalinguistic competence, in order to incorporate the idea, as discussed above, that this part of pragmatics, though different in kind from grammatical competence, nevertheless bears an important similarity to it, in ways that we hope will become more and more evident.

Referring back to Leech's illustration in Figure 1, it may be useful to think of pragmalinguistic competence as the 'interface' between the grammar and the more general principles of communicative use of language. Our focus hereafter will be on the pragmalinguistic competence governing the selection and use of lexical phrases, but we will continue to use the more generally accepted and less cumbersome expression 'pragmatic competence' to refer to this type of competence.

1.2.4 Pragmatic competence and form/function composites

Earlier we referred to lexical phrases as 'form/function composites'. In this section we will look in some detail at this relationship between form and function. We will also look briefly at the question of how it is that only certain lexico-grammatical strings, and not others, come to be selected as conventionalized lexical phrases.

Not only are grammatical strings generated by the syntactic component and performed with all of the limitations mentioned earlier, but only certain of these strings are also selected to play particular functions in particular social contexts — in other words, Leech's 'particular resources which a given language provides for conveying particular illocutions.'

This selection is accomplished by a second competence, then, a particular type of pragmatic competence, which takes specific strings generated by the syntactic component and assigns them functional meanings, so that these strings not only have syntactic shapes, but are capable as well of performing pragmatic acts, as for example the basic forms selected for speech acts such as promising, complimenting, asserting, and so on. Pragmatic competence thus selects the form/function composites required for particular circumstances. These composites, unlike the products of syntactic competence, are not neutral as to speaker or hearer, but are differently selected according to whether the language user is producing a message or comprehending one.

Evidence from first language acquisition (Peters 1983) indicates that lexical phrases are learnt first as unanalyzed lexical chunks. If our arguments are correct, these chunks would also be learnt together with their associated functions in context. This composite form/function nature of lexical phrases at this stage may be illustrated as in Figure 2.

The arrows are intended to represent knowledge of the forms themselves as a matter of grammatical competence, whereas knowledge of the associated function in context is a matter of pragmatic

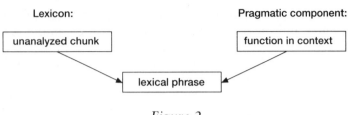

Figure 2

competence. For example, children frequently use a phrase such as *I-want-to-go* as though it were a single, unsegmented unit, [aʸwanəgəʊ]. At the same time, it is used in predictable social situations in which the function of 'request' is clearly associated.

Gradually, in the process of acquiring other chunks with similar syntactic patterning (*I-want-to-get-up, I-want-my-ball, I-want-a-cookie*), the child detaches the pattern from its connection in context, and analyzes and generalizes it into regular syntactic rules. This process may be represented as in Figure 3.

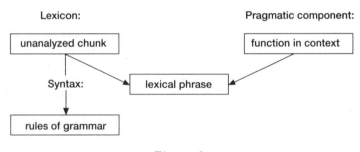

Figure 3

At the same time, however, it is important to recognize that as syntactic rules emerge and become part of grammatical competence, the conventionalized association between the lexical phrase as a chunk and its function in context is retained. This language chunk — analyzed or not — continues to be available for ready access as either a partially or holistically pre-assembled pattern. As such, knowledge of the fixed lexical phrase frames as one kind of dictionary entry is also a part of linguistic competence. As an example of how this might work, consider the lexical phrase frame *if I were* _____ (If I were you/the king/the president, etc.) versus an expression such as *if I were the one that she really wanted to talk to.* Whereas the first is a lexical phrase, the second is generated by regular rules of syntax. That is, the same lexical phrase can also be analyzed by the grammatical rules, and the two similar appearing expressions would be handled differently in grammatical and pragmatic competence. *If I were you* exists as a phrasal constraint assigned a function (expressing advice) by pragmatic competence, while the similar phrase *if I were you* can be produced by grammatical competence (*if*+S+V+O), as evidenced by its generative possibilities, such as *if I were the one she really wanted to talk to* .... A further difference, of course, is that the latter expression does not have a particular associated function.

Just what proportion of the dictionary entries is of this type of pre-assembled unit is difficult to determine, but if Pawley and Syder (1983) are correct, such prefabricated patterns 'form a high proportion of the fluent stretches of speech heard in everyday conversation ... Coming ready-made, [they] need little encoding work', and the speaker can 'do the work of constructing a larger piece of discourse by expanding on, or combining ready-made constructions' (1983:208). Thus, although grammatical competence encompasses the knowledge of the lexical forms and their internal syntax, pragmatic competence accounts for the speaker's ability to continue to access these forms as pre-assembled chunks, ready for a given functional use in an appropriate context.

Such a linguistic model permits sentences to be generated word by word by syntactic competence, but some expressions become conventionalized as more or less unanalyzed composites of form and function by pragmatic competence. One's knowledge of language and one's ability to use it, in other words, include knowledge of how to create sentences 'from scratch' and knowledge of prefabricated patterns (grammatical competence), and knowing how to select and retrieve ready-made form/function composites (pragmalinguistic competence) for appropriate situations or contexts (socio-pragmatic competence).

So far, in discussing pragmatic competence and lexical phrases, we have attempted to clarify the relationship involved between the pragmatic component and the lexicon, but have barely hinted at the relationship between the pragmatics and the syntax. On this point, we briefly mentioned Widdowson's crucial argument that it is just these 'linguistic environments of a lexical kind which have conditioning effects on the applications of syntactic rules, and that knowing this is an essential part of knowing a language' (1989:133–4); and we cited this argument as support for our claim that principles governing the use of lexical phrases (pragmalinguistic competence) are closer in kind to rules of grammar than are principles of appropriateness (socio-pragmatics). Widdowson further argues that variants such as *before you leap, look* are syntactically grammatical yet linguistically ill-formed.

These he compares with syntactically ungrammatical sentences such as *he explained me the problem*. Both, he claims, are the result of the over-application of syntactic rules. That is, though grammatical, expressions like *before you leap, look* are nevertheless 'illegitimate, rule violations, not possible, and the native speaker knows this full well' (ibid.: 133).

We would add that not only are such variants linguistically ill-formed, but they are functionally ill-formed as well. As a lexical phrase composite, *look before you leap* is conventionally associated with the functions of advising or warning. One reason the ill-formed variant sounds odd, it seems, is that the functional association is lost. True, as a grammatical, imperative form it can still be said to have the ordinary imperative meaning of a command. But we recognize it as an odd form that would not normally occur in actual use none the less, and we recognize that its conventionalized function is lost. Apparently, lexical phrase form/function composites place limits on permissible expansions or substitutions, and violations of these limits result in ill-formed structures and in disassociation of the conventionalized form/function relation.

Similar principles apply to lexical phrase frames that allow limited variability, such as *this is a piece of cake*, which is syntactically an ordinary declarative statement, but which as a lexical phrase is a conventionalized sequence with the associated pragmatic function of expressing evaluation of the topic at hand (namely, that X can be accomplished with ease). Allowable syntactic inflections and expansions include *this is/it's going to be/will be a piece of cake*. Some impermissible adaptations (in Widdowson's sense) would be *this is two pieces of cake*, or *this had been a piece of cake*. These impermissible variants are again (a) grammatical, (b) linguistically odd, and (c) dissociated from the pragmatic function of expressing evaluation.

This point is an important one for language teaching, for as Pawley and Syder note,

> It is a characteristic error of the language learner to assume that an element in the expression may be varied according to a phrase structure or transformational rule of some generality, when in fact the variation (if any) allowed in nativelike usage is much more

restricted. The result, very often, is an utterance that is grammatical but unidiomatic, e.g. 'You are pulling my legs' (in the sense of deceiving me), 'John has a thigh-ache', and 'I intend to teach that rascal some good lessons he will never forget'.
(Pawley and Syder 1983:215)

It should also be pointed out that in some cases, a seemingly identical expression in isolation may not always be ill-formed. In such a case, however, the function will still be lost. For example, the completely set, invariant part of the frame discussed above is *this/it BE a piece of cake*. No variations whatever are allowed in the predicate nominal part of the frame as a form/function composite, for example, *this is a piece of baklava*. While this expression may indeed be used as a simple description of a tasty Turkish dessert, it cannot be used for the function of expressing evaluation of a topic in discourse such that *X can be accomplished with ease*. With this type of variation, the function is again entirely lost.

The next obvious question is how this type of violation is to be characterized. One possibility is to assume, with Pawley and Syder (1983), that each lexical entry for a lexical phrase (or in their terms, 'lexicalized sentence stem') will be a 'mini-grammar', which would include a statement of the ways in which 'the lexicalized sequence may be "inflected" and "expanded" and transformed, without changing its status as a nativelike and lexicalized unit' (1983:216–7).

One problem with this approach, though, is that within our lexical phrase perspective, the functional aspect of lexical phrases would not seem to be accommodated. A further problem is that since these constraints on syntactic rules would also presumably be strictly syntactic constraints, one would expect that violating them would result in expressions that are not just linguistically odd, but syntactically ungrammatical as well. We therefore believe that Widdowson's distinction between expressions that are syntactically grammatical and those that are linguistically ill-formed is an important one, and one that descriptions of grammatical and pragmatic competence must attempt to account for.

A more attractive alternative, we suggest, is to assume that the limits of variability on lexical phrases is a part of pragmatic competence. As we have attempted to define pragmatic competence, in the pragmalinguistic sense, it involves the relationship between particular, conventionalized forms and their associated functions in context. If pragmatic competence includes restrictions on the choice of particular syntactic rules that are allowed to apply to these form/function units in context, this might also explain not only why impermissible choices result in linguistically odd expressions, but also why the associated pragmatic function is lost. This can be illustrated by reformulating Figure 3, as in Figure 4, as a more complete representation of the interrelationship of the pragmatic component and the lexicon and syntax. The solid lines indicate processes involved in grammatical competence, and the broken lines those involved in pragmatic competence.

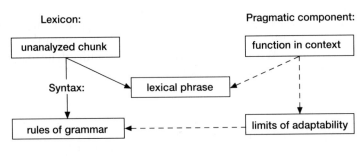

Figure 4

Although limits on lexical substitution have not been considered in the design of Figure 4, these too would, of course, fall under 'limits of adaptability' as part of pragmatic competence in this sense.

It should be mentioned in passing that other types of pragmatic principles also restrict the choice of syntactic rules in context. There are also the types that we have suggested are a part of socio-pragmatic competence. They would include ones that restrict the choice of syntactic rules to those appropriate to a particular context. The difference is that socio-pragmatic restrictions: (a) do not involve specific discourse functions nor interaction of form and function in the sense that pragmalinguistic ones do; (b) they do not involve degrees of idiomatic meaning (for example, the lexical phrase *this is a piece of cake = X can be accomplished with ease*), and (c) they are much more closely involved with aspects of appropriateness to context.

For example, Stalker (1989) discusses pragmatic choices of formal or informal linguistic features 'in order to adjust the social distance between the producer and the receiver' (1989: 182). Appropriateness may also be pragmatic choices made to accommodate previous linguistic context. Green (1989) devotes an entire chapter to the discussion of the choice of syntactic rules based on appropriate context, noting, for example, that rules such as Preposing result in unnatural constructions unless the preposed part is related to previous discourse. Thus, a sentence such as *a gerbil, Mary named after John* seems odd if used as first mention of *a gerbil*, but is entirely natural if used as second mention, as in *Mary went to the pet store and bought several gerbils. One of the gerbils she named after John.* In sum, socio-pragmatic competence would not involve interaction with the grammar at all, except insofar as it restricts the choice of grammatical rules to those which are appropriate to a given context.

1.2.5   Conventions of lexical phrase selection

A remaining question is how pragmatic competence interacts with the syntax to select particular forms as lexical phrases. First, it should be acknowledged that the syntactic forms chosen for particular pragmatic acts are subject to cultural variation. For example, as we will discuss in some detail in Chapter 4, the forms for expressing politeness in one language can be quite different from those used to express the same function in another. Based on this observation, it may be that the selection of a given form in a form/function unit may simply be arbitrary in a given culture. This is essentially the claim made by Pawley and Syder (1983) with respect to lexicalized sequences. For the most part, they consider conventionalized expressions that could in our terms be classified as lexical phrases, but in their discussion they consider discourse functions only in passing. When they do refer to these associated functions, however, they also seem to qualify somewhat the claim for arbitrary selection. Following the claim that lexicalized sequences are an arbitrary choice, they note that 'they may, however, have conversational uses (implicatures, speech act functions, etc.,) in addition to their literal sense, and these additional uses may also be conventionalized and *to some extent* arbitrary' (1983:211, our italics).

A second possibility, then, is that the choice of form may be at least to some degree predictable. In other words, it may be that there are more general principles that predict which of all the forms generated by the syntactic component will be selected, that is, become conventionalized as the form/function composites for pragmatic acts.

One way this might be accomplished is that these principles could be based on (1) syntagmatic simplicity, and (2) paradigmatic flexibility. This is to say that composites which are relatively simple in syntactic pattern yet flexible in the amount of lexical variation they permit may be the ones favored for common pragmatic acts. Take, for example, the question forms that have become conventionalized as indirect speech acts for requests. The basic syntagmatic shape is simply 'Modal + *you* + VP', yet is paradigmatically quite flexible in that the 'slots' for modal and verb can be filled with several modals and a large variety of verb phrases, such as *could you pass the salt?*, *could you hand me that pencil?*, *would you lend me a dollar?*, and so on. A diagrammatic representation is given in Figure 5.

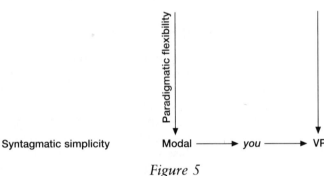

Figure 5

Further, in addition to these set slots, there are also optional slots for adverbial expressions such as *kindly, please*, as in *would you (kindly/ please) lend me a dollar?*. In Chapter 2 we discuss indirect speech acts in more detail, and we illustrate that form/function composites like these allow considerably more flexibility than these simple examples show.

Composites such as 'Modal + *you* + VP' can be compared with the types of expressions which have not been selected as the conventionalized ones for requests. As Searle (1975) notes, a request can be made by saying *can you hand me that book on the top shelf?*, 'but not, or not very easily, by saying "Is it the case that you at present have the ability to hand me that book on the top shelf?" ' (1975: 75). A possible reason a form such as this is not selected is that it is not only syntagmatically more complex, but it resists paradigmatic substitution.

In short, patterns like those illustrated in Figure 5 are easy to acquire and efficient to use, for they permit wide variation of lexical content in relatively simple syntactic frames. Regardless of whether or not this is a characteristic that actually holds for lexical phrases in all cases, the schema presented in Figure 5 nevertheless has profound implications for language teaching, as we will show later.

1.2.6 Processing effort

Further confirmation for our analysis may be related to the notion of 'processing effort'. Wilson and Sperber (1986), referring to Grice's maxim of brevity, state that there is no maxim of brevity. Instead, the intuitions Grice wanted to explain 'are intuitions about processing effort, and in particular, about the fact that a speaker aiming at optimal relevance should spare her hearer any unnecessary processing effort' (Wilson and Sperber 1986: 77). They refer here to word frequency, noting that word frequency affects processing effort in that, in general, the rarer the word, the greater the processing effort. Therefore, in Sperber and Wilson (1988), they conclude that 'processing effort is a negative factor: other things being equal, the greater the processing effort, the lower the relevance' (Sperber and Wilson 1988: 124).

While Wilson and Sperber focus on word frequency, this same explanation seems also to apply to the form/function composites we are considering. Since the basic frames of these composites have become conventionalized, and thus specialized for particular functions, such as requests and so on, they occur in discourse frequently indeed, and since they are very familiar, relatively high-frequency forms, we would expect that the speaker here, too, 'spares the hearer any unnecessary processing effort'.

Of course, while the great majority of lexical phrases have slots that allow variability, some do not. For example, a phrase such as *by the way*, which functions to shift the topic in a conversation, cannot be varied as *beside the way, off the way, by the road*, and so on. The explanation seems to be that the set of invariant lexical phrases are nevertheless especially high in frequency (and perhaps syntagmatically simple as well), and are thus particularly efficient in reducing processing effort. Notice, for instance, that ordinary idioms, *kick the bucket, hell for leather*, etc., do not by any means occur with the same high frequency as *by the way, as I was saying*, and so on. And since only the latter have associated functions (shifting the topic, returning to a previous topic), only they, and not idioms, qualify as lexical phrase form/function composites.[3] It is likely that the factors of very high frequency and reduced processing load are the reasons that the criterion of paradigmatic flexibility has been suspended as these forms have become completely fixed phrases.

1.3 Computer analysis of text

In the past few years, extensive computer analysis of language has been uncovering recurring patterns of lexical co-occurrence. Ever since Firth stated that 'You shall know a word by the company it keeps' (Firth 1957), it has been a practice in linguistics to classify words not only on the basis of their meanings, but on the basis of their co-occurrence with other words, and in this way to search for increasingly delicate word classes. With the help of computers, this search is now taking place over vast quantities of actual language data (Hockey 1980; Sinclair 1987a; Garside *et al.* 1987). For our purposes, this research lends considerable support to the significance and pervasiveness of lexical phrases in language use.

1.3.1   Collocations in computer analysis

A number of recent projects have been collecting large corpora (10–1,000 million words) in order to describe better how language is used in practice (Garside *et al.* 1987), and it is likely there will be more research projects collecting larger corpora in the future. One interesting aspect of these corpora is that they consist of authentic material, full of unexpected and diverse constructions which are often treated as too peripheral or ill-formed to be of much interest for theoretical grammars, and for this reason often require unconventional categories of description. Computers scan all these data, whether central or peripheral, for *collocations*.

Whereas *syntax* deals with general classes of words and their combinations, *collocations* describe specific lexical items and the frequency with which these items occur with other lexical items. Collocations are defined along a syntagmatic, or horizontal, dimension, and a paradigmatic, or vertical, dimension. That is, a collocational unit consists of a 'node' that co-occurs with a 'span' of words on either side. The span consists of particular word classes filled by specific lexical items. This is represented diagrammatically in Figure 6.

If it is the case that the node word occurs with a span of particular words at a frequency greater than chance would predict, then the result is a collocation. The more certain the words in the span are to co-occur with the node, the more fixed and idiomatic the collocation. With completely fixed collocations such as many idioms and clichés, mutual expectancy has become fixed, syntagmatically and paradigmatically ossified, which results in loss of meaning because of elimination of an element of choice. As collocations become less fixed, that is, as more variation becomes possible along both axes, predictability lessens and meaning increases.

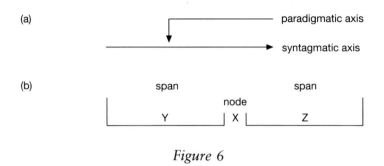

Figure 6

The analysis proceeds by listing all the examples of the node word with the respective spans. In pen and paper analysis, the usual next step has been to delete words in the spans which occur only once, to delete function words, and repeated but rare words that appear only because of the subject of the text. After these procedures, one is then left with possible collocations — strings of words that seem to have a certain mutual expectancy, or a greater-than-chance likelihood that they will co-occur in any text. By deleting articles and other function words, the resulting collocations consist of combinations of the four major syntactic classes, and are usually colorful combinations of one sort or another (*beautiful princess, rancid butter, curry favor*).

Recent computer analyses of data have widened the scope of investigation and search for patterns among function words as well. These analyses show that patterning exists to a striking extent among most closed-set items. Kennedy (1989), for example, shows that two generalized frames for prepositional phrases with *at* — '*at* + (*the*) + Proper N denoting place', and '*at* + Personal Pron' — account for 63 per cent of the occurrences of this preposition.

Lately, procedures for locating collocations have employed statistical techniques. Church and Hanks (1989) propose an objective measure based on the information theoretic notion of mutual information for estimating word association norms. Their proposed measure, the 'association ratio', estimates word association norms directly from computer readable corpora. This ratio is based on 'mutual information', which comprises the probability of observing X and Y together (the joint probability), with the probability of observing X and Y separately (chance). If there is a genuine association between X and Y, then the joint probability will be larger than chance. Word probabilities are estimated by counting the number of Xs and Ys in a corpus and normalizing by the size of the corpus. Joint probabilities are estimated by counting the number of times that X is followed by Y within a span of W words and normalizing by N.

The span, or 'window', the authors choose for their analysis encompasses five lexical items, a setting they feel is large enough to show some of the constraints between verbs and arguments, but not so large as to wash out constraints that make use of strict adjacency. Smaller windows will identify fixed expressions and other short-range relations; larger windows will highlight semantic concepts and other larger-scale relationships. From our own research on academic lectures and other extended discourse, we believe that large windows can reveal important and pervasive co-occurrence relationships that, but for the wide eye of the computer, are otherwise too discontinuous to be noticed. For example, *so/very/too/different . . . from* can be manifested as *very different in age or in any other environmental factor from the rest.* Other frequent disjunctive pairs are *distinctions . . . between, moved . . . through,* and *now . . . so then.* Many researchers think a window of five words is adequate to locate these disjunctive associations, but we have come to believe that even wider windows are necessary to capture these generalizations.[4] We will have more to say about this in Chapter 7.

1.3.2   Collocations in natural language processing

Following the lead of Chomskyan grammars, the computational lexicon has traditionally been viewed as a list of words having specified syntactic and semantic properties, subject to the combinatory rules of a parser/generator. Increasingly, however, the lexicon is thought to include a variety of linguistic knowledge types, not just properties of single words. Becker (1975) was one of the first to suggest that phrases such as *let alone, as well as,* and *so much for,* which in many ways defy traditional textbook analysis, cannot simply be ignored, for they seem to be ubiquitous. He called for the systematic treatment of this large class of idiosyncratic phrases. Current opinion among computational linguists seems to agree that linguistic knowledge cannot be strictly divided into grammatical rules and lexical items; that, rather, there is an entire range of items, some of which are specific and pertain to a small number of instances, and some of which are very general and pertain to a large number of instances. The former are frequently called 'lexical items' and the latter 'grammar rules', but, since elements exist at all levels of generality, it seems impossible to draw a sharp border between them. *Raining cats and dogs* is certainly specific, *John saw the giraffe* is certainly general. Between these two, however, lies a vast number of phrases like *a day/month/year ago, the _____er the _____er*, etc., which have varying degrees of generality and cannot efficiently be placed with either of these two extremes.

In 1984, Wilensky *et al.* proposed a 'phrasal approach', which incorporates entire phrases as well as individual words in the lexicon; and in 1987, Zernick and Dyer went further. They not only include non-productive phrases like *at large, at all*, whose meanings are relatively fixed and cannot be produced from the meanings of their constituents, they also include productive sets of phrases like *at noon/midnight/two o'clock, look/sniff/play at*, whose meanings are less fixed and more general, and can presumably be derived by combining the individual meanings of their constituents. Thus, Zernick and Dyer's large lexicon maintains (a) single words, (b) fixed phrases, (c) all instances of certain variable phrases, and (d) single generalized entries which encompass these sets of phrases. For example, generalized entries for the variable sets above would indicate that many phrases of the form '*at* + TIME' carry the meaning of 'sharp timing'; phrases of the form 'V + *at*' can mean 'aimless activity'. The result is that specific phrases are maintained in the lexicon as compiled, easy-to-access knowledge, while general phrases (which can be the base for various specific phrases) are also maintained to allow the system predictive power to handle instances not previously encountered.

Such multiple lexical storage is also characteristic of recent connectionist models of knowledge, which are beginning to rival dominant symbolic models used in computer analysis of language (Gasser 1990). Connectionist models assume that all knowledge is embedded in a network of processing units joined by complex connections, and accord no privilege to parsimonious, non-redundant systems. Rather, they assume that redundancy is rampant in a model of language, and that units of description, whether these be specific categories such as 'word' or 'sentence', or more general concepts such as 'lexicon' or 'syntax', are fluid, indistinctly bounded units, separated only as points on a continuum.

Research in computational analysis of language thus confirms the significance of patterned phrases as basic, intermediary units between the levels of lexis and grammar. Lexicons that encompass these units are the very sorts that one might expect to be contained by the type of pragmatic competence described above.

1.4   Prefabricated language and language acquisition

If prefabricated lexical phrases are so pervasive a part of adult language, then we would expect to find them also in the language of young children, as part of the overall language system they are in the process of acquiring. Recent studies of language acquisition confirm that this is indeed the case.

These studies show that children pass through a stage in which they use a large number of unanalyzed chunks of language in certain predictable social contexts. They use, in other words, a great deal of 'prefabricated' language in appropriate situations.[5] For example, when children ask the frequent question *what is that?*, they may use it as if its three morphemes were a single, unsegmented unit, *what-is-that?*, just like any single word in their vocabulary. They treat this chunk of language as an unanalyzable unit, often reducing many of its sounds ([hwǝsdæt], [hwǝdæ], etc.) under a single tonic stress, and apparently do not recognize, in the earlier stages of language acquisition at least, that it is a phrase with separate lexical components. And in responding to such questions children might use the phrase *this-is-a X* the same way, as if the first three morphemes also functioned as a unit—in this case, one which identifies a following topic, X, as an answer to the question. Similar chunks that children frequently use are *go-on, give-me, this-is-mine, I-want-to-go, I-know-how-to-do-it*, and so on.

Many early researchers attributed the frequency of these chunks to the relevance of imitation and to the need of memorizing in learning a language. They also saw them, however, as rather a dead end in acquiring the regular, syntactic rules for the language. They thought these prefabricated chunks were distinct from, and somewhat peripheral to, the main body of language, which they saw as the creative product of the systematic rules of competence (Huang 1971; Brown 1973; Clark 1974).

1.4.1   Invariable routines and variable patterns

Hakuta was one of the first to suggest that perhaps these chunks were not so incidental to language acquisition after all. In a study of a Japanese child learning English, he made an important distinction between prefabricated 'routines', which he described as 'unvarying chunks of language' (such as *what-is-that?*) and prefabricated 'patterns', which he described as 'segments of sentences which operate in conjunction with a moveable component, such as the insertion of a noun phrase or a verb phrase' (such as *this-is-a* X) (Hakuta 1974:289). He also suggested that these chunks were not isolated or incidental to the creative rule-forming process, but, in fact, played a role in its development. Children seemed to use these chunks not only as memorized formulas but also as raw material for later segmentation and analysis in developing the rules of syntax.

For example, children may initially use *wannago* holophrastically as a memorized prefabricated routine in certain set situations, and then, after they become aware of similar phrases like *wannaplay* and *wannaget* in other contexts, they begin to analyze this phrase as a pattern with a moveable component, '*wanna* + VP'. As children hear such moveable components in prefabricated patterns, they begin to analyze chunks into their separate pieces, and work their way to the actual rules of syntax.

Hakuta's view of the importance of routines and patterns for language development was later affirmed by Lily Wong-Fillmore. Wong-Fillmore, whose research is generally accepted as one of the most complete studies of prefabricated speech in child second language acquisition, spent nearly a year collecting natural language data from several Spanish-speaking children learning English, and found that prefabricated language constituted a major part of their speech behavior. This led her to put these language chunks at the very center of acquisition and to claim that 'the strategy of acquiring formulaic speech is central to the learning of language', for she, like Hakuta, believes that routines and patterns learnt in the language acquisition process 'evolve directly into creative language' (Wong-Fillmore 1976:640).

Peters, in a study of both first and second language acquisition, takes the argument a step further. She develops principles for determining which of the occurring phrases are actually unanalyzed units, and then describes the process by which children analyze these units 'first to formulaic frames with slots and [then] into the conventional lexical items and syntactic patterns of the language' (Peters 1983:13).

1.4.2   The role of prefabricated language

Not all researchers agree that prefabricated language is so integral to language acquisition; the view that it is only peripheral to the language learning process persists. For example, in an influential article in 1978, Krashen and Scarcella conclude that routines and patterns play only a minor role in language acquisition and are fundamentally different from the 'creative construction process', which is uniquely a matter of analysis into syntactic rule. They feel that such language chunks are 'useful in establishing and maintaining relations, [but] do not serve a primary role in language acquisition' (Krashen and Scarcella 1978:295).[6] They admit the importance of routines and patterns in Wong-Fillmore's data, but suggest that the children in her study were under a great deal of pressure to produce language that far exceeded their linguistic competence, and that, for most of the time, they were exposed to language which was very routine and predictable. The authors claim that these two factors 'are not present in most language acquisition situations' (Krashen and Scarcella 1978:295). We believe, however, that these two factors do indeed characterize language acquisition, especially that which takes place more or less naturally. We will return to this matter shortly.

Most researchers now agree that learners use a large number of prefabricated expressions in acquiring language; they still disagree on the ultimate importance of these expressions, however. Peters points the way towards a possible resolution to the question when she suggests that there are two approaches to language learning which operate simultaneously—'the gestalt approach', in which children attempt to use whole prefabricated utterances in socially appropriate contexts, and 'the analytic one-word-at-a-time approach', in which children construct sentences from 'scratch'. Both approaches, she feels, are necessary forces in shaping first and second languages.

This view is buttressed by certain psycholinguistic research which shows that language learning on all levels takes place in two stages: a stage of 'item-learning' and a stage of 'system-learning' (Cruttenden 1981). In acquiring phonology, children may use sequences far in advance of normal development; for example, they may use particular CCV syllables before they use expected CV or reduplicated CVCV syllables. Cruttenden found children using advanced consonant cluster forms like [sz:] *shoes,* and [dridə] *do it,* before they had acquired the 'earlier' CV forms. Such CCV clusters should be considered phonological idioms comparable to syntactic idioms and, like them, learnt as unanalyzed units. Later on, children re-analyze these phonological chunks and learn to segment and reconstruct them in accordance with the phonemic principle.

The same phenomenon occurs in morphology. For example, children may first acquire the inflected form of a morpheme only as a memorized free-variant of the uninflected form: *daddy's~daddy.*

Later, they learn to segment this morphological idiom into its parts and attach meaning to the inflection.

Thus, it goes for all levels of language, the intonational, semantic and, of course, syntactic levels as well. Children learn to segment a previously unanalyzed unit and then learn to attach meanings to the segmented pieces:

> The evidence shows learning taking place initially on an item by item basis at all levels of language. A child has to learn individual items by straightforward imitation to allow his mind to worry at, and play with (like a dog with a bone), such individual items in order to extract the system from them (like the marrow from the bones). He will begin to extract the system when he recognizes some part of the item being used in another utterance (phonology, intonation, morphology, and syntax) or the whole item being used in different situations or with different referents (semantics) ... there is at least a strong possibility that some form of item-learning is an essential prerequisite to any type of system-learning. (Cruttenden 1981:87)

The research above concerns the language acquisition of children in fairly natural learning situations. Because of infrequent studies of adult learners in similar situations, the amount of prefabricated speech in adult acquisition has never been determined. However, there is no reason to think that adults would go about the task completely differently. In important ways, the language learning situation is the same for adults as for children, and makes it likely that an adult learner would also find prefabricated language an efficient way to begin to acquire a new language system.

For one thing—and contrary to Krashen and Scarcella's comments noted above—a great deal of language that people are exposed to every day *is* very routine and predictable, just as are the situations they encounter. This ritualization, as sociological and anthropological theory have long recognized, is simply characteristic of all aspects of human behavior and its contexts.[7]

For another thing—again contrary to Krashen and Scarcella—learners always feel pressure to produce more than they can, and they quickly become discouraged when they are able to express little of what they wish. It is likely that adults would feel such pressures even more than children. Prefabricated chunks would allow the expressions that they were yet unable to construct creatively from rules, simply because these chunks could be stored and retrieved whole when the situation called for them. Hakuta claims that prefabricated patterns:

> enable learners to express functions which they are yet unable to construct from their linguistic system, simply storing them in a sense like large lexical items. I think it is also important to note that, if learners always have to wait until they acquire the constructional rules for forming an utterance before using it, then they may run into serious motivational difficulties in learning the language, for the functions that can be expressed (especially in the initial stages of learning) would be severely limited. It might be important that the learner be able to express a wide range of functions from the beginning, and this need is met by prefabricated patterns. As the learner's system of linguistic rules develops over time, the externally consistent prefabricated patterns become assimilated into the internal structure.
> (Hakuta 1976: 333)

Adults would even have an advantage over first language learners in making use of prefabricated language, since they would be immediately aware that these units could be analyzed into smaller pieces by the process of segmentation with which they were already adept.

Further, intuitive judgments seem to be in accord with the research evidence. Many people who have learnt a foreign language in naturalistic circumstances remember a period of item-learning followed by one of system-learning, just as described above. For one of the authors, some of the first phrases of survival Spanish, for example, were memorized routines like *quetal*, *megusta*, and *mepareceque*, which later he learnt to break apart into patterns with moveable pieces. Some learners have commented on the almost audible 'crack' when this break occurs:

> Hearing again and again the question *Kore wa nan desu ka?* (What is this?) but never seeing it printed I conceived of *korewa* as a single word; it is spoken without pause. Some lessons later I learned that *wa* is a particle, an unchanging uninflected form, that marks the noun it follows as the topic of the sentence. Interestingly enough I did not, at once, reanalyze my word *korewa* and such others as *sorewa* and *arewa* into noun and particle forms. I did not do that until I started to hear such object forms as *kore o* and *sore o* and *are o* in which *o* marks the direct object. Then the truth dawned on me, and the words almost audibly cracked into *kore*,

sore, and *are*, three demonstratives which took *wa* in the nomina-
tive form and *o* in the objective.
(Brown 1973:5)

Most language learners could, no doubt, share many similar
anecdotes.

We will return to this issue in Chapter 5, where, in connection with
teaching with lexical phrases, we discuss the relationship of prefabrication and acquisition to another characteristic of language
behavior, social interaction.

Notes

1   Of course, rules of grammar can also be exploited to achieve
    particular poetic effects, or other special effects in context. In
    poetry, for example, e. e. cummings is well known for his type of
    grammatical rule exploitation.
2   Incidentally, a consideration of lexical phrases, or in Widdow-
    son's terms 'formulaic chunks', figure prominently in his discus-
    sion of pragmatic competence. Indeed he suggests that
    communicative competence is not so much a matter of knowing
    rules for the composition of sentences and being able to appropri-
    ately employ such rules as it is 'knowing a stock of partially pre-
    assembled patterns, formulaic frameworks, and a kit of rules, so
    to speak, and being able to apply the rules to make whatever
    adjustments are necessary according to contextual demands'
    (Widdowson 1989:135).
3   For this reason we exclude ordinary idioms from further con-
    sideration. This exclusion is also consistent with the view of
    Pawley and Syder (1983), who state that most such units (in their
    terms 'lexicalized sentence stems') 'are not true idioms but rather
    are regular form-meaning pairings' (1983:192).
4   Church and Hanks suggest that it might be interesting to consider
    alternatives to the 'rectangular' window that they describe, alter-
    natives such as triangular windows, or decaying exponential
    ones, which would weight words less and less as they are
    separated by more and more words.
5   Among many other labels suggested have been: 'idioms' (Fraser
    1970); 'holophrases' (Corder 1973); 'praxons' (Bateson 1975);
    'preassembled speech' (Bolinger 1975); 'gambits' (Keller 1979);
    'conventionalized forms' (Yorio 1980); 'sentence stems' (Pawley
    and Syder 1983), and 'composites' (Cowie 1988).

6   Krashen and Scarcella feel that prefabricated speech is closer to the automatic speech of aphasics than it is to normal speech. Such aphasic speech is 'neurologically different from creative language' and probably has a 'fundamentally different mental representation than other kinds of language' (1978:286). There is, of course, a similarity between these two types of speech in that both use stereotypical expressions. But there is also a major difference between them. As Heubner explains, in automatic speech:

> the appropriateness of the utterance to the social context is apparently purely a matter of chance; for the language learner, there is an attempt to match the routine or pattern with the appropriate social and linguistic context ... Studies in first language acquisition and second language acquisition ... leave no doubt that the routines and patterns employed by language acquirers, unlike the automatic speech of aphasics, are sensitive to the contexts in which they are employed. (Heubner 1983:42)

7   Unfortunately, the role of ritualization in language behavior is not yet a frequent topic of investigation. Linguistic studies still tend to ignore stereotyping and standardization in language performance.

2 Formal aspects of lexical phrases

2.1 Introduction

In Chapter 1, we briefly described differing types of lexical phrases as ranging from short, relatively fixed phrases such as *a _____ ago*, to longer phrases such as *the _____er the _____er*, and we argued that pragmatic competence accounts for our ability to access and adapt these phrases in language use. In the present chapter, we look more closely at the nature of lexical phrases, in particular, the nature of the defining features of the various structural types. As a starting point, we look at how the forms themselves are related to the psychological processes of storage and retrieval. Section 2.2 draws on studies of performance for insights into these processes, and for insights into the basic differences in the forms that prefabricated speech takes. Section 2.3 is concerned with formulating specific categories of lexical phrase types. In section 2.4, we examine in more detail the defining characteristics of the various types, and the possible implications of their relative flexibility.

2.2 Prefabricated language and psychological processing

In formulating performance models of language processing, researchers endeavor to offer direct descriptions of psychological categories and processes, attempting to describe languages in terms of how they are perceived, stored, remembered, and produced. These researchers feel that the storage capacity of memory is vast, but that the speed for processing those memories is not (Crick 1979:219), so that we must learn short cuts for making efficient use of this processing time.

Many studies of language processing thus suggest that language is stored redundantly. Words, for example, are stored not only as individual morphemes, but also as parts of phrases, or as longer memorized chunks of speech, and that they are often retrieved from memory in these pre-assembled chunks (Bolinger 1975). One of the earliest findings from memory research was that short-term memory holds a fairly constant number of units (Miller 1956), units which later research has shown likely to be chunks of information, composed of several, rather than single, items. Lexical phrases, no doubt, serve as such chunks for the language user. Even though these chunks may be larger and contain more information than discrete items, their number still remains fairly constant in memory (Simon 1974), and their size increases as we become more familiar with remembered material, permitting us to store and recall more information. A great deal of the learning task is thus to chunk unfamiliar material in meaningful ways and create more effective lexical phrases.

This sort of 'chunking' also characterizes speech production to a surprising degree. Becker, from his work in artificial intelligence on spoken language, feels that the frequency of lexical phrases in performed speech implies:

> that the process of speaking is *Compositional*: We start with the information we wish to express or evoke, and we haul out of our phrasal lexicon some patterns that can provide the major elements of this expression. Then the problem is to stitch these phrases together into something roughly grammatical, to fill in the blanks with the particulars of the case at hand, to modify the phrases if need be, and if all else fails to generate phrases from scratch to smooth over the transitions and fill in any remaining conceptual holes.
> (Becker 1975:72)

It is our ability to use lexical phrases, in other words, that helps us speak with fluency. This prefabricated speech has both the advantage of more efficient retrieval and of permitting speakers (and hearers) to direct their attention to the larger structure of the discourse, rather than keeping it focused narrowly on individual words as they are produced. All this, of course, fits very neatly with results of the computational and language acquisition research, and with our analysis in Chapter 1.

If lexical phrases characterize language acquisition and language performance to such an extent, they would seem to be an ideal unit for language teaching. In Chapters 5 to 7, we present that approach as an alternative to current practice.

2.2.1   Idioms and clichés

The extent of prefabricated speech in performed language now seems far greater than once was thought. Most previous attention in linguistic theory has been directed to idioms, complex bits of frozen syntax, whose meanings cannot be derived from the meaning of their constituents, that is, whose meanings are more than simply the sum of their individual parts: *step on the gas, raining cats and dogs, kick the bucket*. Discussion of these usually concerns their legitimacy in grammatical description, how isolated a phenomenon they are from regular phrases constructed from the generative rules of grammar. Idioms, however, are only one kind of prefabricated speech; there are many other sorts of formulaic fixed phrases that need to be attended to as well.

Clichés, for example, are similar to idioms in that they too consist of patterns that are relatively frozen, but they are unlike them in that the patterns usually consist of larger stretches of language and that their meaning is derivable from the individual constituents: *there's no doubt about it, a good time was had by all, have a nice day*.

2.2.2   Non-canonical phrases

Non-canonical forms are other sorts of patterned phrases, different from both of the above in that their patterns do not have the typical shapes of English structures. *Off with his head, by and large, as it were*, and *waste not, want not*, are examples of such phrases that depart from usual patterns. The command, *off with his head*, for example, contains no verb; *by and large* co-ordinates a preposition with an adjective; *as it were* employs the subjunctive form of the verb without the conditional marker *if*; *waste not, want not* also omits *if* before the conditional phrase.

Like many idioms and clichés, these phrases are sometimes invariable (*by and large, as it were*), but often they are quite flexible, making a particular phrase one of a large set of possible variations. *Off with his head*, for example, is only one variation on a pattern which can also appear as *down with the king, away with all bureaucrats*, and so on. There seems to be a general pattern, 'Adv [direction] + *with* + NP', whose category slots can be filled by different lexical items, with only the preposition *with* remaining constant. These patterns seem to exist somewhere between traditional syntax and lexicon. They are phrases with variable lexicon which are stored and recalled as units; yet, since they deviate so far from normal English sentence patterns, their structure cannot be derived by the traditional rules of syntax.

2.2.3   Variability as points on a continuum

Facts such as these are what lead many linguists to begin to question the traditional sharp distinction between syntax and lexicon, and to search for a framework that could describe all of these data in the same manner. Formerly, most linguists had regarded idioms and other frozen forms as vestigial, isolated units to be dealt with after the regular productive units had been described, and assumed a difference in kind between this patterned speech and more creative speech. But it is more likely that what constitutes a pattern and what does not is relative, a matter of degree instead of kind, for one usually finds a continuum in the amount of variation involved, from more invariable and frozen forms (such as idioms and clichés) to less invariable (non-canonical) forms. In fact, several scholars have argued that there is no sharp break at all between the frozen and the variable, and claim that there is thus no absolute division between morphology and syntax. Wood, for example, argues for the principle of gradience in describing language by showing that semantic compositionality and productivity of form for phrases constitute 'a continuum from complete frozenness to full freedom of combination' (Wood 1981: iii). We feel these studies are worth mentioning in passing, though we take no particular position with respect to idioms and clichés, or other conventionalized forms, unless they can be seen as associated with specific functions.

Whatever the description of patterns, it is generally agreed that the sequence of words in phrases with little variation is more predictable than in phrases with a lot. This is an extremely important fact in communication, one that Oller exploits in his 'grammar of expectancy' (Oller and Richards 1973; Oller and Streiff 1975), and accounts for much of the way we process language. The degree to which words constrain those around them, and the assurance we have that certain words are going to follow certain others, are the facts we use to make sense of language and to create all sorts of subtle variations and surprises. The cliché, *a good time was had by all*, is a relatively frozen pattern, yet *a bad time was had by all*, *a glorious time was had by all*, and *a good time was had by none*, are all possible variations on this basic pattern and each would have its proper effect. The effect comes about because we expect something else, with varying degrees of certainty, in the Adj or in the Pro slots. The same is true for idioms, but since their meaning is tied directly to relatively frozen, frequently unusual combinations of specific lexical items, these units cannot be manipulated quite as easily: *kick the bucket* can perhaps become *kick the bedpan,* but it would be difficult to vary the phrase in many other ways and still have it mean the same thing.

2.2.4 From less variable to more variable

There are other kinds of fixed phrases which are different from idioms, clichés, and non-canonical forms. These are phrases which are quite canonical in shape, which are also variable, more so than non-canonical forms, and whose meaning can also be described by the traditional rules of syntax: *a year ago, as far as I know, could you tell me what time it is?, if I had time, I would show you.* These are, therefore, phrases much like any others in the language. They differ, however, in that they seem to be stored and recalled as more predictable sequences of words than regular constructions. For example, the phrase *a year ago* is a variation on a pattern which functions as a temporal linking device in discourse. Variable lexicon fits into the syntactic frame *a _____ ago,* such as *a day ago, a short while ago, a very long time ago,* to indicate a specific past time. We recognize this pattern and its function even when the lexicon stretches the meaning metaphorically, as in Dylan Thomas's *a grief ago.* Likewise, the sentence *if I had time, I would show you* is a variation on a pattern which functions as a conditional marker, a pattern that is built on the syntactic frame '*if* + *I* + past tense V + X, (*then*) I + Modal + V + Y', or, more abstractly, '*if* + NP + past tense V + X, (*then*) NP + Modal + V + Y'. All of these are similar to other phrases of the language, and it would be difficult, as Wood suggests, to draw an absolute distinction between these patterned sequences and those which combine more freely. All seem only to be different points on a continuum, where some phrases pattern items quite predictably, and others combine them much less predictably, differences only of degree.

When they are described as above, patterned phrases obviously play a much larger part in language than most previous theory has allowed. Just how large a part they *have* played is often unclear, though, since the boundary between habit and rule, which is essentially what is at issue here, has never been clear. The balance of routine and creativity in language is an empirical question which has long been neglected, and only recently have researchers begun to explore this issue carefully.

2.3 Lexical phrases as variable units

Previously, we defined lexical phrases as form/function composites, lexico-grammatical units that occupy a position somewhere between the traditional poles of lexicon and syntax: they are similar to lexicon in being treated as units, yet most of them consist of more than one word, and many of them can, at the same time, be derived from the regular rules of syntax, just like other sentences. Their use is governed by principles of pragmatic competence, which also select and assign particular functions to lexical phrase units.

Lexical phrases, then, differ from other conventionalized or frozen forms such as idioms or clichés mainly in that they are used to perform certain functions. For example, *it's raining cats and dogs*, *kick the bucket*, *powder room* are idioms that appear to have no particular function; *how do you do?*, *a _____ ago*, *the _____er the _____er*, on the other hand, can be used in discourse to perform the functions of greeting, expressing time relationships, and expressing comparative relationships among ideas.

2.3.1 Lexical phrases, collocations, and syntax

It is also important to our discussion to distinguish clearly between lexical phrases and collocations, or ordinary syntactic strings that do not count as lexical phrases. These three terms now need to be differentiated more precisely.

1 *Syntactic strings* are strings of category symbols, such as 'NP + Aux + VP', which are generated by syntactic competence and which underlie all grammatical (canonical) structures of the language.

2 *Collocations* are strings of specific lexical items, such as *rancid butter* and *curry favor*, that co-occur with a mutual expectancy greater than chance. These strings have not been assigned particular pragmatic functions by pragmatic competence.

3 *Lexical phrases* are collocations, such as *how do you do?* and *for example*, that *have* been assigned pragmatic functions, and consist of two main types:

a. strings of specific (non-productive) lexical items, which allow no paradigmatic or syntagmatic substitution. These strings can be both canonical (conforming to a syntactic string) and non-canonical. Examples of the former would be *what on earth*, and *at any rate*; and of the latter, *by and large*, *as it were*;

b. generalized (productive) frames (by far the largest group), consisting of strings of category symbols (or otherwise generally specified syntactic/semantic features) and specific lexical items, which have been assigned a pragmatic function. Examples would be '*a* + N [+ time] + *ago*', and 'Modal + *you* + VP'. These generalized frames underlie specific lexical phrases, such as *a year ago, a month ago*, and *would you pass the salt?, could you shut the window?*, etc. Generalized frames can also be canonical, as the two above, or non-canonical, as in 'Adv [+ direction] + *with* + NP', with adaptations like *off with his head, down with the king, away with all bureaucrats*.

Thus, there are three different sorts of phrasal combinations in the language (aside from idioms, as discussed above). There are those produced by the general rules of syntax and considered regular, freshly created constructions. These have traditionally been the center of most linguistic investigation. Then there are those other two sorts of phrases that are produced more as prefabricated 'chunks' than as newly minted constructions. These have usually been assigned to the periphery of linguistic investigation. Prefabricated phrases are collocations if they are chunked sets of lexical items with no particular pragmatic functions; they are lexical phrases if they have such pragmatic functions.

Because lexical phrases are prefabricated form/function composites, we believe that they are crucial intermediaries between the levels of lexis and grammar and have been too long neglected in linguistic analysis.

2.3.2 Categories of lexical phrase

Given that lexical phrases can be distinguished from collocations or syntactic strings, it is, nevertheless, apparent that a good deal of variation exists among the lexical phrase units themselves. For purposes of description, as well as pedagogy, it is useful to classify them in terms of their structural and functional characteristics.[1] The classifications given below are based on structural criteria, and while taking some account of the function by listing particular functions of individual examples parenthetically, they do not by any means exhaust the range of functions associated with these units. We will give a more detailed account of functions in discourse in the following chapter, and explore a much wider range of the functions associated with various lexical phrases.

Four structural criteria characterize these phrases. The first has to do with their length and grammatical status; the second, with whether the phrase has a canonical or non-canonical shape; the third, whether the phrase is variable or fixed; and the fourth, whether the phrase is continuous or discontinuous, that is, whether it consists of an unbroken sequence of words or whether it is interrupted by variable lexical fillers. In applying these criteria, it is again necessary to think in terms of a continuum, since it is sometimes difficult to distinguish sharp boundaries between categories. For that reason, our discussion of the criteria employs qualifiers such as *usually*, *mostly*, and *often* rather than absolutes like *always* and *never*. Pawley and Syder (1983) speak of the same difficulty in their analysis of language categories: 'Again we would assert that this feature of gradation is a fact of language, and in seeking discrete classes we are in danger of misrepresenting the nature of the native speaker's knowledge' (1983:212). Particular examples cited are from various data collected by the authors.

(a) *Polywords*: (1) Polywords are short phrases which function very much like individual lexical items. (2) They can be both canonical and non-canonical. (3) They allow no variability. (4) They are continuous.

Polywords are associated with a wide variety of functions, such as expressing speaker qualification of the topic at hand, relating one topic to another, summarizing, shifting topics, and so on.

Examples:
(i) canonical:

for the most part	(qualifier)
in a nutshell	(summarizer)
by the way	(topic shifter)
I'll say	(agreement marker)
hold your horses	(disagreement marker)
at any rate	(fluency device)
what on earth?	(marker of surprise)
so long	(parting)
for that matter	(relator)
so to speak	(fluency device)

beside the point	(evaluator)
strictly speaking	(evaluator)
you know	(clarifier)

(ii) non-canonical:

as it were	(exemplifier)
so far so good	(approval marker)
all in all	(summarizer)
by and large	(qualifier)
not on your life	(disagreement marker)
once and for all	(summarizer)
in part	(qualifier)
in essence	(summarizer)
nevertheless	(relator)

Nevertheless, together with *moreover, notwithstanding, however,* and the like, all linking devices (or 'relators') in discourse, are members of a special class of polywords, which are not only perceived as one word but are written as such. They were formerly polyword phrases, but over time have become written as single lexemes, and are now so perceived by English speakers. The common formula for parting, *goodbye*, shares a similar phrasal history. The same sort of chunking is a continuing phenomenon, of course, as shown by such often encountered spellings as *usta* (used to), *gonna* (going to), and so on.

(b) *Institutionalized expressions*: (1) Institutionalized expressions are lexical phrases of sentence length, usually functioning as separate utterances. (2) They are mostly canonical. (3) They are invariable. (4) They are mostly continuous. In the latter two respects, they are, therefore, quite similar to polywords.

Institutionalized expressions are proverbs, aphorisms, formulas for social interaction, and all of those chunks that a speaker has found efficient to store as units. They are used for quotation, allusion, or (frequently) direct use. Some of these may be general phrases used by almost everyone in the speech community (*how do you do?*, *how are you?*), while others may be more idiosyncratic phrases that an individual has found to be an efficient and pleasing way of getting an idea across (*give me a break*, *have a nice day*). They are mainly continuous, but at times discontinuous pairs (*once upon a time . . . and they lived happily ever after*) frame chunks of entire text.

As we will demonstrate below, such discontinuous pairs can be found in all categories of lexical phrase, and they frame all sorts of discourse. Other pairs of institutionalized expressions that can operate this way, for example, are the greeting *how do you do?* and the closing *nice meeting you*, which frame a somewhat formal speech situation, and the more informal greeting *how are you?* and parting *have a nice day*, which frame a casual speech encounter. Pairs such as these function somewhat like bookends of discourse.

Examples:

(i) canonical:

a watched pot never boils	(advice)
the public seldom forgives twice	(warning; disapproval marker)
how do you do?	(greeting)
nice meeting you	(closing)
how are you?	(greeting)
have a nice day	(parting)
once upon a time . . . and they lived happily ever after	(narrative framer)
get a life	(disapproval)
give me a break	(objection)
there *you go*	(approval)

(ii) non-canonical:

what, me worry?	(denial [ironic])
be that as it may	(concession)
long time no see	(greeting)

(c) *Phrasal constraints*: (1) Phrasal constraints are short- to medium-length phrases. (2) They can be both canonical and non-canonical. (3) They allow variation of lexical and phrasal categories (NP, VP, AdjP, AdvP, N, V, Adj, Adv, etc.). (4) They are mostly continuous. As with polywords, phrasal constraints are associated with a wide variety of functions.

In the following examples, the slots indicate the positions filled by paradigmatic substitution, while parentheses indicate optional syntagmatic material, which is not strictly speaking a part of the basic frame.

Examples:	Variations:
(i) canonical:	
a _____ ago (temporal relator)	*a day ago, a year ago, a very long time ago*
to _____ this up (summarizer)	*to tie this up, to wrap this up*
as I was _____ (topic shifter)	*as I was saying, as I was mentioning*
in _____ (summarizer)	*in short, in sum, in summary*
good _____ (greeting)	*good morning, good afternoon, good evening*
see you _____ (parting)	*see you, see you soon, see you later*
dear _____ (greeting)	*dear* FIRST NAME, *dear* TITLE + LAST NAME
yours _____ (closing)	*yours sincerely, yours truly*
_____ as well as _____ (relator)	*this one as well as that one, linguists as well as sociologists*
as far as I _____ (qualifier)	*as far as I know, as far as I can tell*
to make a (very) long story (relatively) short (summarizer)	

(ii) non-canonical:

Adv [direction] *with* _____ (disapproval [strong])	*down with the king, away with all politicians*
you _____ (disapproval [insult])	*you creep, you jerk*
the _____*er the* _____*er* (comparator)	*the sooner the better, the busier the happier*
for better or (for) worse (evaluator)	*for better or worse, for better or for worse*
for _____ (exemplifier)	*for instance, for example*
what with _____ *(and all)* (cause)	*what with this weather and all (we decided not to go); what with her tardiness and the late hour (we have decided to stay)*
oh for _____ (desire [emphatic])	*oh for a good book, oh for a room to call my own*
[Obj Pro] *and* [Poss Pro] _____ (evaluator)	*him and his carelessness, me and my stupidity*

A few phrasal constraints, such as *the* _____*er the* _____*er* and 'Adv [direction] *with* _____', are discontinuous, but most are continuous. Some phrasal constraints permit very limited variation (*for better or (for) worse*), in which there is only an optional syntagmatic expansion, and thus verge on the inflexibility of polywords. Others permit only a limited amount of paradigmatic substitution (such as the exemplifier *for* _____, while others permit a great deal (_____ *as well as* _____). Further, some phrasal constraints such as *see you* _____ permit a null substitution, so that *see you* is a possible variation of this phrase as are *see you later*, *see you soon*, and so on.

The examples above also include instances of phrasal constraints used as the sort of 'discourse bookends' discussed previously. For example, the greeting *good* _____ and parting *see you* _____ frame somewhat casual conversation, and the greeting *dear* _____ and closing *yours* _____ frame formal written text.

(d) *Sentence builders*: (1) Sentence builders are lexical phrases that provide the framework for whole sentences. They contain slots for parameters or arguments for expression of an entire idea. (2) These phrases can be both canonical and non-canonical. (3) They allow considerable variation of phrasal (NP, VP) and clausal (S) elements. (4) They are both continuous and discontinuous.

In the examples below, the slots that contain the variable parameters or arguments are marked by capitalized letters (usually X, Y, and Z) to distinguish these positions from the slots in phrasal constraints. Parentheses again indicate optional material which is not really a part of the basic frame.

Examples:
(i) canonical:

I think (that) X (assertion)	*I think that it's a good idea; I think he ought to do it*
not only X, but also Y (relators)	*not only are most spiders harmless, but they are also beneficial; not only was her mother injured in the accident, but also her father*
my point is that X (summarizer)	*my point in all this is that Hemingway was having a very difficult time getting anything on paper; my point is that gravitational force is by far the weakest*
I'm a great believer in X (evaluator)	*I'm a great believer in putting money away for a rainy day; I'm a great believer in writing the preface and introduction last*
let me start by/with X (topic marker)	*let me start by mentioning a few of the things that are most important; let me start with the physical characteristics of that species*
it's only in X that Y (qualifier)	*it's only in countries below the equator that one sees those constellations; it's only in working through the problem carefully that you can come up with the solution*

Modal + *you* + VP *(for me)?* (request)	*would you help me?, could you lift that for me?*
it seems (to me) (that) X (assertion)	*it seems to me that it's going to take a long time; it seems he left without her*
that reminds me of X (topic shifter)	*that reminds me of the place we went to in Chicago; that reminds me of another reason for doing this*

(ii) non-canonical:

the _____er X, *the _____er* Y (comparator)	*the sooner all this work is finished, the sooner we will all be able to go home; the greater the number of subjects you have, the better the results you will get*

In this last example, one sees how a lexical phrase can be classed differently depending on the filler it takes. *The _____er the _____er* is a phrasal constraint, whose slots take adjectives as fillers (*the faster the better*), but when expanded to encompass clausal categories, symbolized by X and Y, it becomes a sentence builder.

This category contains many more discontinuous lexical phrases than the other three categories. The phrases *not only X, but also Y*, *it's only in X that Y*, and 'Modal + *you* + VP *(for me)?*' are typical of the kinds of discontinuities that exist in sentence builders. Even the relatively fixed portions of these phrases are often separated by an intervening filler, as well. For example, note that in the variations of *not only X, but also Y* cited above, the word 'also' easily separates from the word 'but'. Note also how basically contiguous phrases likewise often permit syntagmatic variation. The parenthetical options in *I think (that) X*, and 'Modal + *you* + VP *(for me)?*' are examples of such expansions.

In sum, polywords, institutionalized expressions, phrasal constraints, and sentence builders each contain canonical and non-canonical lexical phrases, though in the sentence-level categories, the non-canonical instances are not at all frequent. Lexical phrase types differ in grammatical level, in the kind of substitution they allow, and as to whether they are typically continuous or discontinuous. The four lexical phrase types could thus be characterized as shown in Figure 7.

	Grammatical level	Canonical/ Non-canonical	Variable/ Fixed	Continuous/ Discontinuous
Polywords:	word level	both	fixed	continuous
Institutionalized expressions:	sentence level	canonical	fixed	continuous
Phrasal constraints:	word level	both	somewhat variable	mostly continuous
Sentence builders:	sentence level	canonical	highly variable	often discontinuous

Figure 7

Figure 7 makes clearer certain relationships among lexical phrase categories. For one thing, institutionalized expressions and sentence builders are sentence-level counterparts of polywords and phrasal constraints, respectively. That is, along the four dimensions, sentence builders and polywords differ mainly in grammatical level, just as do sentence builders and phrasal constraints. Another characteristic of lexical phrase categories made clearer is that the possibility of variation and the possibility of discontinuity increase as one moves from polywords through institutionalized expressions, phrasal constraints, and sentence builders (see Figure 8).

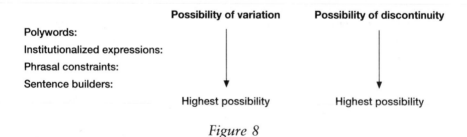

Figure 8

As we will discuss in more detail later, it is these dimensions of variation and discontinuity, with their possibility for generativity and framing, that offer the greatest potential for a lexical phrase approach to teaching. For that reason, we often group institutionalized expressions with polywords in the discussion that follows, since both categories are fixed and continuous, and not as flexible and productive as phrasal constraints and sentence builders.

One fact about lexical phrases is obscured rather than clarified by the categories of Figure 7. That is the fact mentioned previously, that there is no sharp boundary separating these categories, but that the differences among them are frequently ones of degree rather than kind. For example, typical instances of polywords will be completely fixed and continuous, whereas typical phrasal constraints will be moderately variable and often discontinuous. *At any rate*, *by the way*, and *by and large* are thus typical examples of polywords; and *a _____ ago*, *as I was _____*, and *the _____er the _____er* are typical examples of phrasal constraints. Between these prototypes, however, lie many lexical phrases that do not fit exclusively into either category. *So long*, which closely resembles a polyword, strays a bit from the prototype. Although it is continuous, it allows a syntagmatic variation (*so long for now*) and is thus not completely fixed. *For better or worse* also allows a syntagmatic variation (*for better or for worse*), and in this case strays further from the prototype by allowing the variation within the phrase rather than at the end or beginning of the phrase, creating somewhat of a discontinuity. Straying even further would be the phrase *to make a long story short* which, likewise, permits internal syntagmatic variation (*to make a very long story short*); but unlike the above, it permits not just one but several possibilities for this variation (*to make a very rather/extremely long story short*), and thus might be considered less unitary and more discontinuous than the other phrases. It is at the same time more continuous than a typical phrasal constraint like *a _____ ago* since the syntagmatic expansion containing the paradigmatic choice is optional, whereas in the latter phrasal constraint, the paradigmatic choice is an obligatory part of the phrase. The situation, then, is something akin to the representation in Figure 9.

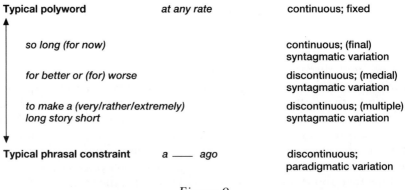

Figure 9

Phrases that permit only syntagmatic variation at the beginning or end of the phrase we classify as polywords; those that permit any sort of internal variation, particularly when there is paradigmatic choice within the variation, we classify as phrasal constraints.

The border between phrasal constraints and sentence builders likewise has no sharp edge. Many sentence builders are in fact amalgams of the two types. For example, *the ____er X, the ____ Y* has the basic form of a phrasal constraint, but in this particular case it is expanded to encompass the arguments X and Y, and for the moment becomes a sentence builder.

We will return to a discussion of segmenting the lexical phrase continuum in the final chapter. No matter how they are categorized however, it should be apparent that all of these types of lexical phrases amount to much more than picturesque phrases of infrequent occurrence, and much more than just isolated curiosities of phatic and 'incidental' language. Lexical phrases are in fact basic to language performance; they are pervasive because they seem to be characteristic of the way we comprehend and the way we speak.

2.4 Issues of form and flexibility

In previous sections, we presented a sketch of types of lexical phrase, and emphasized their pervasiveness in speech production. In this section, we explore a more detailed description of lexical phrase categories, and of the form/function associations outlined in Chapter 1. We look first at examples of sentence builder lexical phrases that are typical of those found in social discourse, namely, indirect speech acts. Indirect speech acts are also of interest because their description has proved to be somewhat problematic in terms of more traditional analyses, and we suggest that a lexical phrase approach leads to a much more satisfactory account. We then examine phrasal constraints, which contrast with sentence builders in that they allow less variation, and which, as less flexible units, appear to be more arbitrary with respect to selection of structures for form/function units. Finally, polywords and institutionalized chunks will be compared on the basis of these criteria. The implications for teaching these various structures are significant, as will be demonstrated in Chapter 5.

2.4.1 Indirect speech acts as lexical phrase sentence builders

Some speech acts are 'direct' speech acts, in which the primary purpose is not really distinct from the literal meaning, and some are 'indirect' speech acts, which contrast sharply with direct speech acts in that the primary purpose is quite distinct from the literal meaning.

Polite requests, for example, are not usually expressed directly by using a performative verb, as in *I request that you pass the salt*, but rather this function is expressed indirectly by asking a yes/no question of the type, *could you pass the salt?* Likewise, offers are normally expressed indirectly by asking a yes/no question of the type, *can I help you?*

Searle (1975) defines an indirect speech act as one 'primary' speech act performed by way of performing another, or 'secondary' one. Thus, *could you pass the salt?* conveys as its primary, though non-literal meaning, a request for you to pass the salt, although it also expresses as its secondary, and literal meaning, a yes/no question concerning your ability to pass the salt. This non-literal, primary meaning expresses the real purpose, or function of the utterance, which is generally referred to as its 'illocutionary force'.

Many indirect speech acts are unconventional, with no particular associated form; a great many others, however, are highly conventionalized, and take the form of lexical phrase sentence builders.

2.4.2   Non-conventional indirect speech acts

Searle discusses first the type of non-conventional speech act found in the reply by B, below, to the proposal made by A.

A: Let's go to the movies tonight.
B: I have to study for an exam.

B's reply would normally constitute a rejection of the proposal to go to the movies, but not in virtue of its literal meaning. The illocutionary force of the indirect speech act resides in B's secondary act of making a statement to the effect that he has to study for an exam. However, statements of this type do not normally convey rejections. Thus, Searle notes, *I have to tie my shoes* or *I have to eat popcorn tonight* would not in a normal context be a rejection of the proposal to go to the movies tonight. For this reason, it is necessary to posit a series of steps that speaker A would follow, at least unconsciously, in order to work out the illocutionary force of B's reply: in response to A's proposal, B stated that he had to study for an exam; A assumes that B is co-operating in the conversation and that, therefore, his remark was intended to be relevant; a relevant response must be one of acceptance, rejection, counter-proposal, etc.; but his literal utterance was not one of these; therefore, he probably means more than he says, and his primary illocutionary point must differ from his literal one.

2.4.3   Conventional indirect speech acts

Non-conventional speech acts are highly dependent on context, and the form they take is thus selected differently, depending on a given context. This type of speech act form, however, contrasts with the type of form that a great many indirect speech acts take. Most of Searle's examples are indirect requests and indirect offers, and the forms they take are often quite conventional. One of his well known examples is the request form: *could you pass the salt?*

Variations on this form are *can you pass the salt?*, *can/could you reach the salt?*, *can/could you hand me the salt?*, and so on. Other common forms he cites for indirect requests and offers include *I would like you to go now, I want you to do this for me, I'd rather you didn't do that, would you be willing to write a letter of recommendation for me?, would you mind not making so much noise?, do you want to hand me that hammer over there?, can I help you?, can I do that for you?, could I be of assistance?, would you like some help?, wouldn't you like me to bring some more next time I come?*

As opposed to statements like B's response, *I have to study for an exam*, sentences like those above are 'standardly' or 'conventionally' used in the performance of indirect directives. As conventionalized forms they are instantly recognized as such, and no series of steps need be posited for the hearer to be able to work out the intended illocutionary force of the utterance.

In our terms, these conventionalized indirect speech acts are lexical phrases of the sentence builder category. As conventionalized forms (for example, *could you pass the salt?*) linked to specific functions (for example, request), they are form/function composites. They are also generally canonical, continuous sentence builders allowing variation of clausal elements (*could you lend me a dime?*, *would you hand me that hammer?*).

2.4.4   Conventionalized sets and basic lexical phrase frames

Indirect speech acts are particularly clear examples of the greater flexibility allowed in the sentence builder category, as compared with other lexical phrase categories. At first glance, it may appear that the 'entrenched' structures for expressing a given indirect speech act form a fairly large set. However, this set may in fact consist of only a very limited number of basic lexical phrase frames, with various fillers in the slots accounting for several variations of the frames. As suggested in Chapter 1, the relative syntagmatic simplicity and

paradigmatic flexibility allowed within a particular frame may provide at least a partial account for why that frame, rather than
another, has come to be selected as one of the favored, conventional
ones for a given indirect speech act. It is part of pragmatic competence that a given frame is assigned a particular functional
meaning.

The question of why one form is selected over another is one that
Searle considered problematic for his theory of indirect speech acts.
In Searle's words, the biggest problem with his analysis is as follows:

> If, as I have been arguing, the mechanisms by which indirect
> speech acts are meant and understood are perfectly general—hav-
> ing to do with the theory of speech acts, the principles of coopera-
> tive conversation, and shared background information—and not
> tied to any particular syntactical form, then why is it that some
> syntactical forms work better than others. Why can I ask you to do
> something by saying 'can you hand me that book on the top shelf?'
> but not, or not very easily, by saying 'is it the case that you at
> present have the ability to hand me that book on the top shelf? . . .
> even within such pairs as . . . 'can you do A?', 'are you able to do
> A?', there is clearly a difference in indirect illocutionary act
> potential.
> (Searle 1975:75)

The answer given is that certain forms tend to become conventionally established as the standard idiomatic forms for indirect speech
acts; that politeness is the most prominent motivation for indirectness, and certain forms naturally tend to become entrenched as
conventional devices for making polite indirect requests, offers, and
so on.

These reasons provide a partial answer, but they do not entirely
explain how it is, nor why it is, that certain forms, and not others,
become entrenched as the conventional devices of indirect speech
acts. If viewed as lexical phrases, however, a more complete explanation might be attempted for why certain forms become entrenched,
and the means by which their forms come to be conventionalized. In
other words, if certain sets of indirect speech acts are seen as lexical
phrases, the pragmatic competence we posited in Chapter 1 to
account for the prefabricated forms and functions of lexical phrases,
may provide considerable insights in attempting to answer the question of why some syntactical forms work better than others.

Searle's examples of requests and offers present a particularly clear illustration of this point. Among the forms that function as requests, for instance, he lists the following questions:

> *could you pass the salt?*
> *can you pass the salt?*
> *can you reach the salt?*
> *are you able to reach the book on the top shelf?*
> *will you quit making that awful racket?*

Seen from a lexical phrase perspective, however, these five sentences have only one (basic) form, namely, the lexical phrase frame suggested in Chapter 1,

Modal + *you* + VP?

with the variations accounted for by the different fillers used in the modal and verb slots. Other question forms listed for requests include:

> *would you mind not making so much noise?*
> *would you kindly get off my foot?*
> *would you be willing to write a letter of recommendation for me?*

But these sentences, too, are simply variations of the same basic lexical frame. These variations show that the frame is somewhat more flexible than we have indicated so far. The basic frame, 'Modal + *you* + VP?' can be modified to allow for versions like these, with parentheses indicating optional slots:

Modal + *you* (*mind/kindly/be willing to*) + VP?

The expressions in the optical slot are various politeness 'markers'. In addition to those given from Searle's list, the most common P-marker in this slot is 'please'.

Other variations of the same frame can also be seen in the list Searle gives:

> *have you got change for a dollar?*
> *do you want to hand me that hammer?*
> *aren't you going to finish your cereal?*

The only differences illustrated by these examples are that auxiliaries other than modals can also occur in initial position, and negation is possible. Again, a slight modification of the lexical phrase frame allows for this greater flexibility in slot and filler options. It also serves to reveal the fundamental similarities in the form of these eleven requests:

Aux *(not)* + *you (mind/kindly/be willing to)* + VP?

Indirect requests can also be made by uttering a certain type of statement form. Searle lists a number of these conventionalized statement forms, but they too can be reduced to one basic lexical phrase frame. Among those he lists in the set

I would like you to go now
I want you to do this for me
I would rather you didn't do that.

The relationship between the request statements in this particular set is revealed in the frame

I $\begin{Bmatrix} want \\ would\ like/rather \end{Bmatrix}$ *you (to) (not)* VP *(for me).*

Other variations related to this frame are

I hope/wish you will/would (do) X (for me).

The remainder of the examples given for requests can, likewise, be reduced to a very limited set of lexical phrase frames.

The examples Searle gives for offers fit into similar patterns, as, for example:

can I help you?
can I do that for you?
could I be of assistance?

which can be reduced to the lexical phrase frame

Modal + *I* + VP *(for you)?*

Based on Searle's analysis, it would appear that one basic difference between the question forms for requests and the question forms for offers is that the former are 'hearer-based' (Modal/*want* + *you*), whereas the latter are 'speaker-based' (Modal + *I*). It should be mentioned, however, that in one respect the patterning indicated by these particular data may be somewhat misleading. Research done by, among others, Brown and Levinson (1978), and Blum-Kulka and Levenston (1987) indicates that, at least for English, the preferred forms for the most polite requests may be just the opposite. Assuming that requests usually threaten the hearer's face, the forms that avoid naming the hearer as the performer minimize this imposition. If so, then the most polite requests would be speaker-based, as in *could I borrow your pen?* rather than *would you lend me your pen?*

Whatever the most polite or less polite forms may be, the point we wish to make here is that Searle's examples for requests and offers illustrate that the basic, relatively simple syntactic frames for sentence builder lexical phrases are, nevertheless, quite flexible in that the slots and fillers allow for a variety of actual utterances. Thus, we suggest that, at least in many cases, this simplicity and flexibility may help to explain why it is that a certain lexical phrase frame becomes the conventionalized form for a given function. The use of a limited number of prefabricated frames for these functions helps to explain Searle's puzzle as to why it is that 'some syntactical forms work better than others' as indirect speech acts. Just as other lexical phrases have been selected as the conventionalized, or entrenched forms for particular functions, so have those for indirect speech act functions, such as requests and offers. Evidently, the ones that become conventionalized for these common, frequently occurring functions, are those with simple syntagmatic frames that, while easy to learn and store initially as lexical phrase chunks, still allow for considerable paradigmatic slot/filler variation for a particular utterance.

Sentence builders other than indirect speech acts may be explained by these principles as well. Take for instance, the frame

it's only in X that Y

with noun phrase and gerund phrase expansions of X, and clausal expansions of Y, such as

it's only in Venice that you see gondolas
it's only in running uphill that I get out of breath.

It may at first appear that the basic frame could just as well be something like

only X has Y.

If so, however, a good deal of flexibility would be lost, since X and Y in this frame would allow only noun phrase substitutions, not gerund or clausal ones. Thus, a reasonable paraphrase of the first type of expansion would still be possible, but the second one would not, as seen below:

only Venice has gondolas
*only running uphill has I get out of breath.

Instead, a paraphrase of the second expansion above would require an entirely different structure, such as *only when I run uphill do I get out of breath.*

Thus, just as with indirect speech acts, it seems that with other sentence builder lexical phrases, 'some syntactical forms work better than others' as well.

We recognize, of course, that these tentative suggestions provide only partial answers at best, and that the pairing of form and function remains to some extent arbitrary, as acknowledged in our discussion in Chapter 1. For example, it appears that the common greeting *how do you do?* could just as well be *how is your health?* This arbitrary aspect is perhaps best illustrated by functions that have clearly differing forms in different cultures. In Chinese, for instance, one of the commonest greetings is not *how do you do?*, but rather *have you eaten/had lunch/dinner (yet)?* Similarly, whereas *see you* ___ (*see you later/soon/next week*, etc.) is a common parting expression in English, in Spanish *God go with you* is common.

Thus, simplicity and flexibility can be seen as factors that influence selection of particular *types of forms*, but the pairing is still to some degree arbitrary in any given culture. That is, the overall shape of lexical phrase frames is characteristically simple yet flexible, but the actual form selected from a range of likely candidates in a form/function pairing seems otherwise somewhat arbitrary. In the next section, we will suggest that these factors vary, however, depending on the category of the lexical phrase in question.

2.4.5   Distinctions in variability and lexical phrase types

Sentence builders are distinguished from phrasal constraints mainly in that the latter allow less variability, and this variability is at the lexical or phrasal level rather than the clausal level. Since by their nature, lexical and phrasal substitutions allow for less variation than those at the clause level, the phrasal constraint frames impose more rigidity. For example, *by pure* ___ allows very limited substitutions in the noun slot, for example, *by pure coincidence, by pure chance*, as can be seen by the (pragmatic) strangeness of phrases like *?by pure accident, ?by pure fortune*. As noted in Chapter 1, phrases like the latter are entirely grammatical, of course, but what they have lost is their idiomatic quality and their associated function of expressing relationships between topics in discourse (detailed discussion of this function, and the function of lexical phrases in general, will follow in Chapter 3). Put another way, these unidiomatic phrases are like any other phrase generated from scratch by the ordinary syntactic rules of the grammar. Another example would be *hey, wait a* ____, which allows the temporal noun substitutions *hey, wait a minute, hey, wait a second*, but not *?hey, wait an hour/day/month*, etc.

Likewise, slots for other lexical categories are relatively limited in phrases of the phrasal constraint category. The verbal slot in *as far as I* ____, for instance, is limited in the sense described above to *as far as I can tell, as far as I know*, since even those verbs with a similar meaning such as *?as far as I can say, ?as far as I ascertain, ?as far as I realize*, etc., result in loss of associated function (expressing evaluation), and render the phrase unidiomatic.

A few phrasal constraints do allow somewhat more flexibility than the examples discussed thus far. An obvious example is *a* ____ *ago*, which admits substitution of several common nouns which express a duration of time, for example, *a minute/hour ago, a week/month/year ago*. Even in this case, though, certain others seem to be disallowed (for example, *?a second ago, ?a decade ago, ?a millennium ago*).

With lexical phrases like these less flexible ones, the selection for a conventionalized form/function unit may be seen as more arbitrary than for sentence builders, such as indirect speech acts used for requests, offers, and the like, as discussed in the previous section. There seems to us no obvious reason, for example, that *as far as I* ____ has been selected as a culturally authorized lexical phrase unit, rather than, say, *to the extent that I know/can tell*, or again, *hey, wait a* ____ (*hey, wait a minute/second*) rather than *I object to that/this*. Even with phrasal constraints, though, there are still a number for which it can be argued that simplicity and flexibility play a part to some degree. Take, for example, phrasal constraints such as *listen* ____, or *if I were* ____. It seems to us difficult to find alternative phrases that have the same simplicity and yet allow some degree of flexibility. The closest possibilities might be for the former something like *here's a warning*, which lacks flexibility, and for the latter *here's some advice (for you/the king/president)*, which would allow flexibility in the optional slot, but which would then lack the same simplicity.

To sum up thus far, the influence of syntagmatic simplicity and paradigmatic flexibility on the choice of lexical phrase frames is difficult to assess. We have tried to illustrate that these factors seem to have at least a limited role in explaining why it is that sentence builder frames, and to a lesser degree phrasal constraint frames, come to be the ones chosen as forms for culturally agreed upon, idiomatic lexical phrase form/function units. But, as also suggested in

the previous section, to the extent that the choice of linguistic structure can be seen as arbitrary or not, this factor can be characterized
at best as points on a continuum, from less arbitrary (sentence
builders) to more arbitrary (phrasal constraints).

Further, if we compare polywords with these other two categories,
it becomes clear that according to the criteria discussed above they
are more arbitrary yet than phrasal constraints. While most are quite
short and simple (*for the most part, on the other hand, in a nutshell,*
and so on), they allow no flexibility at all. So, for example, *for the
most part* cannot be *?for the least part, ?for the most portion; on the
other hand* cannot be *?on the other foot, ?on the other arm;* or *in a
nutshell* cannot be *?in a peanut shell, ?in a clam shell.* Similar
remarks hold for institutionalized chunks. Although they are texts of
clausal length, they too, are nevertheless quite short and simple relative to normal clausal shapes, for example, *a watched pot never boils,
how do you do?, once upon a time.* And, like polywords, as inflexible
units they would appear at a point on the more arbitrary end of our
continuum.

In addition to the issues discussed in the preceding sections, there
are a number of other factors which relate to the selection and use of
lexical phrases. For example, Leech (1983) discusses factors relating
to politeness, such as the selection of *could* versus *can* as politeness
markers in request forms. He argues first that an expression like *can
you take me home?* is more polite than *will you take me home?* on
the grounds that the latter allows little freedom to refuse, whereas the
former avoids this impoliteness at third remove, because it gives the
hearer an 'out' in that he or she is able to decline the request on the
grounds of being unable to do so. However, if *can* is replaced with
the unreal form *could,* as in *could you take me home?,* the request is
even more polite. The reason given is that 'the adoption of the unreal
form is, of course, yet a further stage in the avoidance of commitment', for by replacing *can* by *could* the speaker gives the hearer yet
'another excuse for not complying with the request: the past-tense
modals signify a hypothetical action by [the hearer], and so in reply,
[the hearer] can in theory give a positive reply to the question
without committing himself to anything in the real world' (Leech
1983: 121).

Politeness markers may also be 'stacked' within basic lexical
phrase frames. Those mentioned earlier include the optional material
in the basic request frame

Aux + *you (mind/kindly/be willing to)* + VP?

However, still others such as *terribly* or *possibly* may be stacked within the optional slot, as in *would you mind terribly picking up my dry cleaning?, would you possibly be willing to drive my dog to the kennel?* For each added marker (for example, *could* + *possibly* + *be willing to*), hearer options are increased, and thus also the degree of politeness.[2]

Other factors that, of course, influence the choice of particular politeness markers include a variety of social factors such as speaker/hearer relationship, the context of utterance, and so on. As social factors, they involve culture-specific appropriateness conditions that would fall under socio-pragmatics in the model given in Leech (1983), as discussed in Chapter 1. While a detailed investigation of such factors goes beyond the scope of this book, we mention social relationships and features of context as two factors that we believe merit further investigation in future research. For example, degree of politeness is related to the degree of formality required, and thus, the more distant the social relationship between speaker and hearer, the more politeness markers we would expect to be required.

An example of a context requiring more formal politeness markers would be that of bearing bad news, regardless of the speaker/hearer relationship. In the context of a speaker being called upon to be the bearer of news about a relative's death, the function of expressing sympathy would not be expressed in blunt, direct speech act terms such as *your father passed away this morning*, but rather the indirect *I'm (very) sorry to (have to) (be the one to) tell you that your father passed away early this morning*. In this case, the basic lexical phrase sentence builder *I'm sorry to tell you/hear that X*, which has the function of expressing sympathy, is expanded by the three optional politeness markers in parentheses, with each adding another layer of politeness that in such cases also increases the depth of sympathy expressed. Only the proposition *your father passed away early this morning* occurring in the X clausal slot conveys the information portion of the entire expression.[3]

Notes

1 'Lexical phrase' is a term we first encountered in Becker (1975). Labels for the following categories are also his, but we have greatly modified the content of these categories for the purposes of this book.

2 Leech (1983) remarks that explicit markers such as *possibly, mind, kindly, please* are 'pragmatically highly specialized

towards the function of indicating "on the record" politeness' (1983:121). For further discussion of politeness factors, see also Brown and Levinson (1978).

3   Davison (1975) argues that these markers do not involve politeness at all, but simply provide a more indirect way of expressing bad news. However, as Leech (1983) points out, any act that is an imposition on the hearer requires indirect politeness markers. Given this view, surely the bearing of bad news is an imposition in the sense that it is presumably information that the hearer would rather not receive.

3   Functional aspects of lexical phrases

3.1   Introduction

Speaking a language means conversing in it, and comprehending a language means understanding phrases, not as isolated bits of grammatical structure, but as parts of the general ebb and flow of the surrounding discourse. In this chapter we deal with the functions of lexical phrases in both spoken and written discourse. A further aim is to illustrate that lexical phrases are effective and essential guideposts in sorting through material that is otherwise often confusing and contradictory to second language learners.

We begin with a more specific identification and illustration of lexical phrase types as they are related to particular functions. Next, following a discussion of some of the general issues in discourse analysis, we look specifically at aspects of spoken discourse, and then of written discourse.

3.2   Functions of lexical phrases

What follows is an attempt to group lexical phrases according to function in a way that will reflect the requirements of spoken and written language and, at the same time, be pedagogically useful. These groups are not traditional grammar categories by any means, nor are they semantic ones; instead, they represent various categories of meaning and pragmatic characteristics of discourse and conversational structure that exist in many different types of situations. They are somewhat similar in aim to Wilkins' notional–functional categories, where emphasis is on the lexicon needed to perform specific speech 'functions' for common situations (Wilkins 1976). We emphasize that ours are intended to be pedagogical as well as theoretical categories, devised for use as practical instruments for the classroom, but also, we feel, adhering closely to current work in discourse analysis and speech act theory.

We refer to these groups as 'social interactions', 'necessary topics', and 'discourse devices'. Under social interactions we list lexical phrases that are markers describing social relations. Necessary topics are those topics about which learners will be asked, or ones they will need to talk about frequently. The third group, discourse devices, are types of lexical phrases that connect the meaning and structure of the discourse.

Lexical phrases are parts of language that often have clearly defined roles in guiding the overall discourse. In particular, they are the primary markers which signal the direction of discourse, whether spoken or written. When they serve as discourse devices, their function is to signal, for instance, whether the information to follow is in contrast to, is in addition to, or is an example of, information that has preceded. Among others, markers like *on the other hand, in contrast to ____, however, nevertheless, but look at X, but how about X*, signal contrast; *in addition, moreover, another thing is X*, signal addition; *for example, for instance, X, something like that, it's like X*, signal exemplification, and so on.

Discourse devices are thus phrases that connect the meaning and structure of the discourse. As such, they serve specific pragmatic functions that differ from other categories of lexical phrases, as, for instance, those that function to maintain social interactions such as expressing gratitude (*thanks very much/a lot (for X)*), requests (Modal + *you* + VP), and so on.

To illustrate these distinctions, we list typical examples of each below. These examples do not represent an exhaustive list, of course, but they do suggest some of the kinds of lexical phrases that a new speaker will need to make use of to achieve a minimum level of expressive and pragmatic ability in the language. Students at more advanced levels, or those learning a language for special purposes, would require practice with additional categories and different lexical phrases. The lexical phrases that follow include invariant polywords and institutionalized expressions, and variable phrasal constraints and sentence builders.

3.2.1   Social interactions

Social interactional markers, those that describe social relations, consist of (a) categories of conversational maintenance, and (b) categories of functional meaning relating to conversational purpose.

(a) *Conversational maintenance* (regularities of conversational interaction that describe how conversations begin, continue, and end).

Summoning:	*excuse/pardon me* (sustained intonation); *hey/hi/hello, (NAME), how are you (doing)?; lookit; I didn't catch/get your name; do you live around here?; hello, I'm + NAME; good morning/afternoon/ evening, (how are you?); what's up?*[1]
Responding to summons:	*hi/hello, (NAME); how are you (doing)?; what's going on/happening?; hello, I'm + NAME; (I'm) fine, thanks, (and you)?*
Nominating a topic:	*what's X?; (by the way) do you know/remember X?; have you heard about X?*[2]
Clarifying:	
(1) audience:	*excuse/pardon me?; what did you mean by X/when you said X?*
(2) speaker:	*what I mean/I'm trying to say is X; how shall I put it?; let me repeat*[3]
Checking comprehension:	*all right?; (do you) understand (me)?*
Shifting a topic:	*(say,) by the way; this is (a bit) off the subject/track, but X; where were we/was I?; oh that reminds me of X*[4]
Shifting turns:	*(well,) so OK; excuse/pardon me; could I say something here?*[5]
Closing:	*well, that's about it; I must be going; (it's been) nice talking to you/meeting you; I've got to run/go/do X; I mustn't keep you any longer*[6]
Parting:	*goodbye; see you later; (well) so long (for now)*

(b) *Conversational purpose* (types of speech acts, i.e. functions that describe the purposes for which conversations take place).[7]

Expressing politeness:	*thanks (very much); (please,) if you don't mind*
Questioning:	(rising intonation), *do you X?; is/are there/it/they X?*
Answering:	*yes, (there/it/they is/are) (X); no, (there/it they is/are not) (X)*
Requesting:	Modal + Pro + VP (i.e. *would you (mind) X?*); *may I X?*[8]
Offering:	Modal + Pro + VP (i.e. *may/can I help (you)?*); *would you like X?*
Complying:	*of course; sure (thing); I'd be happy/glad to*
Refusing:	*of course not; no way; I'd rather you X; I'm sorry but (I'm afraid/I think that) X*
Complimenting:	NP + *BE/LOOK* + (intensifier) + Adj; *I* + (intensifier) + *LIKE/LOVE* + NP[9]
Asserting:	*it is (a fact/the case that) X; I think/believe that X; it's said that X; word has it that X; it seems X; I read (somewhere) that X; there is/are/was/were* X[10]
Responding:	
(1) acknowledging (simple reinforcers):	*(and then) what happened (next/then/after that)?*
(2) accepting:	*(yeah,) I know; (oh,) I see, no kidding*
(3) endorsing:	*yes, that's so/correct/right; I absolutely/certainly/completely agree; (that's) a (very) good/excellent point; there you go; that's great*

(4) disagreeing:

yes, but (I think that) X; I don't (really) agree (with you/X)[11]

Expressing gratitude:

thanks (very much/a lot) (for X); I (really) appreciate your thoughtfulness/kindness/doing X

Expressing sympathy:

I'm (very) sorry about/to hear (about) X; (wow), that's/how terrible/awful; what a shame/pity/terrible thing[12]

3.2.2 Necessary topics

These lexical phrases mark topics about which learners are often asked, or ones that are necessary in daily conversations.

Autobiography:

my name is ____; I'm from ____; I'm (a) ____ (years old)[13]

Language:

do you speak ____?; how do you say/spell ____?; I don't speak ____ very well; I speak ____ (a little)

Quantity:

how much/big is ____?; (not) a great deal; lots of ____

Time:

when is X?; what time X?; for a long time/____ years; a ____ ago, since X; at/it's ____ o'clock; on ____ day; the ____ before/ after ____

Location:

where is ____?; what part of the ____?; across from ____; next to ____; to the right/left (of ____); how far is ____?; ____ blocks (from ____)

Weather:

is it going to X? it's (very) ____ (today)!; I'm ____

Likes:

I like/enjoy ____ (a lot); I don't like/enjoy ____ (at all); I'd like to X; ____ is lots of fun; (what) do you like to X?

Food:

I'd like (to have) ____/to make a reservation (for ____); the check; a table for ____; serve breakfast/ lunch/dinner

Shopping:

how much is ____?; I want to buy/see ____; it (doesn't) fit(s); (not) too expensive; a (really) good/ bad buy/bargain; ____ cost(s) (me/you/them) ____ dollars

3.2.3   Discourse devices

Discourse devices are lexical phrases that connect the meaning and structure of the discourse.

Logical connectors:

as a result (of X); nevertheless; because (of) X; in spite of X

Temporal connectors:

the day/week/month/year before/ after ____; and then; after X then/ the next is Y

Spatial connectors:

around here; over there; at/on the corner

Fluency devices:

you know; it seems (to me) that X; I think that X; by and large; at any rate; if you see what I mean; and so on; so to speak; as a matter of fact[14]

Exemplifiers:

in other words; it's like X; for example; to give you an example

Relators:

the (other) thing X is Y; X has (a lot)/doesn't have (much) to do with Y; not only X but also Y

Qualifiers:

it depends on X; the catch is X; it's only in X that Y

Evaluators: *as far as I know/can tell; there's no*
                                     doubt that X; I'm (not) absolutely
                                     sure/positive/certain (but) ____; I
                                     guess; at least; at all[15]

Summarizers: *to make a long story short; my*
                                     point (here) is that X; OK (level
                                     intonation)

3.2.4   Forms of lexical phrases in functional groups

All formal categories of lexical phrases discussed in the previous
chapter are represented in the three functional groups. For teaching
purposes, the four formal categories may be reduced to three, with
institutionalized expressions being incorporated into the polyword category, since institutionalized expressions are more or less
sentence-length polywords. We illustrate from examples above,
employing the three formal categories: polywords, phrasal constraints and sentence builders:

Social interactions

Polywords: (shifting a topic)   *by the way*
                        (checking comprehension)   *all right?*

Phrasal constraints: (clarifying: audience)   ____ *me?*
                        (parting)   *see you* ____

Sentence builders: (clarifying: speaker)   *what I mean is X*
                        (nominating a topic)   *do you know X?*

Necessary topics

Polywords: (quantity)   *a great deal*
                        (shopping)   *(not) too expensive*

Phrasal constraints: (autobiography)   *I'm from* ____
                        (quantity)   *how much is* ____?

Sentence builders: (likes)   *what do you like to X?*
                        (time)   *what time X?*

Discourse devices

| Polywords: | (exemplifier) *in other words* |
| | (fluency device) *at any rate* |

| Phrasal constraints: | (evaluator) *as far as I* ___ |
| | (logical connector) *as a result of* ___ |

| Sentence builders: | (evaluator) *there's no doubt that* X |
| | (summarizer) *my point here is* X |

3.2.5   Lexical phrases in other languages

Lexical phrases are not phenomena restricted to English, by any means. They exist in the same abundance and perform the same conversational functions in other languages as they do in English, and they can therefore be exploited no matter what the language being taught. We list in the Appendix (at the back of this book) a few representative lexical phrases from the three categories above, first in Chinese, then in Spanish, and Russian, and hope the reader will see that the pervasiveness and universality of these phrases make them an appropriate structure of study for *foreign*-language, as well as ESL, classrooms.

Not only do they occur in the same abundance and perform the same functions in other languages, they also occur with strikingly similar characteristics and category types. In basic structure, they commonly occur as lexical phrase frames with slots for various fillers; in type they are found in the full range from the invariant polywords to the variable phrasal constraints and sentence builders; and in function they also exhibit the full range of social interactions, necessary topics, and discourse devices.

In addition to the examples given in the Appendix, in the present section we illustrate these similarities with a few representative lexical phrases from the three categories, first in Chinese, as an example of a non-Indo-European language, and then in Spanish, and Russian. To make the comparison of functions clearer for each type, the translations indicate the pragmatic function of the phrases rather than their literal meaning. The slot/filler frames show that the forms correspond to the patterns also found in English.

Chinese:

Social interactions

Polywords:	(summoning) duibuqi, *pardon me/us*; (shifting a topic) shunbian ti yixia, *by the way*; jiu zhe yang, *so, OK*
Phrasal constraints:	(parting) hui (tou) jian, *see you later*; (refusing) juedui buxing/meimen, *no way* (checking comprehension) you wenti mei you?, *OK?/all right?*
Sentence builders:	(complimenting) (wo) (zhen/hen) xihuan X, *I (really) like X*; (ni) (zhen/hen) + Adj, *you're really very* + Adj (gratitude) xie xie (ni) (de) (X), *thanks (very much) (for X)*

As in English, the Chinese polywords are completely fixed (duibuqi, *pardon me/us*; shunbian ti yixia, *by the way*; jiu zhe yang, *so, OK*), phrasal constraints are relatively short lexical phrases with low variability (hui (tou) jian, *see you later*; juedui buxing/meimen, *no way*; you wenti mei you? *OK?/all right?*), whereas sentence builders are usually frames for complete sentences, amenable to the regular rules of syntax ((wo) (zhen/hen) xihuan X, *I really like X*; (ni) (zhen/hen) + Adj, *you're really very* + Adj; xie xie (ni) (de) (X), *thanks (very much) (for X)*). And like their English counterparts, the Chinese lexical phrases have similar functions, in this case, the social interactional functions of shifting topics, summoning, parting, refusing, checking comprehension, complimenting, expressing gratitude.

The examples of necessary topics and discourse devices given below illustrate similar correspondence in frame, type, and function.

Necessary topics

Polywords:	(shopping) tai gui le, *too much*
Phrasal constraints:	(location) nabian/duimian _____, *across from* _____; zai na/shenma difang?, *where is (place)?*
Sentence builders:	(likes/dislikes) (wo) xiang/yuan yi . . ., *I'd like to . . .*; X hen you yisi/qu ji le, *X is lots of fun*

Discourse devices

Polywords: (fluency devices) wulun ruhe, *at any rate*

Phrasal constraints: (evaluators) ju (wo) suo zhi er yan, *as far as I can tell*;
(temporal connectors) di er tian/natian yihou ——, *the day after* ——

Sentence builders: (qualifiers) zhe you lai/qujue yu X, *it depends on X*; zhi you zai X zhong Y cai, *it's only in X that Y*

For necessary topics and discourse devices, lexical phrases in Chinese express similar functions with similar frames, from less variable to more variable. The sentence builders show that these lexical phrases are again parallel to their English counterparts in their contrast to phrasal constraints and polywords. As in English, they are often of sentence length, highly variable, with slots for parameters or arguments ((wo) xiang/yuan yi . . ., *I'd like to* . . .; X hen you yisi/qu ji le, *X is lots of fun*; zhe you lai/qujue yu X, *it depends on X*; zhi you zai X zhong Y cai, *it's only in X that Y*).

  As a further illustration of these correspondences, we include a few brief examples from Spanish and Russian. A much broader range of these social interactions, necessary topics, and discourse devices, with a few representative examples illustrating the functions in each, is given in the Appendix. The Appendix is included in order to illustrate that the full range of categories is similar in other languages, and that foreign language teachers as well as ESL teachers could begin to organize the lexical phrases in a given language along these lines.

Spanish:

Social interactions

Polywords: (summoning) ¿qué tal?, *what's up?*
(shifting turns) bueno pues, *well, so OK*

Phrasal constraints: (summoning) buenos/as días/tardes, *good morning/afternoon*
(parting) hasta ——, *until/see you* ——

Sentence builders:	(complying) me gusta/gustaría (mucho) X, *I'd like (very much) to X* (refusing) no tengo ganas (de X), *I don't want to do/feel like doing X* (questioning) ¿hay X?, *is/are there X?* (offering) ¿quiere(s) X? *do you want X?*

Necessary topics

Polywords:	(quantity) a patadas *a lot*
Phrasal constraints:	(time) hace poco/mucho tiempo, *for a short/long time*; desde (hace) _____, *since* _____ (shopping) ¿cuánto (es/cuesta/vale _____)? *How much (is _____)?*
Sentence builders:	(likes/dislikes) (no) me/le gusta(n)/apetece(n) (mucho) (nada) (X), *I/you (don't) like X (very much) (at all)*

Discourse devices

Polywords:	(logical connectors) por eso, *therefore*; (fluency device) si mal no recuerdo *if I remember correctly*
Phrasal constraints:	(temporal connectors) al principio/final de _____, *towards/at the beginning/end of* _____; el _____ pasado, *last* _____ (i.e. winter/autumn/spring, etc.) (spatial connectors) al/a la _____, *at the* _____ X (i.e. corner, center, etc.) (fluency devices) si me entiende(s)/comprende(s), *if you get what I mean*
Sentence builders:	(qualifiers) X depende de Y, *X depends on Y*; con tal que X, *provided that X* (assertion/fluency device) me parece que X, *it seems to me that X*

Russian:

Social interactions

Polywords:

(summoning) v čem delo?, *what's up?*
(parting) do skorogo, *so long*

Phrasal constraints:

(summoning) dobrij den'/večur/utro, *good morning/afternoon*
(shifting turns) nu (čto že), *well, so OK*
(complying) konečno/razumeetsja, *of course/it goes without saying*

Sentence builders:

(questioning) X tam?, *is/are there X?*
(requesting) u vas/tebja est' X?, *do you have X*
(offering) (vy) xotite/ty xočes X?, *do you want X?*
(gratitude) (bol'šoe) spasibo (za X), *thanks (very much/a lot) (for X)*

Necessary topics

Polywords:

(shopping) sli škom mnogo, *too much*

Phrasal constraints:

(time) nedolgo/dolgo, *for a short/long time*;
s tex por kak X, *since X*

Sentence builders:

(likes/dislikes) mne (ne) (očen') nravitsja X, *I (don't) like X (very much)*; mne xotelos by X, *I would like to (do) X*

Discourse devices

Polywords:

(shifting a topic) meždu pročim, *by the way*

Phrasal constraints:

(temporal connectors) v načale/konce X *towards/at the beginning/end of X*; prošloj/zimoj/osen'ju/vesnoj), *last X (i.e. winter/autumn/spring, etc.)*
(spatial connectors) v X, *at the X (i.e. corner, center, etc.)*
(summarizers) v celom/obščem/summe, *in sum*

Sentence builders:

(fluency devices) mne kažetsja čto X, *it seems to me that X*
(qualifiers) X zavisit ot Y, *X depends on Y*; pri uslovii čto X, *provided that X*

3.3   Lexical phrases in conversational discourse

Comprehending and producing a language means understanding how the parts of language fit together as parts of a discourse. Social interactions and discourse devices are the basic pragmatic organizers and provide patterns for the framework of the discourse; necessary topics, introduced here basically for their pedagogical usefulness, provide patterns for the subject of discussion. Figure 10 gives a diagrammatic representation of this relationship.

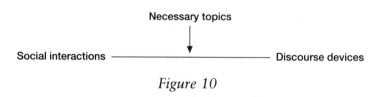

Figure 10

Beyond that, lexical phrases do not operate in exactly the same way in all sorts of discourse. Social conversation is primarily a matter of maintaining social relationships, and lexical phrases of social interaction and necessary topics predominate, with discourse devices having a lesser role. In this section, we concentrate on lexical phrases in conversation. In section 3.4, we turn to types of discourse in which the primary purpose is transmitting information rather than maintaining social relationships, and in which discourse device lexical phrases predominate rather than those of social interaction or necessary topics.

3.3.1   Patterns in conversation

Despite the predominance of certain types of lexical phrases in conversation, most conversational encounters, if they are not of the briefest, phatic sort, are composed of a patchwork of patterns from all three of these categories. For example, one of the most basic interactions at the beginning of a conversation is to get the attention of the person one is talking to. When that person responds to the summons, the next step is to get the partner to attend to the topic of discourse; one then begins to offer information about the selected topic. In this way, the participants co-operate to build a conversation. After the purpose of the conversation has been satisfied, the participants close the dialogue, and part.

The following is a relatively simple, reconstructed dialogue which illustrates some typical lexical phrase functions in conversation (with labeled lexical phrases):

A: *Excuse me?* (sustained intonation) (summons: SI)

B: *Yes, may I help you?* (response: SI)

A: *Can you tell me where the Saturday Market is please?* (request: SI) (location: NT)

B: *I'm not sure but I think* (assertion: SI) (evaluator: DD) (fluency device: DD) *it's three blocks over, next to the Burnside Bridge.* (location: NT)

A: *Pardon me, the Burnside Bridge?* (audience clarification: SI)

B: *It's just three blocks to your right.* (location: NT) *You can't miss it.*

A: *OK, well,* (closing: SI) *thanks very much.* (politeness: SI)

B: *OK then,* (acknowledge: SI) *So long.* (parting: SI)

Person A initiates the conversation by summoning the attention of B with the lexical phrase *excuse me?*, spoken with sustained intonation. B responds to the summons, and A makes a request, *can you tell me where the Saturday Market is please?* B asserts an answer which also functions as an evaluator and fluency device, and which precedes two short lexical phrases that describe location, *three blocks over*, and *next to the Burnside Bridge*. A indicates that the location is not understood by asking for clarification, *pardon me, the Burnside Bridge?* B then clarifies by giving a more explicit location marker, *three blocks to your right*. A then moves to close and expresses politeness. B acknowledges, and responds with a phrase for parting. Of the various lexical phrases in this exchange, only *I'm not sure but I think* functions as a discourse device.

3.3.2   Interconnected functions

The somewhat more involved conversation given below involves a larger variety of typical functions. This longer reconstructed dialogue illustrates, in greater detail, the interconnected functions of lexical phrases of social interactions, necessary topics, and discourse devices.

A: *Hey, Sally. What's up?* (summons: SI)

B: *Hi, Bill. How are you doing?* (response: SI)

A: *Pretty well, thanks.* (response: SI) *By the way,* (topic shift: SI) *did you hear about my new car?* (topic nomination: SI)

B: *No kidding,* (response: SI) *a new car?* (clarification: SI)

A: *Uh huh.* (response: SI) *I bought an old Volvo.* (shopping: NT) *the day before yesterday.* (time: NT)

B: *Hey, that's great.* (response: SI) *How much did it cost you?* (shopping: NT)

A: *It seems to me that it was a really good buy,* (assertion: SI) (evaluator: DD) (fluency device: DD) (shopping: NT) *and what's more,* (conjunction: DD) *there isn't anything wrong with it* (assertion: SI)—*as far as I can tell,* (evaluator: DD) *at any rate.* (fluency device: DD)

B: *Yeah, it's a beauty;* (response: SI) *you were lucky to find it.* (assertion: SI) *Oh, guess what?* (topic shift: SI) *Word has it that Jack just got a big promotion.* (assertion: SI) *Did you hear about it?* (question: SI)

A: *Yes, I heard.* (answer: SI) *The other thing I heard is that he gets to move into a fancy big office* (relation: DD) *on the top floor.* (location: NT)

B: *No kidding, that's great.* (response: SI) *Well, I've got to run now.* (closing: SI) *See you later.* (parting: SI)

A: *Well, then,* (closing: SI) *so long for now.* (parting: SI)

A's remark beginning with *it seems to me that X* is typical of the complex utterances that often occur after a topic has been established and information is being presented about it. Evaluators, fluency devices, and other discourse devices begin to play some part in the evolving conversation. Of the twenty-four lexical phrases in this exchange, five are discourse devices. Moreover, the lexical phrases themselves begin to serve several purposes simultaneously.[16] For example, the beginning of A's utterance, *it seems to me that X*, bears a multiple function: it marks a social interaction, for it is a routinized way of making an assertion, and at the same time it serves as a couple of discourse devices—as an 'evaluator', because it marks the assertion as personal opinion, and as a 'fluency device', because it is a bigger piece stitched into the discourse than the similar phrase, *it was X*. Being a bigger chunk, it gives the speaker more time to plan for the next routine, and thus promotes fluency.

In purpose, it is very similar to the assertion-evaluator that participant B used in the previous conversation. *I'm not sure but I think* is one of the expanded forms of the lexical phrase *I'm (not) (absolutely/pretty) sure/positive/certain (but I think) (that)* X, and certainly allows B more time to gather thoughts than would a minimal form of the same lexical phrase, such as *I think* X, or simply the bald assertion, *it is* X.

It would be unreasonable for a teacher to condemn such fluency devices as linguistic crutches or as verbose, empty filler, for they serve an extremely important function, especially at the beginning and intermediate stages of language learning, of promoting fluency, and of thus motivating learning.

Fluency devices serve not only to give the speaker time to plan subsequent discourse and to promote fluency, they can also serve to distance the speaker from potentially unpleasant information. As squid elude their foe under a cloud of ink, so speakers avoid attack under a cloud of lexical phrase fluency devices. During a (recorded) meeting of the Portland State University Faculty Senate in 1989, the sensitive subject of reduced faculty salaries found its way onto the agenda, and a representative from the Governor's office came to explain what the state had in mind for the University. The representative began with details of the state of the economy and of the legislative process, but as he neared more local matters he began to be less specific. Finally, when the question of faculty salaries could no longer be avoided, the representative began:

> Now having said that, I want to share with you what is on my own mind and, at the same time, I want to make it perfectly clear that, in this context at any rate, I'm one of those who thinks that—and this is purely a personal opinion, and one in fact I'm not sure that the Governor would share—to make it clear that in this climate there may be a general need for reduction.
> (PB, PSU Faculty Senate, 2.6.89)

Such expertise in the use of fluency devices, and of oral formulae in general, rarely goes unrewarded.

3.4   Lexical phrases in transactional discourse

Earlier, various kinds of lexical phrases were illustrated as they function in ordinary conversation. In what follows, the focus will shift from conversation to other types of discourse in which discourse devices play a much larger role than they do in conversation, and correspondingly, social interactional and necessary topic lexical phrases play a smaller role.

3.4.1   Interactional versus transactional discourse

Conversation, interpreted by listening, and written language, interpreted by reading, are to some extent different kinds of discourse. Social conversation is viewed as basically *interactional*, used for working out social relationships, and the resulting discourse is characterized, both in form and function, by this interactional nature. Writing, on the other hand, is basically *transactional*, used for transmitting factual information rather than maintaining social relationships.[17] Thus, its characteristic shape is different.

   Part of knowing a language is knowing how to produce and comprehend interactional and transactional discourse. Production involves two processes, speaking and writing production; likewise, comprehension involves two processes, listening and reading comprehension. Although the processes involved in production and comprehension involve essential similarities from a cognitive point of view, a matter we will take up in Chapter 7, it is important to distinguish the differences in terms of content and shape. Certain features of interactional and transactional discourse are part of both of these processes, but as a general rule conversation deals more with interactional features, whereas written discourse deals more with transactional ones. As we shall see, these remarks with respect to written discourse also hold for certain types of spoken discourse whose purpose is not basically social, such as academic lectures, teacher/student conferences, committee meetings, and the like.

3.4.2   The role of discourse devices

It seems reasonable, then, that since social conversation is mainly interactional, and since written and other sorts of non-social discourse are mainly transactional, they require different sorts of lexical phrases. Namely, the former requires mainly social interactional lexical phrases, and the latter mainly discourse device lexical phrases, because it is the particular function of discourse devices to indicate the overall direction and organization of the informational content of the discourse. Part of pragmatic competence is knowing the functions assigned to lexical phrases that are appropriate to social conversation versus those appropriate to discourse that is basically non-social, and knowing how these functions are differently codified by the various types of lexical phrases.[18]

As noted earlier, however, while interactional and transactional discourse require different categories of lexical phrases to some extent, neither requires exclusively one type or the other. For example, in the conversation given in section 3.3.2, in which the majority of lexical phrases (twenty-four) were of the social interactional and necessary topic categories, a few discourse devices (five) were also interspersed as aids in marking the direction and flow of the overall discourse. In later sections, a more explicit comparison of data from social discourse and from transactional discourse will illustrate the converse tendency for the transactional discourse, in which the majority of lexical phrases are discourse devices that serve an organizing function for the flow of information being transmitted, but in which a few social interactional markers are also interspersed.

3.5   Transactional spoken discourse

Up to this point, the spoken discourse of conversation has been characterized as mainly interactional. However, although social conversation is indeed basically interactional, that is, formed through social interaction, this is not necessarily so for other kinds of spoken discourse. As mentioned briefly in the previous section, other kinds may be basically transactional, or a combination of the two.

The discourse of academic lectures, for instance, is basically transactional in that it is primarily used for transmitting information, but it is secondarily interactional in that it is also used for social maintenance, as with greetings before the lecture begins and partings when the lecture is over. Indeed, although teachers and students are well aware of the transactional nature of discourse in academic lectures, convention dictates that at the very least brief greetings such as *good morning* or *good afternoon* are to be exchanged before the lecture begins. If a teacher were to stride into a classroom, face the students and begin immediately with a topic marker, say *today I want to talk about X*, the student reaction would undoubtedly be one not only of surprise, but also of considerable unease. On the other hand, if a teacher were to prolong the interactional phase by chatting on for fifteen or twenty minutes about the weather, the participants' health, or other topics of social maintenance, the reaction might again be either surprise, or in this case, perhaps restlessness or resentment instead.

Similarly, the discourse of teacher/student conferences, of study groups, of committee meetings, of political meetings, of lectures, of various types of public speeches, of giving directions, of explaining how to do something, and so on, is primarily transactional, though to varying degrees containing interactional discourse as well.

In the previous sections, we outlined the distinction between types of discourse, interactional versus transactional, and between types of lexical phrases that characterize them, social interactional/necessary topics versus discourse devices. Social conversation is basically interactional, and makes more use of social interactional/necessary topic lexical phrases; writing and other non-social discourse is basically transactional, and makes more use of discourse device lexical phrases. But what about spoken discourse that is more transactional than interactional? What characteristic discourse devices occur? It might be expected that spoken discourse that is transactional would parallel written transactional discourse in the form of the discourse devices that occur, but this is not generally the case. In the next section, we explore these differences in greater detail.

3.5.1   Characteristics of discourse devices in spoken transactional discourse

Although transactional spoken discourse and transactional written discourse share the primary purpose of transmitting factual information, and although discourse markers function in the same way in both, it does not follow that these discourse markers are necessarily identical in form. In data collected by the authors, the similarities in the function of lexical phrase markers in transactional spoken and transactional written discourse are not always mirrored by corresponding similarities in the structure of these phrases. Rather, in these two types of discourse the forms of the discourse devices also differ to some extent.

The exact characteristics that typify this distinction in form are somewhat difficult to isolate, however, and in any case are to be found only in some, but not all discourse devices. The features that distinguish at least some of the forms found in these types of discourse seem to be (a) the presence or absence of idiomatic meaning, and/or (b) variability of the lexical phrase frame. For example, in spoken transactional discourse, as in social conversation, one is more likely to find more idiomatic and more variable lexical phrases such as *the upshot is* ____, *but how about* ____?, *the first shot out of the barrel*, whereas in written transactional discourse fixed polyword expressions like *as a result, nevertheless, to begin* are more common.

In addition to this difference in the form of discourse devices that tend to occur, there are, of course, many other differences in spoken and written discourse that are well beyond the scope of this book. As one example, another difference is that in spoken language the syntax in general is typically less structured than in written language, as pointed out by Brown and Yule (1983). This more loosely structured syntax may include false starts, such as *I don't want . . . uh, I would rather have . . .*, repetitions such as *I would rather have . . . rather have this one here*, and various sentence fragments like *got a match?, a troublemaker, that boy, no bananas today.* The speaker may also produce a large number of lexical phrase fluency devices, such as *it seems (to me) that X, you know, by and large, at any rate.*

The point here, with respect to lexical phrases, is that transactional spoken discourse is still spoken discourse, and for the most part it is characterized by the same types of discourse markers found in social conversation, rather than by those found in writing. Undoubtedly, the reason is that in teacher/student exchanges, in study groups, in committee meetings, or in lectures, for instance, maintaining social relationships is also important, even though the primary purpose is conveying factual information.

3.5.2   Spoken versus written discourse devices

These differences between lexical phrases in spoken versus written transactional discourse are often quite striking, and they include those found in markers of logical connection, temporal connection, exemplification, and summary, among others.[19]

Logical connectors:

written	spoken
as a result, therefore	*so, this means that X; the upshot is X; so then ____; what happens is X*
moreover	*that's not all; what's more; not to mention (that also)*
nevertheless, however	*but look at X; but how about ____?; but then again; well yes but ____; I still think that X*

Temporal connectors:

written	spoken
to begin	*let me start with X; the first shot out of the barrel; the first thing is X*
and next	*and then there's X; and how about ____?; another thing is X*
a final/last point	*last but not least; one final thing/point here; before I stop let me add X; the last thing is X*

Exemplifiers:

written	spoken
for example, in other words	*X, something like that; it's (a little) like X; look how X does this; take a look at X; take something like X; maybe if I show you X, that'll clear it up*

Summarizers:

written	spoken
in summary, in conclusion	*remember that this means X, that's (about) all there is to it; in effect ____; to make a long story short; the point is that X; what I'm trying to say is X; in a nutshell; that's about the size of it; OK so* (level intonation)

These examples illustrate marked differences in structure and idiomaticity, despite the similarities in function of these spoken and written lexical phrases in signaling the direction of the discourse. Most noticeably, they illustrate in more detail the difference mentioned briefly above, that the spoken phrases are often somewhat more varied in syntactic complexity. Again, however, bear in mind the qualification that these differences are a matter of degree, for many lexical phrases found in written texts we examined are also common in spoken discourse, including at least some of those given above such as *however, for example, in other words*. On the other hand, many of those we found to be common in spoken discourse do not normally occur in written discourse at all, as for instance: *the*

upshot is X; that's not all; so, this means that X; well yes but ____*;
the first shot out of the barrel; and how about* ____*?; X, something
like that; and so on.*

Other features of discourse devices that are more characteristic of
spoken language are the type of lexical items of which they are
composed, and their morphological shape, as seen in these examples.
The spoken discourse markers can often be distinguished by the
occurrence of such items as *so, well, OK, thing*, idiomatic words and
phrases like *upshot, first shot out of the barrel, the size of it, nutshell*,
and contractions like *there's, it's, that's, I'm*—items perhaps
considered too informal, too conversational to be appropriate for
written discourse. It seems, then, that although transactional spoken
discourse parallels written discourse in the primary purpose of
transmitting factual information, it does not entirely parallel written
discourse in the forms that its discourse devices take.

A further difference between the spoken and written transactional
modes is that lexical phrase markers in spoken discourse serve
additional functions which are not normally found in written texts.
Two of these functions are fluency devices and markers of asides (see
also Chapter 4).

fluency devices

you know; as far as I'm concerned; as you know; well of course
____*; as far as I can tell; by and large; for the most part; it seems
to me that* ____*; as I was saying; I want to say that* ____

asides

*where was I?; (I guess) I got off the track (here); (I guess) X is
beside the point; I'm getting ahead of myself (here); forget about
X; X's not really important; let's get back to the point*

Texts for second language learners, especially writing and reading
texts, usually provide more opportunity for learning the discourse
markers necessary for the comprehension of written discourse. What
is lacking is this same opportunity for learning spoken discourse
markers. Undoubtedly, this gap occurs largely because our second
language research has thus far not provided us with enough
information concerning these structures. It is our hope that the
research findings presented here will help to fill the gap in this long
neglected area.

We will return to detailed examples of spoken transactional
discourse in the following chapter.

3.6   Transactional written discourse

In certain respects, writing is a kind of language production not unlike spoken discourse. The question we raised earlier is whether it is similar enough to speaking to be characterized by the same sort of lexical phrases. What we suggested was that transactional writing shares many of the features that we have described earlier for transactional speech, and though perhaps differing in the amount of information that is interactional and transactional, it employs many of the same sorts of functions and phrases, even though, of course, one difference we noted was that in spoken discourse many of the discourse devices tend to be more conversational in style, whereas, in written discourse they tend to be more formal. Indeed, lexical phrases seem to characterize written language almost as pervasively as they do spoken language. In Chapter 7, in which we turn to teaching written discourse, we will illustrate these phrases and their functions by examining three kinds of writing that most ESL students at the university level become familiar with: a formal paper, an informal letter, and a business letter.

At first, it would seem that the premeditated quality of written language might preclude *any* prefabricated, lexical phrases at all, for the careful planning that is often necessary for writing would seem to filter out such fixed patterns and let through only sentences formed word by word. Secondly, it would seem that the purpose of writing is transactional rather than interactional. Writing, most of us feel, is used for relating facts and conveying other sorts of information rather than for maintaining social relationships, so that even if there were lexical phrases in writing, they would serve none of the interactional functions we have described for conversation.

In this chapter, however, we have suggested that neither of these seems to be the case, either in writing or in the transactional spoken discourse in teacher–student conferences, academic lectures, meetings, and so on. We briefly alluded to the function of lexical phrases in written discourse, noting that although they tend to be more formal in writing, they still maintain relatively similar transactional and interactional functions. Indeed, for all the exhortation from writing teachers for students to avoid cliché and other sorts of prefabrication, writing is full of the sort of set, chunked patterns we have described for speaking. See, for example, the list comparing written and spoken lexical phrases in the previous section. These phrases range from fixed polywords (*for the most part*; *on the other hand*; *as it were*), to relatively fixed phrasal constraints that tie together discourse (*for (an) example/instance*; *at first/the start/onset/ beginning*; *the one(s) that/who/which* X), to larger rhetorical sentence builders for presenting an argument (*whereas X, then Y*; *X is different from/similar to Y in that/because Z*; *this paper/article intends/is designed to* X). Written language, just as spoken, draws from a stock of ready-made phrases which exist in a continuum from the entirely fixed, to the more variable, to language that is newly constructed word by word.

3.6.1   Patterns in writing

Just as spoken language may be both transactional and interactional, so also may written language. Writing starts with dialogue just as speaking does, for it is also directed towards an audience; and even though the dialogue between writer and audience is, in this case, unspoken and distanced, it still forms the context in which words have meaning and strategies for comprehension operate. Writing is still a social event, affected by the social roles of the participants and the purpose of the communication, and serves to bond writers the same way as conversations bond speakers in a speech community. Faigley (1985), for example, describes a 'discourse community' as a group of persons held together by the fact that its members share among themselves *written* exchanges. Informal letters, thank-you notes, and personal writing of this kind are obviously the most interactional sorts of writing, for their main purpose is one of maintaining social relationships.

Other writing, however, even though it is based on the interaction between speaker and audience, is used primarily for the working out and transference of information rather than for maintaining social relationships. Newspaper articles, essays, scientific reports, reviews, and most of the writing required of students in a university, have the purpose of conveying factual information to the reader. In short, writing occurs in a general interactional frame, in the sort of 'discourse community' suggested above, yet its specific, immediate purpose is often transactional.

3.6.2   Characteristics of discourse devices in written discourse

Because most writing is still a mix of the interactional and transactional, the lexical phrases that characterize it reflect this dual purpose. Just as in spoken transactional discourse, lexical phrases that predominate are those that function as discourse devices to signal the overall direction and organization of the discourses, but those for necessary topics and conversational purpose also occur. In signaling the overall direction and organization of the discourse, the discourse devices function to mark high-level transactional information, such as exemplification, relationships between topics, evaluations, qualifications, asides, and so on, and indicate its flow through the discourse. Lexical phrases of conversational maintenance, though playing a much smaller role in writing than in speaking, do not disappear. They are still used to summon the audience before the body of the text begins, as well as to prime and nominate the topic, and to close the discourse. The other maintenance phrases, those for clarifying, checking comprehension, and shifting topics are carefully built into the body of the text and resemble discourse devices more than social interactions.

In the previous section, we noted that the discourse devices in spoken and written discourse are often quite distinct. Likewise, the actual lexical phrases used for these 'purpose' and 'maintenance' functions in writing are usually somewhat distinct from those used in conversation. For example, to nominate or shift a topic in conversation, common lexical phrase markers are such as *(by the way) do you know/remember X?* and *guess what?* These, however, do not usually appear in transactional discourse. Instead, we are more likely to find topic markers and shifters like *let me start with X, what I'd like to do is X*, and so on. Likewise, frequent conversational clarifiers are *how should I put it?, what I mean/I'm trying to say is X*, but in writing these become less personalized *(in this paper/article) X means/signifies/is considered to be/is taken to mean Y*, and many come to resemble exemplifiers, such as *that is to say, what that means is X*, and *in other words*. We will return to a discussion of these particular phrases in our discussion of academic lecture discourse in Chapter 6.

The reason that lexical phrases of maintenance are so different in writing and speaking has to do with the nature of the relationship between the participants in the interaction. Writers are removed from their audience in a way that speakers are not from theirs. Speakers and hearers work jointly, in a rather spontaneous, unplanned manner, to establish meaning inside the immediate context in which the interaction takes place. They can thus rely on shared signals, such as those provided by clarifiers and reinforcers, to regulate the speed and content of the message. Writers do not have such proximate relationships with readers, however, for they write in solitude, anticipating the reaction of their eventual audience. Writing is rather like a conversation in which speakers assume the role of audience in order to judge how much background information and clarifying material needs to be supplied for the message to be properly interpreted. Unlike speakers, writers cannot rely on features of the surrounding context to provide information, nor can they count on sharing assumptions with their readers. They must make certain that the message they write is self-contained and removed from the physical circumstances in which it is written. For that reason, written language is more *explicit* than spoken language. It also has a tendency to be more distant and detached from its audience. The result is that speech is basically fragmented and involved, writing integrated and detached (Chafe 1982).

3.6.3   Integration

Speakers use very small chunks of language when they construct conversations, usually no more than two or three lexical phrases joined to form a response or question, whereas writers, with time to edit and sculpt, produce longer and more complexly integrated utterances. The integration that characterizes written language occurs generally through complexity of noun groups, conjoined parallel phrases, sequences of prepositional phrases, and relative clauses (Brown and Yule 1983). It is particularly signaled by macro-organizers that function to signal clearly distinct levels and patterns of co-ordination and subordination, as described above.

Integration, then, is characterized by complement phrases of assertion which are often preceded by macro-organizers which evaluate the assertion (sentence builders such as *most researchers agree that X, it was important (for them) to X*) by nominalized phrases (*exposure to, assessment of*), and pairs of parallel grammatical categories (*shocked and stunned, on or about, cease and desist*) that operate rather as polywords; by phrasal constraint logical connectors (*as a result of _____, in spite of _____*); by impersonal evaluators (sentence builders such as *as X would have us believe, more important than X (is Y)*); and by subordinate clauses. Conversational fragmentation, on the other hand, contains few logical connectors and little subordination, and is, instead, marked with devices of time and location (*in a few _____, on/over _____*) and intersentential linking conjunctions (*and/but/or*). Such intersentential co-ordination tends to encourage a 'clause-chaining' style in unrehearsed, oral language (Pawley and Syder 1983), which shows up in relatively short lexical phrases that exhibit little structural integration with earlier or later constructions and tend to be tacked on to preceding phrases as the talk unfolds.

3.6.4 Detachment

Writing is also characterized by detachment. Since writing cannot depend on the immediate physical context to flesh out meaning in its message, and since its purpose is often transactional and its subject impersonal, it contains language that exhibits its distance from both writer and audience. This detachment is manifested by such agent-less, passive phrases as *is reflected in, has been noted (by X)*, and by certain literary phrasal constraints, such as *the utmost of* _____, and *is conducive/tantamount to* _____. Conversational involvement, on the other hand, produces lexical phrases of self-reference, such as those evaluators and lexical phrases of assertion that signal the communicator's mental processes (*I wish/feel/realize (that) X*), polywords indicating clarification (*you know, I mean*), and certain fluency devices (*things like that, and so on, at any rate*), phrases also characteristic of speaking and of informal writing.

Notes

1 Many summonses begin with 'pseudo-apologies' (Wardhaugh 1985: 124), expressions such as *excuse me, sorry to bother you, I didn't mean to interrupt but*. When the person to whom the remark is addressed acknowledges with a 'reprieve' — *(oh), that's OK/all right* — the 'intruder' then gets to the topic.

   There are many other ways to summon attention: requests for a certain amount of time (*got a minute/second?*) or object (*got a match/light?*); phrases for role-marked situations (*may I take your order? can I help you? and how are we doing today?*); and self-initiated introductions (*hello, I'm + NAME*).

2 After B responds to A's summons, A does not often go directly into the topic without first framing what will follow by 'topic priming'. If a narrative is to be the topic, A may preface it with a lexical phrase like *I want to tell you something/about X, did I tell you (about X)?*; if a joke, the phrases *have you heard the one about X?, stop me if you've heard this one*; and if simply personal, then lexical phrases of asserting are used, *personally, I think (that) X, if you want my opinion (about X)*.

   Topics will be more difficult for adults to recognize than for children. Children's lives are mostly constrained to the here and now, whereas adults must recognize topics that are much more varied and unpredictable. At the same time, however, adults have learnt strategies that children do not seem to have learnt to the same degree for predicting what the entire discourse or the topic might be like.

3   The easiest (and probably most frequent) way to ask for clarification is to say *huh?* Another is to echo the part that has not been understood with rising intonation. Most adult learners have many different strategies to help clarify the topic; that is, they have learnt to ask for repetitions or clarification in a number of ways.

4   Topic shift is no easy matter, for it almost always occurs when all participants think that the current topic has run its course. New topics are usually linked to previous ones with such phrases as *that reminds me of the time/X, now that you mention it, speaking of that*, or phrases that attempt to return to a previously nominated topic, *to get back to what I was saying, what I was trying to say was (that) (X)*. When a new topic is not related to previous ones, it is introduced by phrases which explicitly mark that fact: *this is really off the subject but X*, etc.

Topic shift may also signal dramatic illocutionary effects, as for example in B's refusal to answer A's question: A: *how old are you?* B: *I'm a very wise person* (Richards 1980).

5   This is a general category that includes interruptions and other such misplacement markers. To repel interruptions, participants usually resort to compounding and subordination to produce chained expressions, or to filling pauses with fluency devices so as not to allow a turn-over. See note 14 for further discussion.

6   Closing must be a co-operative activity, and is one in which we offer some form of compliment (*it's been great/wonderful/fun talking to/seeing/running into you*), or we try to leave the impression that we really want to carry on, but some external condition is forcing our hand (*well, (I've got to get) back to work, I must/I've got to be going, (guess) I'd better let you go, (because I know you're busy)* (Wardhaugh 1985: 156–7).

7   'Speech acts' here are defined more narrowly than they usually are in the literature since they do not include the interactional markers of conversational maintenance. For a detailed discussion of speech act theory, the reader is referred especially to Austin (1962), Searle (1969, 1976, 1979), and Searle and Vanderveken (1985).

8   Ervin-Tripp (1976) argues that non-literal directives—which are the unmarked form for requests between adults—have the routinized sentence frame of 'Modal + *you* + Feasible Action', such as *would/could/can you do X*), and, therefore, do not have to be interpreted by inference on every occasion of utterance.

There are three basic kinds of requests in English: (1) questions, such as Ervin-Tripp's, and others like *do you have the time?*; (2) statements, *I wonder how we are doing for time*, and (3) imperatives, *tell me the time*. Direct imperatives are usually avoided for the reason that the more one's request impinges on someone else, the more delicate and less bald it must be (Tannen 1986). See also Chapter 2.

9   The linguistic forms used for expressing compliments in US middle-class adult society appear to be extremely limited. Over half of nearly 700 compliments collected in a recent study fit the two sentence frames above; and if one adds a third frame, 'Pronoun + *BE* + (intensifier) *(a)* Adjective + Noun Phrase' *(that's really a great tie)*, then 85 per cent of the data can be accounted for! (Manes and Wolfson 1981).

Teachers must prepare for a great deal of intercultural diversity in this speech act, however, in the forms of compliments, in their frequency and in appropriate responses to them.

10   In general conversation, assertions are usually blunted somewhat so that there remains room for maneuver and for saving face. Instead of using straightforward assertion, frames like *it is (a fact/the case that) X, X is right/wrong*, we usually use hedged forms. Personal point of view prefaces, for example, *(personally, I think X, in my opinion)* allow one to assert information without making one responsible for the complete accuracy of it. More indirect forms *(it may be that X, I've heard (tell/it said) that X)* also succeed in distancing the speaker from full responsibility for the assertion. Since these phrases often indicate the degree of commitment speakers have to their assertions, *(as far as I can tell, frankly, to be perfectly honest)* they serve at the same time as 'evaluators', one of the discourse devices. See note 15.

11   Although feelings may run high, strong disagreement is not characteristic of conversation. Phrases that indicate mild disagreement *(I wouldn't say that exactly, yes, but (I think that) X)* are much more frequent than those that suggest clear dissent *(you're/that's wrong/ridiculous)*.

12   Other speech acts, with a few of their characteristic lexical phrases, that a teacher may think valuable to practice are:

Complaining: *sorry, but there's a problem, I hate to mention this, but* X.

Excusing: I *didn't know/realize that* X, *it slipped my mind.*

Denying: *it isn't my fault, I'm not to blame for* X.

Apologizing: *I'm (really/very) sorry about* X, *I won't let it happen again, I offer my (sincerest) apologies.*

13   Learners need to be prepared to talk about a small number of topics they know they will be asked about. The most frequent questions will have to do with who they are, what they do, and where they are from.

14   Essentially, these phrases buy time to help one gather one's thoughts. They not only promote fluency, but also indicate to the hearer that one has not given up, thus serving to rebuff interruptions (turn shifts).

15   Evaluations are closely tied to asserting, for they are phrases that indicate how dogmatically one views the world. Most people avoid certain evaluators like X *is (absolutely) certain/definite* because these make them seem inflexible. They choose instead phrases which allow them and their audience more room for maneuver (*sort/kind of, looks like,* X *may/could be that* Y.) Many such 'evasive' phrases (*in some ways, it depends, that's a difficult question*) are ways of expressing politeness at the same time.

16   It is not unusual that a single lexical phrase should have multiple functions. Speech act theory has also had to allow for the fact that many categories cannot be defined as non-arbitrary and discrete types. Other kinds of multiple function lexical phrases will be discussed in Chapter 4.

17   'Interactional' and 'transactional' correspond to other terms that have been used to describe the same distinction: 'emotive'/ 'referential' (Jakobson 1960); 'interpersonal'/'ideational' (Halliday 1970), and 'social-expressive'/'descriptive' (Lyons 1977). See Brown and Yule (1983) for further discussion.

18   It seems to us unfortunate that language course texts do not usually make these distinctions. ESL reading texts, for instance, focus on presenting the formal discourse devices needed for the

comprehension of reading, and writing texts, likewise, focus on those needed for production. There are, however, no corresponding conversational devices presented in any systematic way for spoken discourse.

It is unlikely that this gap represents any unconscious bias towards 'standard' forms on the part of textbook authors, since ESL texts do often present lessons which include at least a scattering of conversational forms, particularly in grammar or conversation texts. Even in grammar texts for advanced or upper-intermediate students in which most of the examples are more formal, a certain number of idioms or slang terms are included. Fingado *et al.* (1981), for instance, provide dialogues at the beginning of each chapter that illustrate idiomatic phrases such as *crash a party, a drop in the bucket, make it on my own.*
19   Some of these examples also appear in Chapter 2, but there written discourse is not taken into consideration.

4   The organizing function of lexical phrases

4.1   Introduction

The previous chapter included a brief investigation of the role of discourse devices in transactional spoken discourse. Chapter 4 looks in more detail at the essential functions of discourse devices, focusing especially on their role in organizing overall patterns of the informational content. Further areas of inquiry include: how these various lexical phrases produced in transactional discourse help to guide comprehension, how pervasive they are, and how many different types occur. One of the key points mentioned earlier is that lexical phrase discourse markers are not limited to the simple function of signaling relations between adjacent sentences. A much more important function is that of signaling the overall direction of a given discourse.

4.2   Macro-organizers

Markers of the overall direction of discourse we refer to as *macro-organizers* since they signal the organization of high-level information: marking topics, shifts in topic, summary of topic, exemplification, relationships between topics, evaluations, qualifications, and asides.

They are, of course, mostly transactional. They also include two categories that overlap with social interactional markers, marking a topic and shifting a topic, but with the difference that as transactional markers, they also function distinctly as macro-organizers, that is, as markers of the direction of the discourse and the relationships among the parts of the factual content.

As such, they are to be distinguished from markers of social interaction. The difference between the two is quite marked, and it is one that second language learners need to be aware of in order to improve comprehension of transactional discourse. In the following sections of 4.2 and 4.3, we first examine in detail the nature and function of macro-organizers, and then return to a more detailed discussion of the distinction between macro-organizers and markers of social interaction.

4.2.1 The signaling function of macro-organizers in transactional discourse

The text that follows illustrates the signaling function of lexical phrase macro-organizers in transactional discourse. It is (an abbreviated version of) a recorded student/teacher conference; it is thus typical of a basically transactional spoken discourse, with interactional discourse interspersed. Discourse device macro-organizers are underlined, and are also labeled as 'MO'; social interaction markers are not underlined, but are labeled as 'SI'.

(1) S: Hi, (SI) can I come in now? (SI)

(2) T: Oh hi there, (SI) come on in. (SI)

(3) S: Sorry I'm late . . . the bus was, I waited a long time, uh . . ., the bus was late. (SI)

(4) T: Oh that's too bad . . . and this rain too, awful day, just awful. (SI) Anyway, it's OK, we still have time. (SI)

(5) S: Thanks, good (SI) . . . I was, I'm really sorry. (SI)

(6) T: It's OK . . . (SI) how about the paper, the draft I left in your [mail] box? (SI)

(7) S: Yeah, right here . . . here it is. (SI)

(8) T: What I wanted mainly to talk about was, (topic marker: MO) uh . . ., was your part on the review of the literature. It seems to me that (evaluation: MO) here . . . you just list things, that here you list all this stuff you read, but you don't really discuss it.

(9) S: Huh? I'm not sure what you mean. I do discuss it . . . see, in this part here, I talk about it.

(10) T: Well, you sort of do. (qualification: MO) Here, you say that . . . ah yeah, you say these theories are the leading ones, in the current literature these are important. However, (relationship: MO) that's not all you need to say here, you need to say that these are competing theories, or at least (qualification: MO) say why they're different, and also (relationship: MO) you need to say which you choose to base your study on. Not only that

(relationship: MO) you have to say why you support that one . . . you need to say why. OK? Do you see?

(11) S: Yeah, I guess so . . . OK I'll try.

(12) T: <u>OK so</u> (level intonation, no pause; summary: MO) you <u>need</u> to do more than just list these and tell that they're important, you need to discuss them more and say why you're basing your study on a certain one. OK, now, . . . (falling intonation + pause; topic shift: <u>MO) I also</u> <u>wanted to talk to you about</u> (topic shift: MO) your <u>hypotheses. I don't think</u> (evaluation: MO) they are written well <u>enough, ah</u> . . ., they're not quite clear enough. <u>How about 1 and 4?</u> (exemplification: MO) <u>They seem to me</u> (evaluation: MO) to contradict each other.

(13) S: Oh . . . yeah, that isn't what I mean . . . I guess maybe they do . . . I guess so.

(14) T: <u>OK so</u> (level intonation, no pause; summary: MO) you <u>need</u> to state each one more clearly. Get right to the point . . .[1]

Although this discourse is basically a transactional one, concerning a draft of the student's thesis, the exchanges in (1–7) are all social interactional. They include typical summons and response greetings, *hi, oh hi there*; request and compliance, *can I come in now?*, *come on in*; apology and acceptance, *sorry I'm late, it's OK*; gratitude *thanks, good*; and question and answer, *how about the paper . . .?, yeah, right here . . .* All of these are social interactions which provide the framework of conversational maintenance and conversational purpose. Without them, the transactional phase of the discourse, beginning with (8), would seem abrupt, awkward, and rude.

The transactional phase begins in (8) with the teacher, who marks the first topic with the macro-organizer *what I wanted mainly to talk about was X*. After the teacher expands on the topic, evaluating (*it seems to me that*) the problem of the student's lack of discussion, and after the student expresses some confusion in (9), the teacher responds in (10) by qualifying her previous statement, marked by the phrasal constraint *(you) sort of ____*. The qualifier is also classified as a marker of high-level information, an important guidepost in that it signals a modification of what the speaker has previously stated about the topic. *Sort of* can sometimes be used simply as a hedge, but in this case it genuinely qualifies information given previously by the speaker: the student did in fact discuss the theories; she just did not discuss them in the required manner. The macro-organizer function of qualifiers is perhaps clearer with common qualifier markers like *or at least*, the second qualifier the teacher uses in (10). Other common qualifiers are *it depends on X, the catch (here) is, it's only in X that Y*.

The other macro-organizers in (10) are all 'relators', that is, those lexical phrases that signal relationships between high-level information. *However* signals a contrast between what the student has written as opposed to what is still necessary to write on this topic; *and also* and *not only that* signal addition of similar material, namely essential sub-topics that must be added to the discussion on the review of the literature. At the end of (10) the teacher pauses for a check on the student's comprehension, *OK?, do you see?*, and returns to transactional discourse only after the student's affirmative response, *yeah, I guess so* in (11).

In (12) the speaker returns to transactional discourse by summing up the points made previously, signaling summary with the macro-organizer *OK so*, spoken with level intonation and no pause. This lexical phrase marker is distinctly different in function from the next one that follows, the second MO in (12), *OK, now, . . .*, spoken with falling intonation and pause (falling intonation indicated by commas and pause by three dots). The latter is not a signal of summary, but rather of topic shift: it signals the close of the previous topic and the shift to a new topic, namely, the student's hypotheses. In data collected by the authors, these two lexical phrases, with distinctly different functions, are especially frequent in transactional discourse.[2]

4.2.2   Double markers

In this particular discourse, the topic shifter *OK, now, . . .* in (12), is immediately followed by another topic shifter, *I also wanted to talk to you about ____*, with the effect that the topic shift is marked twice. While double markers for topic shifts, summaries, and so on, are not uncommon, single markers are more common. When double markers do occur, they are often combinations involving *OK so* or *OK, now, . . .* as the first member in the pair, though these phrases occur as single markers as well. In (12), for instance, *OK, now, . . .* alone, that is, *OK, now, . . .* (falling intonation + pause) *your hypotheses* would also be sufficient to mark the topic shift.

It seems reasonable to assume that the *so* and *now* members of the phrases also contribute to distinguishing between the functions of summarizing versus topic shifting, for it does not seem that this difference is signaled by intonation alone. That is, the phrase *OK now*, spoken with level intonation and no pause, does not occur in our data at all, and if it did it is hard to imagine how it could signal summary. The meaning of *now*, as with other time words like *first*, *next*, and the like, would normally be associated with shifting forward to a new topic or item. Conversely, the semantics of *so* seem compatible with summarizing but not with moving forward to a new topic. It is furthermore relatively common to find *so* and *now* ellipted in these phrases, with the same intonation pattern remaining intact, and with no resulting difference in meaning or function. Thus, *OK* with *so* ellipted and with level intonation and no pause can be used to signal summary, and *OK* with *now* ellipted and with falling intonation and pause can be used to signal topic shift. For non-native speakers these functions are not at all evident from the forms of either the full phrases or the ellipted versions, and it is thus especially important that teachers be aware of the need to include them in classroom instruction and practice.

Three other macro-organizers occur in (12), *I don't think X*, which signals the speaker's evaluation of previously mentioned material, *how about X?*, which signals exemplification of previously mentioned material, and *they seem to me (to) X*, which signals evaluation of the examples just pointed out. Following a statement of acceptance by the student in (13), in (14), the teacher sums up points discussed on the second topic, the summary this time signaled by *OK so*, spoken with level intonation and no pause, as a single marker of summary.

4.3   Levels of discourse: co-ordination and subordination macro-organizers

Up to this point, macro-organizers have been analyzed as though they appeared in linear order in a discourse. Transactional discourse, however, whether spoken or written, does not typically proceed in a linear fashion. Macro-organizers are categorized as such because their function is to signal high-level information, but this information is not on a single linear plane. In the framework of the discourse fragment discussed above, for instance, there are basically two topics: the review of the literature and the hypotheses in the student's thesis. The discussion of each is followed by a summary. These form a co-ordinate level, equal in importance. The other information is on a subordinate level: contrast and addition of important material, sub-topics relating to the review of the literature, evaluation of previous material, and examples to illustrate previous material.

In order to reflect this division of the high-level information, macro-organizers may be distinguished further as co-ordinate, or *global* markers, and subordinate, or *local* markers. Global macro-organizers are those which signal the introduction of a topic at the beginning of a discourse, the shift to a new topic, and the summary of a topic. Local macro-organizers also mark sequencing or importance of high-level information, but they do so at specific points *within* the overall framework set by the global macro-organizers. They include markers of exemplification, relations between topics, sub-topics, or other subordinate material, evaluative comments, qualification of previous material, and asides. The categories given below reflect this distinction between global and local markers.

Global (co-ordinate) macro-organizers:

Topic markers

what I (mainly) wanted to talk about/tell you about was X; let's look at X; what do you think of X?; have you heard/did you hear about X?; let me start with X; the first thing is ____

Topic shifters

OK, now, . . .; (with falling intonation + pause); *that reminds me of X; I'd like/I wanted to ask you about X; by the way; this is off the subject but X*

Summarizers

OK so; so then (both with level intonation, no pause); *in a nutshell; that's about it/all there is to it; remember that this means X; in effect; to make a long story short; what I'm trying to say is X*

Local (subordinate) macro-organizers:

Exemplifiers

how about X?; X, something like that; it's like X; in other words; for example/instance; to give (you) an example

Relators

none the less; however; and also; not only X but (also) Y; it has to do with X; same way here; but look at ____; *the other (thing) X is Y*

Evaluators (commitment to a point of view)

I think/don't think that X; as far as I know/can tell; (there's) no doubt that X; I'm absolutely (positive/certain/sure) that X; X might not work

Qualifiers

it/that/you sort of ____; the catch is; it depends on X; it's only in X that Y; it doesn't mean that X; that's true but X; at least in ____

Asides

where was I?; I guess I got off the track here; I guess that's beside the point; I'm getting ahead of myself here

In short, this additional division into global and local macro-organizers is necessary in order to distinguish main topics from the explanations, sub-topics, examples, relations, etc., which serve as development and support for the topics. Local organizers are thus, in a sense, subordinate to global organizers. If we picture a discourse in outline form, the main topics and their summaries form, say, the left margin capital A, B, C, and so on, and the subordinate explanations, sub-topics, examples, relations, form the indented 1, 2, 3, etc.

The categories of macro-organizers differ somewhat from the categories discussed in the previous chapter, section 3.5, concerning differences between written and spoken discourse. Some general categories, such as logical connectors, are subsumed under the categories given here, since as macro-organizer signals in transactional discourse, they serve the more specific functions of relators, evaluators, or qualifiers. Likewise, temporal connectors appear as topic markers and topic shifters.

With respect to the nature of the categories included within the global co-ordinate the local subordinate levels, we justify including the category relators as macro-organizers because they signal sequencing, restatement of important points, and comparison or contrast of topics or ideas. Of course, some of these can also be used for low-level links between adjacent sentences, but that is not a concern here. Evaluators are included because they signal the relative importance of topics, examples, and other points. Asides signal the converse, that is, they signal which information is not important. For second language learners especially, it is equally essential to know which information is important to pay attention to, and which is not.

Referring back to the lexical phrase types defined in Chapter 2, discourse devices that function as macro-organizers range from polywords such as *OK so,   OK, now, . . .,   in a nutshell*; to phrasal constraints like *as far as I know/can tell, how about ____?,   X, something like that*; and sentence builders like *what I (mainly) wanted to talk about/tell you about was X, it's only in X that Y, I'm absolutely (positive/certain/sure) that X.*

4.3.1   Levels and patterns: macro-organizers versus interactional discourse markers

In the previous discussion we examined the role of macro-organizers in signaling levels of discourse. In particular, we looked at ways in which they do more than just signal the relationship between one piece of discourse and another. As the discourse progresses, they impose patterns of organization, patterns including levels, that facilitate top-down processing in the comprehension of transactional discourse. In this section, we look at how these patterns of organization are a particular feature of transactional discourse that distinguishes it from interactional discourse.

In terms of the categories set up in the first part of this chapter, macro-organizers appear to have the same functions as the discourse devices in conversation, and of social interactional markers. As macro-organizers in transactional discourse, however, the range and extent of these functions are markedly different from those occurring in social interactional discourse. For example, two of these sets of global macro-organizers fall in with two of the categories that also appear as markers in social interactions, namely, marking a topic (*I wanted (mainly) to talk about/tell you about X*), shifting a topic (*that reminds me of X*). As noted earlier, in transactional discourse they function distinctly as macro-organizers in that they signal the direction of the discourse and the relationships among the parts of the factual content.

An equally important function is to further mark the parts of the content as to co-ordinate and subordinate levels. That is, global discourse devices function as markers of co-ordinate-level main topics and summaries of these topics, whereas local discourse devices function as markers of subordinate-level supporting material. Examples of local discourse devices include exemplifiers (*how about ____?*), relators (*it has to do with X*), qualifiers (*it depends on X*), evaluators (*I think that X*). They have the same *basic* functions as discourse devices in conversation (signaling summary, examples, relations, etc.), but again, the range and extent of these functions are different.

These functional aspects, then, are key features that distinguish macro-organizers from the otherwise similar discourse devices that appear in social interactional discourse. That is so because in interactional discourse, these markers do not normally function to signal clearly distinct levels and patterns of co-ordination and subordination, as they do in transactional discourse, nor do they mark inter-relationships in the content in such a structured way. In ordinary social interactions, the primary purpose is not transmitting factual information but expressing social relations and personal attitudes, and thus, whatever content is conveyed is presented in a looser, less structured form, one in which a clear pattern of the interrelationships of factual content and of co-ordinate and subordinate levels cannot easily be discerned.

These differences show up clearly if we compare a typical interactional conversation, such as the one given in Chapter 3, with the transactional portion of the discourse fragment given earlier in the present chapter. Social interactional markers are designated as SI, discourse devices as DD, and transactional macro-organizers as MO; the discourse markers relevant to the organization of content are underlined.

Conversation: (primarily interactional)

A: Hey, Sally. What's up? (summons: SI)
B: Hi, Bill. How are you doing? (response: SI)
A: Pretty well, thanks. (response: SI) By the way, (TOPIC MARKER: SI) did you hear about my new car? (topic nomination: SI)
B: No kidding, (response: SI) a new car? (clarification: SI)
A: Uh huh. (response: SI) I bought an old Volvo the day before yesterday.
B: Hey, that's great. (response: SI) How much did it cost you?
A: It seems to me that (EVALUATOR: DD) it was a really good buy, (assertion: SI) and what's more, (conjunction: DD) there isn't anything wrong with it (assertion: SI) — as far as I can tell, (EVALUATOR: DD) at any rate. (fluency device: DD)
B: Yeah, it's a beauty; (response: SI) you were lucky to find it. (assertion: SI) Oh, guess what? (TOPIC SHIFTER: SI) Word has it that Jack just got a big promotion. (assertion: SI) Did you hear about it? (question: SI)
A: Yes, I heard. (answer: SI) The other thing I heard is that

(RELATOR: DD) he gets to move into a fancy big office (assertion: DD) on the top floor.

B: No kidding, that's great. (response: SI) Well, I've got to run now. (closing: SI) See you later. (parting: SI)

A: Well, then, (closing: SI) so long for now. (parting: SI)

Teacher/student conference: (primarily transactional)

T: What I wanted mainly to talk about was (TOPIC MARKER: MO) your part on the review of the literature. It seems to me that (EVALUATOR: MO) here you just list things, that here you list all this stuff you read, but you don't really discuss it.

S: Huh? I'm not sure what you mean. (clarification: SI) I do discuss it . . . see, in this part here, I talk about it.

T: Well, you sort of do. (QUALIFIER: MO) Here, you say that these theories are the leading ones, in the current literature these are important. However, (RELATOR: MO) that's not all you need to say here, you need to say that these are competing theories, or at least (QUALIFIER: MO) that they are different theories, and also (RELATOR: MO) you need to say which you choose to base your study on. Not only that (RELATOR: MO) you have to say why you support that one . . . you need to say why. OK? Do you see? (comprehension check: SI)

S: Yeah, I guess so (response: SI) OK I'll try.

T: OK so (level intonation, no pause; SUMMARY: MO) you need to do more than just list these and tell that they're important, you need to discuss them more and say why you're basing your study on a certain one. OK, now, . . . (falling intonation + pause; TOPIC SHIFTER: MO) I also wanted to talk to you about (TOPIC SHIFTER: MO) your hypothesis. I don't think (EVALUATOR: MO) they are written well enough, they're not quite clear enough. How about (EXEMPLIFIER: MO) 1 and 4? They seem to me (EVALUATOR: MO) to contradict each other.

S: Oh yeah, that isn't what I mean . . . I guess maybe they do, I guess so. (accepting: SI)

T: OK so (level intonation, no pause; SUMMARIZER: MO) you need to state each one more clearly. Get right to the point . . .

One of the clearest differences between the two types is that in the transactional discourse the speaker responsible for imparting the factual information is the one who uses most of the macro-organizers. The teacher uses the topic marker (*what I wanted mainly to talk about was X*), topic shifters (*OK, now . . ., I also wanted to talk to you about X*), summarizers (*OK so*), exemplifiers (*how about _____?*), qualifiers (*sort of _____, or at least*), evaluators (*it seems to me that X, they seem to me X, I don't think X*), and relators (*however, and also*). The student's contributions are asking for clarification (*huh?, I'm not sure what you mean*), responding (*yeah, I guess so*), and accepting (*I guess so*).

In the interactional discourse, on the other hand, speaker A uses a topic shifter (*by the way*) in order to nominate a topic, and speaker B then also uses a topic shifter (*oh, guess what?*). At the same time, speaker B is also using it as a means of taking a turn in the conversation. Unlike transactional discourse, neither speaker uses two or more topic shifters to switch to a new topic before the hearer has made some contribution to the previous topic. During the exchange on the first topic, speaker A uses two evaluators (*it seems to me, as far as I can tell*), and during the exchange on the second topic, speaker B uses a relator (*the other thing X is Y*). In contrast, the teacher in the transactional discourse uses a full array of discourse markers, including those like summarizers, which do not normally occur in interactional discourse, and exemplifiers, which are at least much less frequent in interactional discourse.

These differences in the way the markers occur and in the frequency with which they occur result in distinct differences in the pattern of the overall discourse. Transactional discourse is much more highly structured, with clear co-ordinate and subordinate levels, and with more clearly patterned relationships within the subordinate levels; interactional discourse is more loosely structured, with much less patterned relationships. Put another way, social interactional discourse is 'random', whereas transactional discourse is usually 'planned'. One major reason is that in the types of transactional discourse considered here the string of factual information is often lengthy and requires an organized framework, discernible to the hearer, in order to facilitate comprehension. Macro-organizers are the primary markers of this organizational pattern. As the discourse progresses, they signal the way in which the factual information is being organized.

The markers in interactional discourse do not function in the same way. Instead, they function mainly to maintain the social interaction. They do occur as signals to the hearer that a topic is being changed, that a piece of information is being evaluated or being related to another piece, but their use is kept to a minimum because social interactional discourse does not normally involve lengthy chunks of factual information that require a clearly organized framework to aid the hearer in comprehension.

These differences can be illustrated more graphically by listing the markers from the discourse fragments in the form of an outline.

Conversation

A. Topic marker   *by the way*
    1. Evaluator   *it seems to me that* _____
    2. Evaluator   *as far as I can tell*

B. Topic shifter   *oh, guess what?*
    1. Relator   *the other thing I heard is that*

Student/teacher conference

A. Topic marker   *what I mainly wanted to talk about was X*
    1. Evaluator   *it seems to me that X*
    2. Qualifier   *(you) sort of* _____
    3. Relator   *however*
      a. Qualifier   *or at least*
    4. Relator   *and also*
    5. Relator   *not only that*

B. Summarizer   *OK so*

C. Topic shifter   *OK, now, . . . I also wanted to talk to you about* _____
    1. Evaluator   *I don't think*
    2. Exemplifier   *how about* _____*?*
      a. Evaluator   *they seem to me*

D. Summarizer   *OK so*

For these reasons we use the term 'macro-organizer' to refer only to the topic markers and shifters, summarizers, exemplifiers, relators, evaluators, and qualifiers as they function to signal the organization of transactional discourse. For these categories as they function in interactional discourse, we use the more general terms 'discourse device' and 'social interactional marker'. Similarly, we reserve the terms 'global' and 'local' only for macro-organizers.

4.3.2   Category divisions

Because of the framework of most transactional discourse, including the global/local levels of information, the category labels of macro-organizers reflect divisions into functions that are somewhat different from most traditional ones. Given our perspective on functions, the divisions are different because the functions themselves impose the particular categories. Traditional categories of 'connectors', for instance, distinguish between logical connectors, temporal connectors, and spatial connectors. These traditional categories are among those we list as dicourse devices in conversation. But with respect to transactional discourse, these category labels do not reveal whether their members function as macro-organizers or not, nor whether they function to signal co-ordinate as opposed to subordinate information. Yet, depending on context, these connectors sometimes function as macro-organizers, and sometimes only as signals of low-level relations between adjacent sentences; and if macro-organizers, their co-ordinate or subordinate function depends on how they 'divide up' the discourse.

As an example, the logical connector *however* may function as a macro-organizer to signal a contrast between high-level information, as *however* does in the recorded discourse of the teacher/student conference given earlier. In this case, it signaled the contrast between what had already been written on the topic of the literature review, and the necessary sub-topics still to be written. On the other hand, *however* may signal only a low-level contrast between adjacent sentences, as in the following discourse fragment taken from a discussion of a disagreement between a department head and a dean:

> I think he's bitten off more than he can chew this time . . . don't quote me on that, however.

In this case, *however* signals only a contrast between adjacent sentences, and not a contrast between sub-topics or other high-level information.

Connectors that often function as macro-organizers, whether logical, temporal, or spatial, are grouped under the general heading 'relators', along with other macro-organizers that serve the similar function of signaling high-level relations in a discourse, namely, those like *and also, not only that (but)* ____, *it has to do with X, same way here*, and so on. The other categories involve similar considerations, and are thus meant to reflect the most representative examples and the most inclusive of the particular functions in question.

The main consideration in transactional discourse thus far has been the analysis of those markers that signal pieces of high-level information in discourse and the relations between these pieces, and very little has been said about signals of low-level information. In section 4.4, we will return to a more detailed discussion of the importance of distinguishing between the two.

4.3.3 Processing strategies: top-down and bottom-up

As Chaudron and Richards (1986), among others, have pointed out, macro discourse markers are important because they facilitate 'top-down' processing by initiating the hearer's or reader's expectations and predictions about the discourse, expectations and predictions which are then confirmed and supported by the use of successive discourse signals. Top-down processing also makes use of real-world knowledge and reference to various previous experience which help shape the listener's or reader's expectations and help him or her to make predictions and inferences about what will follow in the discourse. For example, on encountering the topic of 'taking a language exam', the listener or reader refers to knowledge about participants and their roles and purposes in the situation, and the typical procedures followed by language teachers, typical participation by students, and the consequences involved.

Top-down processing is in contrast to 'bottom-up' processing, which refers to processing based on incoming data that is analyzed, categorized, and interpreted on the basis of information in the data. Bottom-up processes analyze small bits of discourse such as individual lexical items, which are analyzed by assigning them grammatical status on the basis of syntactic and morphological cues, or such as the syntax and the meanings of lexical items, which serve as the basis for assigning topics.

Although comprehension is viewed as a combination of both bottom-up and top-down processing, top-down processing is critical because it 'enables the listener or reader to by-pass some aspects of bottom-up processing' (Chaudron and Richards 1986:113), and because it allows much faster, more efficient comprehension of the intended message. Hence, the crucial role of macro-organizers in facilitating top-down processing in comprehension cannot be over-emphasized. These remarks apply to both global and local macro-organizers, for local markers also signal sequencing or importance of high-level information, even though this information is subordinate with respect to the overall framework set by the global, main topic markers.

4.3.4   Textbook models

While typical listening comprehension models in the current literature often emphasize the importance of top-down processing, this emphasis is not necessarily found in language texts intended for the classroom. ESL models, for instance, too often assume that all details must be attended to, that small details must be discriminated.[3]

In a top-down, discourse model, however, the listener may begin with small discriminations, but once the topic is identified, can then begin to predict on the basis of past discourse, shared information, and real-world knowledge. Second language speakers can learn to make these predictions based not just on details, but on larger units — units which are often signaled by global or local macro-organizers. Otherwise, they may become so preoccupied with phonic/morphologic/syntactic detail that important parts of the macro-structure message are lost.

As one example, ESL teachers often complain that even advanced-level students sometimes have difficulty in understanding directions. This is especially so for directions, say, for homework assignments that are given orally, but it also applies to written directions for homework assignments, or for exam questions. The problem may well be that students have learnt to rely too heavily on bottom-up processing, on attending to the details in the incoming data, such as individual lexical items and their meanings, and have not been given sufficient instruction and practice with the discourse devices which signal the direction of discourse and the relations within its macro-structure.

4.4   Micro-organizers

Macro-organizers, as signals of high-level information in trans-actional discourse, whether spoken or written, are distinguished from signals of low-level information often found in interactional discourse, such as *uh huh*, *well*, *I see*, *yeah*, *sure*, which are often used simply as pause fillers (see Meyer *et al.* 1980), and which facilitate bottom-up processing by giving the hearer more time to process a given piece of discourse. Other types of these low-level signals, or *micro-organizers*, are lexical phrase fluency devices such as *you know*, *it seems to me*, used by speakers to allow more time to plan for the next routine, thus promoting fluency. Still others include conjunctions, which serve to indicate relations among adjacent sentences. Although some are single-word conjunctions like *and* and *but*, others are lexical phrase discourse devices such as *however, and then, and so, on the other hand*, and *moreover*. These micro-organizers are not to be confused with local macro-organizers, which function as signals of high-level information such as exemplification, evaluation, qualification, and the like, information that serves as supporting examples, explanation, clarification, etc., for the main topics in the discourse.

The main difference is that, as intersentential connectors, micro-organizers do not signal divisions or relations among high-level pieces of information like global topics, sub-topics, summaries, or local examples, evaluations, qualifications, and so on. They signal only low-level relations between clauses or between adjacent sentences. An example, mentioned briefly above, is the discourse fragment taken from a discussion of a disagreement between a department head and a dean:

> I think he's bitten off more than he can chew this time ... don't quote me on that, however.

The lexical phrase *however* does not signal a contrast between main topics or related ideas in the conversation. That is, the topic under discussion, namely, a certain action of the department head, is not shifted to a new topic at all, that is, not shifted to the topic of quotation in itself. After the speaker's evaluation of the topic is given, as signaled by *I think, however* signals only that this evaluation is not to be quoted, as opposed to the normal transactional (or interactional) discourse situation in which the hearer is free to quote from information given by the speaker.

4.4.1   Macro/micro distinctions

In their important study, Chaudron and Richards (1986) explored the effects of discourse markers on the listening comprehension of second language learners. Chaudron and Richards also make the macro/micro distinction between discourse signals, and they found that macro-organizers, or in their terms 'macro-markers', did lead to better recall of the content in video taped natural lectures (presented to ESL university students), whereas 'micro-markers' did not.

Their video taped lectures were presented in four different versions: the first was a 'baseline' version which did not include any special signals of discourse organization or linking between sentences; the second contained micro-organizers of intersentential relations only; the third contained macro-organizers signaling major

propositions within the lecture; and the fourth contained a combination of macro- and micro-organizers. The four versions were then
assigned at random to different classes in the subject groups. Their
results, which were consistent across groups of pre-university and
university students, illustrated that the higher-order macro-
organizers signaling major transitions and emphasis in the lectures
were a significant factor in successful recall of the lecture.

They suggest that the reason that micro-organizers do not aid the
learner's retention of discourse content is that they probably do not
add enough content to make the subsequent information more
salient or meaningful. On the other hand, macro-organizers aid the
learner's retention of discourse content because they are explicit
expressions of the organization of the information presented.

Their study is especially significant in that it illustrates the importance of distinguishing between macro- and micro-organizers, and it
underscores the importance of focusing on macro-organizers in
second language classroom activities and instructional materials.
One major reason is that, as mentioned earlier, macro-organizers
facilitate top-down processing.

In our lexical phrase approach we further divide macro-organizers
into global- and local-level categories. In Chapter 6, this distinction is
shown to be especially crucial in the comprehension of academic
lectures, and particularly so for second language learners.

4.4.2   Macro/micro forms and functions

Another difference of the lexical phrase approach is in categorizing
macro-organizers according to their various discourse functions.
Although previous studies have subdivided micro-organizers into
functional categories, no previous attempt has been made to similarly
subdivide macro-organizers into functional categories. Chaudron
and Richards, for example, list five categories of micro-organizers:
segmentation markers such as *well*, *OK*, *now*; temporal markers
such as *at that time*, *and*, *after this*; causal markers such as *so*, *then*,
because; contrast markers such as *both*, *but*, *only*; and emphasis
markers such as *of course*, *you can see*, *you see*. But since macro-
organizers are the ones that second language learners need most to
learn, it is even more important that they be sorted out according to
discourse function.

The lexical phrase approach also yields somewhat different results
with respect to the macro/micro distinction itself. Although
Chaudron and Richards refer to function, the macro/micro distinc-

tions they make appear to be based more on form, that is, length of phrase or syntactic complexity, or perhaps both. The micro-organizers are all short, non-complex phrases, ranging from one word to four; the macro-organizers are mostly long, syntactically complex phrases, the shortest being a three-word phrase.

As we indicated in the previous chapter, both form and function must be considerations in a complete description of language in spoken transactional discourse, and that form alone is not a reliable criterion. It was found that the lexical phrase polyword *however*, for instance, did function as a micro-organizer in contexts where it signaled the relation between adjacent sentences, but it also functioned as a macro-organizer in contexts where it signaled the relation between high-level pieces of information like sub-topics. The micro-organizer function of *however* was illustrated by the sentence, *don't quote me on that, however*, linking this sentence as a contrast to a previous statement, and the macro-function of *however* was illustrated in the fragment taken from a teacher/student conference in which *however* signaled a contrasting relationship between high-level information.

4.4.3 Phrase length

Our reassignment of some of these phrases into more than one category in no way diminishes the importance of the Chaudron and Richards study. The differences are mentioned here only because our categorization of some of these phrases might otherwise be confusing, given the somewhat different framework of a lexical phrase perspective. To give a more specific illustration of the major role that form seems to have played in their study, of the twenty-six micro-organizers listed, more than two-thirds are one-word markers: *well, OK, now*, etc., for segmentation; *so, then, because*, for causal; and so on. With one four-word exception, *on the other hand*, for contrast, the remainder are all two- or three-word lexical phrases: *after this, for the moment*, for temporal; *of course, you can see*, for emphasis; and so on.

In contrast, of the twenty-five macro-organizers, more than two-thirds range in length from four words to nine words: for example, *the next thing was, one of the problems was, you probably know something about that already, what I'm going to talk about today is something*. Some of their examples are realigned below to illustrate some of these differences.

Micro-organizers	Macro-organizers
as you know	*you probably know that*
	you probably know something about that already
	we'll see that
now	*the next thing was*
	you can imagine what happened next
	our story doesn't finish here
OK	*this/that was how*
	what we've come to by now was that
after this	*what (had) happened (then/after that) was (that)*
you can see (emphasis)	*here was a big problem*
	it's really very interesting that

Thus, to the extent that length of phrase may be a factor in distinguishing, in part, among lexical phrases, it appears to be associated mainly with the codification of spoken versus written style, and not with the codification of macro-organizers versus micro-organizers.

In this respect, it is important to bear in mind that the syntactic complexity or length of a given lexical phrase as it is actually realized in discourse utterances, is not necessarily a factor in *assigning* a particular function to a particular lexical phrase. That is, as outlined in Chapter 1, a seemingly complex, lengthy phrase is generally only the manifestation of a syntagmatically simple yet paradigmatically flexible lexical phrase frame. For example, in the fragment of interactional discourse given earlier, the simple lexical phrase frame *the other (thing) X is Y* is realized as *the other thing I heard is that . . .*, but as we shall see in later chapters, this same frame is variously realized as *the other thing I think I should mention is that . . ., the other person involved in this affair is . . . .*

4.4.4   Dual functions

As the discussion above suggests, while the data from transactional discourse indicates that length of phrase or syntactic complexity are factors that may in some cases further distinguish among types of lexical phrases which serve the same function (or different functions) in discourse, these factors do not always indicate what type of function a lexical phrase performs. Polywords such as *however*, and two-word lexical phrases like *OK, now, . . ., OK so*, can function as macro-organizers signaling topic shift or summary, as shown in the teacher/student discourse fragment given earlier. Other two-to-three-word lexical phrases also very often serve as macro-organizers, the difference in function sometimes determined by context.

As emphasized in earlier chapters, the syntactic scope of lexical phrases is quite variable: they range from short phrases to phrases or full clauses of widely varying lengths—though, of course, based on relatively simple basic lexical phrase frames.

The polyword *however* was given earlier as an illustration that some lexical phrases can serve a dual function as either macro-organizers or micro-organizers, depending on context. The alignment of the phrases in the two columns above provides further illustration of lexical phrases that can serve a dual function. Some phrases in the left-hand column, listed as micro-organizers, can, in addition, serve the same function as the right-hand column macro-organizer counterparts, and sometimes vice versa. That is, *as you know* does not appear to be distinct in function from *you probably know that* or *you probably know something about that already*. Conversely, *the next thing was* or *you can imagine what happened next* could just as well serve the same function as *now*, which is categorized as a micro-organizer signaling segmentation. Similarly, *after this* and its macro-organizer counterpart, *what (had) happened (then/after that) was (that)*, seem to differ only in length and complexity, not necessarily in function. The same appears to hold for *you can see* and its counterparts. Again, in the comprehension of discourse, the function of a lexical phrase cannot always be determined by form alone.

In sum, the lexical phrase approach focuses more on function as the criterion for distinguishing between micro- and macro-organizers. Some lexical phrases function either as micro- or as macro-organizers only; others function as both. Thus, while phrases like *however* can serve as one or the other, depending on intonation, others like, say, *by and large* seem to function only as macro-type fluency devices.

This approach also provides a heuristic for assigning specific functional categories to the macro-organizers themselves—a type of categorization not previously attempted in the literature.

In Chapters 3 and 4, we have focused on the functions of lexical phrases in discourse, and on their organizing role in transactional discourse. In the following chapters in Part Two, we turn to practical classroom application, and suggest ways in which students' knowledge of lexical phrases can lead to dramatic improvement in speaking, listening, writing, and reading skills, particularly in the problem areas of conversing in extended discourse, of listening and note-taking in academic lectures, and of advanced writing and reading.

Notes

1　In this abbreviated version, the more lengthy discussion of further topics and the closings and partings are not included. The portion provided is intended to serve only as illustration of the various functions of macro-organizers.

2　While *OK so* as a marker of summary may occasionally occur in interactional discourse, *OK, now, . . .* as a marker of topic shift apparently does not. The reason, perhaps, is that *OK, now, . . .* with falling intonation and pause would seem too abrupt and authoritative for social discourse.

3　This is in contrast to current models in ESL texts on reading. Many reading texts are based on processing models which emphasize the importance of both kinds of processing, and which are incorporated into schema theory.

PART TWO
Applications for language teaching

5 Teaching spoken discourse: conversation

5.1 Introduction

In Chapter 5, our concern will be teaching lexical phrases as production, and our emphasis will be that teaching speaking means teaching conversation rather than teaching isolated pieces of phonics and syntax, and that conversation is discourse that is formed through social interaction. Thus, the focus will be on lexical phrases as they function in conversation. Likewise, in Chapters 6 and 7, the emphasis will be on teaching lexical phrases for comprehension and production, and the function of lexical phrases in discourse will be basic to our analysis of comprehension and of writing and reading.

Learning to comprehend and produce a language means understanding how the parts of language function as parts of a discourse. In other words, learning to speak means learning to converse. Students need to learn words and sentences not as isolated, planned answers to classroom exercises, but rather to learn how to use these structures to create the flow and purpose of a spontaneously unfolding conversation.

As noted earlier, the language that makes up social conversation serves primarily an interactional function of expressing social relations and personal attitudes, but it also serves a secondary, transactional one of expressing 'content'. Conversations are joint productions, in which participants constantly take account of one another and adjust their speech to fit the contours of the social situation in which the conversation is taking place. Conversational language thus mirrors the way speakers check on how well they are being understood, how hearers claim and prove their understanding of what is being said, and how both keep the conversation going. In order to converse successfully then, participants must not only have facts about the topics they wish to discuss, they must also know how to manipulate these facts in socially and grammatically acceptable ways. This includes knowing which lexical phrases are appropriate in casual conversation in informal situations with friends and acquaintances, and which are appropriate in formal situations with strangers, with those in authority, and so on.

A significant amount of conversational language seems to be highly routinized as prefabricated utterances, for reasons that are not surprising. As we have seen in previous chapters, it is the nature of performed speech to be composed of chunks of language like these. It is also the fact that conversations occur within highly conventionalized boundaries, and employ a number of stereotyped and standardized procedures for characterizing the entailed social interactions. Lexical phrases provide easy access to these social interactions, for they are 'ready-to-go' for particular situations that are frequent and predictable, and are easily recognizable as markers of these situations.

5.2   Advantages of teaching lexical phrases

Lexical phrases offer many advantages for teaching conversation. As was suggested in Chapter 1, they allow for expressions that learners are yet unable to construct creatively, simply because they are stored and retrieved as whole chunks, a fact which should ease frustration and, at the same time, promote motivation and fluency. These phrases also ought to prove highly memorable, since they are embedded in socially appropriate situations. More importantly yet, they provide an efficient means of interacting with other speakers about self-selected topics, which is another characteristic that should certainly engender social motivation for learning the language, as well as guaranteeing feedback to help speakers test how accurately they have constructed their responses.

And since most are also analyzable by regular rules of syntax, they can later be segmented and new patterns constructed in such a way that students are led to an understanding of the syntactic rules of the language. Thus, teaching with lexical phrases seems to offer a 'middle ground' that avoids the pitfalls Widdowson (1989) warns us of: too heavy a reliance on either structural models of competence, or communicative models of appropriate use.

Lexical phrases also, it may be remembered, seem to provide the raw material itself for language acquisition. In Chapter 1 it was suggested that anyone who learns a language in a relatively natural environment, adults as well as children, seem to pass through a stage in which they string memorized chunks of speech together in certain frequent and predictable social situations. Later, on analogy with many similar phrases, they break these chunks down into sentence frames that contain slots for various fillers.

Some linguists feel that the process of segmentation continues until learners have worked their way to individual lexical items and the specific, competence-based rules for their combination. Now, whether the actual grammatical rules are learnt this way is still a controversial matter, and, if one analyzes them solely as structures, then there would be no reason to suppose that lexical phrases would necessarily lead to such grammar rules. But, if we see these phrases also as formulaic units of social interaction, then their centrality in language acquisition becomes more likely. Many linguists now believe that social interactions come before the syntactic structures and provide the basis for them.[1] Infants learn what language is used for before they learn how to speak it; children learn the conventions that make utterances into speech acts before they learn how to frame the utterances as grammatical sentences. Hatch makes the general observation that:

> It [has been] assumed that one first learns how to manipulate structures, that one gradually builds up a repertoire of structures and then, somehow, learns how to put the structures to use in discourse. We would like to consider the possibility that just the reverse happens. One learns how to do conversation, one learns how to interact verbally, and out of this interaction syntactic structures are developed.
> (Hatch 1978:404)

The structures one first uses to 'do conversation' are invariable lexical phrases, manipulated as pieces of function and meaning in predictable social interactions.

Scollon (1979) suggests more specifically how the process might work. In the following conversation:

Child: That dog.
Adult: What about the dog?
Child: Big.
Adult: Oh, the dog is big.

the adult responds to the child's selection of *dog* as topic by asking for a comment about it. The child provides the information *big*, and the adult then models how these two semantically-linked elements of topic and comment are structurally-linked as subject and predicate in an English sentence. Scollon argues that these semantically-linked constructions provide the basis for the longer syntactically-linked structures that develop later. Second language learners seem to make use of the same strategy, even though they have already mastered a syntactic system. One might suppose that these learners would immediately begin to make basic syntactic links in accordance with sentence structures in their native language, yet research shows that most initial structures conform to the semantically linked ones (Hatch 1978). Second language learners, like first language learners, apparently learn the rules of conversational interaction before they learn the rules of sentence structure. They also learn the lexical phrases that codify the functions associated with these rules, such as appropriate greetings and partings, expressing politeness, complimenting, and so on, for acquiring this pragmatic competence is a basic part of language learning.

There are many motives for teaching with lexical phrases. Even if we do not yield to the argument that conversation precedes syntax, there remain all the other reasons why socially motivated lexical phrases are an integral part of language acquisition. How might they, then, be exploited in the classroom?

5.3   Teaching conversation with lexical phrases

In devising teaching methods and techniques, it is important to consider both how learners learn, and why they learn.

5.3.1   How learners learn a language

Since a common characteristic of acquiring language is the progression from routine to pattern to creative language use, one method of teaching lexical phrases would be to get students to use them the same way; that is, by starting with a few basic fixed routines, which they then would analyze as increasingly variable patterns as they were exposed to more varied phrases. There is nothing wrong with memorizing some essential chunks, especially at the beginning stages of language learning.

More specifically, such a method might be put to work as follows. Pattern practice drills could first provide a way of gaining fluency with certain basic fixed routines (Peters 1983). The challenge for the teacher would be to use such drills to allow confidence and fluency, yet not overdo them to the point that they become mindless exercise, as has often been the unfortunate result in strict audiolingualism. The next step would be to introduce the students to controlled variation in these basic phrases with the help of simple substitution drills, which would demonstrate that the chunks learnt previously were not invariable routines, but were instead patterns with open slots. In general, this suggests that one should teach lexical phrases that contain several slots, instead of those phrases which are relatively invariant — sentence builders, rather than polywords or phrasal constraints. For example, in teaching formulas for sympathy, one would find the lexical phrase, *I'm (very) sorry (to hear (about) X)*, more useful than the rather inflexible, *I'd like to express my sympathy (about X)*. The range of variation would then be increased as students became more adept at using the phrases, allowing them to analyze the patterns further. The goal would not be to have students analyze just those chunks introduced in the lessons, of course, but to have them learn to segment and construct new patterns of their own on analogy with the kind of analysis they do in the classroom. It is when students learn this that creative control of the new language begins.

This approach bears some obvious resemblances to the one assumed in Wilkins' (1976) notional-functional syllabuses, but our concerns in teaching lexical phrases result in a considerable difference in emphasis. Wilkins, for example, provides certain semantic and pragmatic categories, and finds exponents of these categories for language teaching. These can be single words or idioms. Our emphasis here, on the other hand, is functional rather than notional. The reason is that lexical phrases are an integral part of social interaction, as we have stressed throughout. Further, we feel that the descriptions and categories we have devised will be more useful for teaching purposes. For instance, the three major categories of functional types that we have established seem less arbitrary, for they are chosen for their immediate relevance to the teaching situation. Then too, the lexical phrases we emphasize for teaching purposes can be flexibly expanded, and are thus useful devices in teaching variations which may be appropriate to specific contexts. This flexibility is also important because lexical phrases can be expanded further as lessons become more advanced, a result that is very much in accord with Wilkins' insistence on cyclical ordering of lessons.

Of course, conversations are social events rather than grammar exercises, so there must be more than structural analysis. We not only have to focus teaching methods on *how* learners go about learning language, we need also focus on *why* they learn it; and as we have seen, people learn language as a part of a social interaction in which they have something they want to say.

5.3.2   Why learners learn a language

To include this interactional dimension, we must design beginning lessons to treat a single, predictable situation centered on some needed communicative function, and offer a few simple but variable lexical phrases for dealing with that situation. Later materials would introduce the students to sets of more complex phrases that could also be used to express the same function, a kind of 'theme and variation' (Peters 1983:113), whose range of variation would broaden as learners became more skilled. These phrases would thus be presented in a cyclical rather than linear fashion, much as Wilkins suggests for his notional-functional syllabus (Wilkins 1976:59), so that students would return to the same functions throughout the course and learn to express them in an increasingly sophisticated manner. To use a previous example: in teaching the function of expressing sympathy, we would begin with a lexical phrase in its minimally expanded form, *I'm sorry*, and then in later lessons cycle back to more expanded versions of this phrase, such as *I'm very sorry to hear that X*.

Again, however, it is equally important that this practice take place within varying situations, so that students are provided with the opportunity to acquire the pragmatic competence necessary in limiting particular structures to appropriate use in given contexts. For example, in a context in which a friend loses a book, it is enough to express sympathy in this situation by using the form *I'm sorry*. But, in a context in which a friend loses a close family member through death, the unexpanded version of this lexical phrase would be inadequate indeed, and perhaps seem insincere; instead the expanded version *I'm very sorry to hear that X* would be deemed socially appropriate and sincere.

5.3.3   Teaching activities

Many communicative language teaching activities would provide a framework for introducing these phrases, especially those exercises that have students consciously plan strategies for interacting with others, such as DiPietro (1987) and various others describe. It is important to note that a lexical phrase approach allows for adaptation of existing work dealing with interactional aspects of language learning and does not require starting all over from scratch. For such interaction, students very early on will need to practice phrases for conversational maintenance, particularly those for nominating and clarifying topics; speech acts, like expressing politeness, requesting, questioning, and responding; and they will need to connect utterances and fill pauses with discourse devices to give their conversations coherence, to give themselves a feeling of fluency, and to let their partners know they are trying and have not given up.

Keller describes activities for second language learners that attempt to deal systematically with turn taking, topic nomination, closings, openings, and a few other categories of conversational interaction in a series called gambits (Keller 1979). In one such activity, students practise interrupting their partners. Students have a list of phrases described as 'interrupters', (which we include as 'turn shifters')—*excuse me for interrupting, but, I might add here, may I ask a question?*, and so on—and a list of phrases that direct a return to the topic ('topic shifters', in our terms)—*anyway, to return to, where was I going?*, and so on. Participant A begins by using one of the interrupter phrases, and B answers, trying to get back to the topic as quickly as possible by using one of the topic shifters.

One of the best frameworks for teaching use of lexical phrases would be through *exchange structures*, which describe expected sets of successive utterances in conversation.[2]

A summons is usually followed by a response, for example, a closing by a parting, an assertion by an acceptance or disagreement. A few of the exchange structures that would be immediately useful for language learners to practice are listed below. Since context constrains the forms selected for particular exchanges, at least two examples of exchanges are given in each set, the first involving a typical informal exchange between two friends, the second, a more formal exchange between acquaintances or strangers. These exchanges should be practiced in the various contexts so that students will learn to associate particular forms as appropriate to particular contexts. We present more complete conversational contexts for informal and formal exchanges in the section dealing with indirect speech acts that follows.

(a) summons–response

Hi, how are you (doing)? — (I'm) fine, thanks (and you?)
Good morning/afternoon/evening. — Good morning/
afternoon/evening.

Here, as in the examples that follow, the more syntagmatic options that are chosen, generally the more polite and formal the effect, even in a basically informal exchange. *Fine, thanks* seems less formal than

I'm fine, thanks, which itself seems less formal than *I'm fine, thanks, and you?.*

(b) nominating a topic–clarifying (by audience)

> (By the way) do you know/remember X? — Excuse/pardon me?
> I'd like to suggest/mention X. — (Excuse/pardon me but) what do you mean by X?

Here, the second example of clarifying achieves greater formality by 'stacking' lexical phrases, that is, by stringing together two or more lexical phrases that serve the same function. Such 'stacking' often serves to increase formality. This strategy is quite common, as the further discussion in section 5.4 illustrates in some detail.

(c) closing–parting

> (It's been) nice talking to you. — (Well), so long (for now).
> It's been nice talking to you, but I must be going. — Goodbye.

In the second example of closing, above, formality has been achieved by filling syntagmatic options and stacking similarly functioning lexical phrases (i.e. *it's been nice talking to you* and *I must be going*).

(d) question–answer

> Are there Xs? — Yes/no there are (not) (Xs).
> Do you X? — Yes/no I do (not) (X).

The question–answer exchange is certainly one of the most basic exchanges for any language learner, and the two examples above contain common lexical phrases for informal as well as formal contexts. Exchange forms typical only of more formal contexts can be constructed by the usual method of stacking, i.e. *do you think that there are Xs?*, etc. (Arrows indicate same-speaker progression.)

(e) nominating a topic → checking comprehension

> (By the way) do you know/remember X? → OK/all right (so far)?
> I'd like to suggest/mention X. → (Do you) understand?

(f) asserting–accepting

> Word has it that X. — No kidding.
> It seems (to me) that X. — I see.

(g) asserting–endorsing

I read/heard somewhere that X. — Yes, that's so/right/correct.
I think/believe that X. — I absolutely/certainly/completely
agree.

(h) asserting–disagreeing

There is/are/was/were X. — Yes/well, but (I think that) Y.
It is a fact/the case that X. — I don't (really/quite) agree with
you/X).

These exchanges should be practiced with necessary topics, those
that students will most frequently encounter in their current linguistic lives, and with the appropriate linking devices of discourse, to give
their conversations coherence and fluency.

It is also important that they be practiced with sufficient variation
in the forms to guide students towards eventual analysis of the syntax. This approach has much in common with one proposed in
Widdowson (1990:96), who suggests that we might consider presenting language as lexical units and then 'creating contexts which constrain . . . the gradual analysis of the [grammar]'. In this way, he says,
'the grammar would not be presented as primary but as a conse-
quence of the achievement of meaning through the modification of
lexical items'.

In sum, lexical phrases are integral to conversation, for they provide the patterns and themes that interlace throughout its wandering
course. These phrases are essential even for rudimentary 'communicative competence', yet texts that present conversational language do
not do so in any systematic way that would permit learners to form
connected, functional discourse. We hope that this chapter helps
provide such a way.

5.4   Indirect speech acts

In Chapter 2, indirect speech acts were illustrated as typical of the
kind of sentence builder lexical phrases found in social discourse.
Indirect speech acts are also particularly relevant for teaching conversation, we feel, not only because they are so numerous and occur in a
variety of functions, but also because as sentence builders they allow
greater possibility for variation and practice with appropriate forms
in appropriate contexts.

Because of the flexibility of these frames, in other words, students do not have to contend with a bewildering array of expressions that convey the same function; rather, they can be shown that for a given function, a basic indirect speech act frame serves as the basis for an entire set of expanded expressions. They can learn this frame, and they can learn to expand it as a set of alternatives for conveying that same function. As with learning other lexical phrases, students can begin with a few basic ones, together with their functions, then practice several alternatives based on the same slot-and-filler frames.

At the same time, it is crucial that students also learn which forms are socially appropriate for which contexts. For example, as indicated above, they need to learn which are the most polite ones to use with strangers, and which are appropriate to use with peers or intimates. Based on studies such as Brown and Levinson (1978) and Blum-Kulka and Levenston (1987), contexts devised for practice should, therefore, take into account that, for English at least, the preferred forms for the most polite requests appear to be speaker-based ones such as 'Modal + *I* + VP', though the hearer-based form (Modal + *you* + VP) is also common for less formal situations with peers or close friends.

This type of practice would be especially helpful for students whose native language may have grammaticized the request function in just the opposite order with respect to degrees of politeness. In the Blum-Kulka and Levenston study, for instance, it was found that for requests in Hebrew, although the non-native learners (who were native English speakers) tended to use more speaker-oriented requests, the native Hebrew speakers tended to use more hearer-oriented requests. That is, presumably because avoiding mention of the hearer as performer minimizes the imposition on the hearer, learners used considerably more speaker-oriented forms such as *could I borrow your notes?* than did native speakers, who showed greater preference for hearer-oriented forms such as *could you lend me your notes?*.

Aside from the form of the basic frames themselves, it would also be important for students to be given practice with appropriate politeness 'markers' in the optional slots of such frames. The reason is that each politeness marker adds another level of indirectness, and the more indirect the speech act the more polite it is. With requests, for example, Leech (1983) points out that the degree of politeness is increased 'by using a more and more indirect kind of illocution' and that 'indirect illocutions tend to be more polite (a) because they increase the degree of optionality [for the addressee], and (b) because the more indirect an illocution is, the more diminished and tentative its force tends to be' (Leech 1983:108).

Thus, even the hearer-based request frame 'Modal + *you* + VP' can be used as a very polite request in formal contexts with strangers or authority figures if appropriate levels of indirectness have been added in the optional slots. A single politeness marker such as *possibly* may be used, adding only one more level of indirectness, or additional ones like *be willing to* may be stacked up, adding another level, in a manner similar to the type of stacking discussed in the previous section. The progression from less polite to more polite can be illustrated as shown in Figure 11.

Could you write me a letter of recommendation?

Could you possibly write me a letter of recommendation?

Would you possibly be willing to write me a letter of recommendation?

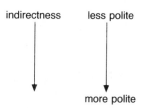

indirectness　　less polite

more polite

Figure 11

In addition to the stacking of politeness markers within the optional slots of the basic frame, even more levels of indirectness can be added by stacking other lexical phrases on top of this frame, as would be appropriate for contexts in which the speaker feels that the request may well be an unwanted imposition on an addressee who may be, say, a person of authority such as a teacher or administrator. Taking the most polite form from the list above, *would you possibly be willing to write me a letter of recommendation?*, and stacking the (optionally expanded) frame *I'm sorry (to have to) to* VP, *but X* in initial position, results in the very indirect and very polite request, *I'm sorry to have to ask/bother you, but would you possibly be willing to write me a letter of recommendation?*.

The result of this stacking option not only adds further degrees of politeness, but also distances the speaker from the request itself, for the stacked lexical phrase in initial position has the function of marking the request as one the speaker is reluctant to make. This 'reluctance' marker lexical phrase is very similar to the polite form that is used for the function of expressing sympathy when bearing bad news. As illustrated in Chapter 2, the basic frame *I'm sorry to tell you that X*, may variously be expanded as *I'm (really) (very) sorry (to have to) (be the one) to tell you that X*. Since the bearing of bad news is an imposition in the sense that it is information that the hearer would rather not receive, it therefore requires indirect politeness markers that imply reluctance on the part of the speaker. Thus, students should be given practice not only with variously expanded forms of polite indirect speech acts for appropriate occasions of use, but also with the most polite stacked forms for contexts in which the speaker is reluctant to make a request, be the bearer of bad news, and so on.

In addition to indirect speech acts, some of the speech acts discussed in earlier chapters were direct speech acts. Examples of direct speech acts were given in conversational purpose categories like expressing politeness, questioning, and answering. *Thanks very much*, for instance, is a straightforward expression of politeness, *do you play tennis?*, *are they here yet?* direct questions, and *no, I don't*, *no, they're not* direct answers to such questions. It is, of course, important that, just as with indirect speech acts, direct speech acts be incorporated into classroom practice with variations of the lexical phrase frames for particular functions in appropriate contexts.

However, it is indirect speech acts, rather than direct ones, that are especially difficult for language learners, and that, therefore, should be given more emphasis in classroom practice. As Schmidt and Richards note:

> Instances of communication breakdown and misunderstanding among non-fluent users suggest they frequently operate primarily at the surface structure level, identifying propositional content where it is marked directly by lexis or grammar, but often missing indirectly marked speech acts and functions.
>
> (Schmidt and Richards 1980: 145)

5.4.1   Universal functions and language-specific forms

With respect to teaching, then, an especially important point is Searle's cautionary note that indirect speech acts are not universal. The reason is that 'in indirect speech acts the speaker communicates to the hearer more than he actually says by way of relying on their mutually shared background information, both linguistic and nonlinguistic' (Searle 1975: 61–2). To some extent at least, the same may apply to lexical phrases in general, because although the processes involved in storing and retrieving lexical phrases are thought to be universal, the phrases themselves frequently differ from one language to another. That is, although we illustrated earlier that lexical phrases are quite similar across languages in that they have basic frames with slots for fillers, and in that they serve the same pragmatic functions, the lexicon and syntax of these frames are often quite different. Nevertheless, direct speech acts and many other lexical phrases present no special difficulties for learners because their functions are relatively apparent from the forms. For indirect speech acts (and certain others which we will discuss in Chapter 6), just the opposite is true.

As an example of how indirect speech acts may differ, consider the differences in the form of the following requests in Chinese and Spanish, as compared with their English counterparts.

Chinese:	(ni)	Meiyou	yijian	ba		ruguo	X
	(you)	not have	opinion	Q-PRT		if	X

Do you mind if I X?

Spanish:	¿Quieres	darme	la sal,	por	favor?
	want	give me	the salt,	for	favor

Could you give me the salt, please?

Put another way, the functions of indirect speech acts occur in all languages, but the forms they take are often language-specific. In the Appendix, we have attempted to indicate the range of speech acts and other lexical phrase functions in other languages.

On this point, however, it should be mentioned that Brown and Levinson (1978, 1989) argue not only that '[strategies] of making indirect speech acts appear to be universal' (1989: 36), but also suggest that, based on comparisons of English, Tamil, and Tzeltal, the linguistic forms are also often parallel. That is, forms can be parallel in the sense of being cognate at a general level of encoding, though differing in particulars. For example, various languages may use past tense forms as a means of indirection by distancing the speaker from the proposition expressed. Nevertheless, various other researchers have shown that it is misleading to assume that the forms of indirect speech acts are parallel across languages.

Schmidt and Richards (1980), for instance, maintain that 'even if speech act strategies are to a certain extent universal . . . learners of new language still need to learn . . . the particular conventionalized forms in the new language' (1980: 140). A clear illustration of an especially compelling reason for this is given in Nelson (1984). Comparing request forms in English and Japanese, she demonstrates that while the question form below,

Ashita	made	matemasu	ka?
tomorrow	until	can-wait	Q

Can you wait until tomorrow?

is a polite request in Japanese as well as in English, the negative question form,

Ashita	made	matemasen	ka?
tomorrow	until	can-wait-NEG	Q

Can't you wait until tomorrow?

is even more polite in Japanese. In English, however, it is not polite at all. At best it is impolite, and in some contexts would be downright rude. (On the differences in illocutionary force of negative question forms, see also Leech (1983).)

Thomas (1983) discusses various other types of examples in which the linguistic forms are language-specific. In illustrating the reasons for cross-cultural pragmatic failure of non-native speakers, she points out, for example, that while *can you X?* is a highly conventionalized form in English, likely to be interpreted by native speakers as a request to do X, rather than a question as to one's ability to do X, in other languages, such as French and Russian, just the opposite is true. Certainly, students ought to be guided to an awareness of these cross-cultural distinctions.

This difference in forms with respect to indirect speech acts is what Qin (1983) had in mind when he reported that one of his Chinese students was puzzled at being taught that in English a question like *could you pass the salt?* functions as a request to pass the salt to the speaker. The student's response was that the practice dialogue illustrating this request was not logically composed because, since the speaker asks a general question, the hearer should begin his or her answer with *yes* or *no*. Qin makes the point that teaching English as a foreign language will never be effective unless it includes the teaching of such culture-specific forms for the various functions. We, of course, agree with Qin, but would add that the same applies to the ESL classroom, and to any foreign language classroom as well.

Based on these studies, indirect speech acts, rather than direct ones, would seem to pose the greatest difficulty for language learners, since not only do the forms differ across cultures, but also the functions are not readily apparent from the form. However, we would like to emphasize that the importance of teaching these form/function composites extends not only to indirect speech acts but to various other lexical phrase forms and functions as well. Even for phrases whose functions are transparent, students still need to learn the appropriate forms, as the examples below illustrate for transparent, direct speech acts expressing politeness and complimenting, respectively, in Chinese:

Xie   xie   ni.
thank thank you
Thank you very much.

Wo hen   xihuan   X.
I   very   like   X

I really like X.

5.4.2   Teaching indirect speech acts

Although we have outlined the types of difficulty that indirect speech
acts pose for students, we have done so mainly to emphasize the
importance of teaching them. The real difficulty for students comes
when they are not taught at all. The phrases themselves, however, do
not pose any particular problems for classroom teaching. To the
contrary, because they are lexical phrase sentence builders, and
because sentence builders allow greater paradigmatic flexibility in
any given form, they also allow greater opportunity for practice with
variations that are appropriate for particular contexts, as illustrated
above. Knowing these form/function associations, and knowing the
contextual constraints on the choice of form, is all part of pragmatic
competence. And if students are to become fluent and to converse
effectively and appropriately, they need to work towards attaining
pragmatic competence as well as grammatical competence.

The technique of stacking lexical phrases should certainly add to
the student's feeling of confidence and fluency. Seemingly complex
forms such as the request, *I'm sorry to have to bother you, but would
you possibly be willing to write me a letter of recommendation?* are
based on two simple frames: the request frame 'Modal + *you* + VP',
stacked together with the reluctance marker frame, *I'm sorry to VP,
but X?*. Since students begin with practicing the basic frames, gradually learning to expand the optional slots by stacking, and in the final
stage learning to stack the two phrases themselves, by the time this
final cycle is reached little effort is required to produce the expanded
polite form. And since each type of expansion has been practiced in
association with an appropriate context, such as speaker/friend,
speaker/stranger, speaker/authority figure + imposition, and the like,
students are also guided towards gaining knowledge of the form/
function associations necessary for attaining pragmatic competence.

As with other lexical phrases, one of the best frameworks for
teaching would be through the exchange structures that describe
expected sets of successive utterances, as outlined above. With

indirect speech acts, however, it should be stressed that the functions are not readily apparent from the forms, and the structures should be practiced so as to stress the particular functions. For example, useful exchange structures for second language learners would include polite forms for request–comply (*Could I borrow your pen? — Sure, go ahead*); invitation–acceptance (*Would you like to come to my party? — Yes, thanks a lot*); invitation–refusal (*How about going to a movie with me? — I'd really like to but . . .*); offer–acceptance (*Can I help you with X? — Yes, thanks very much*); offer–refusal (*Can I give you a lift? — Thanks, but . . .*); suggestion–response (*Why not try working with a tutor? — OK, I'll give it a try*), and so on.

However, as we have stressed throughout, it is equally important that these exchange structures be set within appropriate contexts, and these contexts will need to be simulated in the classroom.[3] For example, for the request–comply pair, beginning practice could be with the unexpanded basic frame 'Modal + *I* + VP', which would be appropriate to use with peers or intimates.

Context #1:

Student A and her friend, Student B, are seated in the classroom before a test. Student A discovers that she has forgotten her pen. Seeing that her friend has two pens, she requests to borrow one and her friend complies.

Student A: Could I borrow your pen?
Student B: Sure, go ahead.

When students are ready for more complex forms, the next step would be to introduce controlled variation with simple substitution practice that would demonstrate that the chunks learnt previously were patterns with open slots rather than invariable routines. Variations could be *could I see your lecture notes?*, *can I have a piece of candy?*, which would also lead students to a focus on the form, and to guide them towards analyzing the grammar of the basic frame.

Later on, the next cycle for the various functions could include different contexts that would illustrate variations that are specific to these contexts, and thus how context determines the choice of form.

Context #2:

A is seated at the bus stop waiting for the bus to the market. She looks in her bag for her pen so that she can make a list of items she needs to buy, but discovers the pen missing. Seeing a pen in the pocket of B, a stranger seated next to her, she requests to borrow the pen and he complies.

A: Could I possibly borrow your pen?
B: Of course, here it is.

During this kind of practice, it should be pointed out to students that politeness markers like *possibly* are required with the more indirect forms used with strangers.

When students become more advanced, the final stage in the cycle would include the more complex forms. In this stage, variations with stacked politeness markers and reluctance phrases could be introduced as required in contexts such that the speaker feels that a stronger imposition on the addressee is being made.

Context #3:

A is ready to leave for an appointment for a job interview when he discovers that his car has a flat tire. Just then B, his new neighbor whom he has met only once, walks to the driveway and gets in his car. A desperately wants to keep his appointment for the interview, but realizes that a request for a ride from B would probably be considered an imposition since B may be going in a different direction. After greeting B and explaining about the tire and the interview, A makes the request and B complies as follows:

A: I'm very sorry to bother you, but could I possibly ask you to give me a ride downtown?
B: Of course, I'll be glad to.

Again, students need to be made aware that because the imposition on the addressee in this case is much stronger, the request must be made more indirectly by stacking politeness markers such as *possibly* and *ask you to*, plus the reluctance marker *I'm very sorry to bother you*.

Within these contexts, the simple dialogues illustrated here can be expanded into longer conversations, thus placing emphasis on conversation as discourse that is formed through social interaction. For example, the dialogue illustrated above could begin with the summoning–response (followed by the explanation), and continued with such exchange pairs as gratitude–response, and so on.

A: Excuse me (NAME).
B: Yes, what can I do for you?
A: I just discovered that I have a flat tire, and I'm late for an important appointment. I'm very sorry to bother you, but could I possibly ask you to give me a ride downtown?
B: Of course, I'll be glad to.

A: Thanks very much. You saved my life.
B: Not at all, it's no trouble.

In summary, given this approach to classroom practice, the successive stages cycle lexical phrases in such a way that the differing contexts for given functions demonstrate constraints on choices of form, thus providing input needed for acquiring pragmatic competence. At the same time, variations in the open slots of the basic frames reveal the recurring pattern of the syntactic shape, thus providing input needed for acquiring grammatical competence.

This chapter has been concerned with teaching conversation, with the types of lexical phrases that need to be included in that instruction, and with suggestions for teaching activities that can enhance learning. Chapter 6 will also be concerned with practical teaching application, but the focus will be on listening comprehension.

Notes

1   Some linguists who have also studied language acquisition feel that such a thing is unlikely, however. 'It is difficult to demonstrate', Hakuta states, 'how the specific rules of grammar might be derived from conversational analysis' (Hakuta 1986: 129).

2   We use 'exchange structure' to indicate a minimal interactive unit of discourse, and as such it encompasses similar terms like 'adjacency pairs' (Sacks *et al.* 1974), 'interchange' (Goffman 1971), and 'exchange' (Sinclair and Coulthard 1975).

3   With respect to contrived situations such as these, one currently held assumption is that language in the classroom must be authentic rather than contrived, if students are to learn to communicate naturally. This view is open to question, however, for reasons that Widdowson (1990) makes quite clear. He argues that,

Authenticity of language in the classroom is bound to be, to some extent, an illusion. This is because it does not depend on the source from which the language as an object is drawn but on the learners' engagement with it. In actual language use . . . meanings are achieved by human agency and are negotiable: they are not contained in text . . . So the situations which are to stimulate the use of the language being learned will have to be contrived in some way, and the learners will have to co-operate in maintaining the illusion of reality (Widdowson 1990: 44–5).

6 Teaching spoken discourse: listening comprehension

6.1 Introduction

This chapter will deal with classroom application of the lexical phrase approach in teaching comprehension, in particular, that area of comprehension which causes college-bound second language learners the most difficulty—the comprehension of academic lectures. However, although the chapter is directed towards this specific problem, we wish to emphasize that this approach is equally useful for teaching comprehension in general.

In Chapter 4, we outlined the functions of macro-organizers in discourse. One of the most important applications of macro-organizer functions in comprehending discourse is in the area of the comprehension of academic lectures by second language learners. This area is one that has long been neglected, and has only recently been addressed in any seriousness. As Lebauer (1984) notes, 'a problem common to many students in advanced listening comprehension and note-taking classes is that, in spite of apparent fluency, they still have difficulties understanding the points made in lectures' (1984:41).

To compound the problem, many students are not aware that they are having serious comprehension difficulties in lecture classes. They believe that they understand what the lecturer is saying, and they do not realize that they are missing many of the important points. Consequently, they are shocked and dismayed to discover that they are unable to achieve a passing grade. As one college-bound student complained to one of the authors, he had spent years studying a second language, in this case English, in order to attend college in the US, he had spent another year and a half studying English after he arrived in the US, he was relatively fluent in conversing with native speakers in basic social situations, and yet he was failing courses in which there was a lecture format. At the same time, he insisted that he was able to understand the lectures, and therefore was completely at a loss as to why he was failing the exams. However, a discussion of his lecture notes revealed that what he was missing was a sense of the flow and direction of the lecture, and a sense of what counted as important information and what did not.

6.2   Lexical phrases in academic lectures

After viewing instructional materials for courses in listening comprehension, and after examining the type of discourse that occurs in academic lectures, it is our belief that non-native speakers have difficulty because, although they do study markers that signal the direction and the categorization of written discourse, these markers tend, for the most part, not to be those that commonly occur in typical academic lectures. In other words, they tend to be micro-organizers, or even macro-organizers of the more formal, literary type that occur in written texts or in formal speech, such as *however, in addition, on the contrary*, etc., and not of the more informal—sometimes highly informal—conversational type that are more often found in actual lectures. Furthermore, in the instructional materials the distinction between micro- and macro-organizers is rarely recognized.

In this chapter, these problems are examined from a lexical phrase approach. Based on numerous recorded natural lectures on a variety of topics, as well as pre-recorded video lectures, our analysis focuses on how macro-organizers function in academic lectures as an aid to comprehension, on how many and what type occur, depending on the style of the lecturer, and on how the findings might suggest ways in which students' knowledge of macro-organizers can lead to improving listening comprehension. We then turn to the teaching of lexical phrase macro-organizers for the comprehension of academic lectures.

6.2.1   Macro-organizer functions in academic lectures

For the most part, academic lectures conform closely to the description of speech production discussed in previous chapters. They are primarily transactional and they are full of formulaic phrases that serve as much more than clichéd expressions or pause fillers. These phrases, in particular the macro-organizer type of phrase discussed in Chapter 4, function as important directional signals for working one's way through the information in the lecture, as they indicate how the information in the lecture is organized and, just as important, how it is to be evaluated. As evidenced in our corpus, they tend

to be more pervasive and provide more signals of the overall structure than those found in social discourse or even in other non-lecture
types of transactional discourse such as meetings, study groups, conferences, and so on.

The discourse of academic lectures, like other basically transactional discourse, is a combination of the transactional and the interactional. In academic lectures, there is relatively little interactional
discourse interspersed, the interactional phases consisting chiefly of
greetings, and sometimes other social maintenance discourse such as
brief exchanges about the weather, at the beginning of the lecture,
and of partings and other leave-taking exchanges at the end of the
lecture. Since lectures begin with an interactional phase, second
language learners need to be aware of those macro-organizers which
commonly occur as topic markers, and which serve the dual function
of signaling the end of the interactional phase and signaling the topic
to be discussed at the beginning of the transactional phase.

In the transactional phase of the lecture format various other
macro-organizers occur periodically, and students must learn to
listen not only for the meanings of words, phrases, and sentences, of
the content of the lecture, but also for these organizational markers
that serve to frame the general outline that the content fits into, and
that indicate how the parts are interrelated.

The many common and recurring macro-organizers in various
styles of lectures fit naturally—according to function—into the discourse categories discussed in Chapter 4. Furthermore, because of
their formulaic nature, groups of these lexical phrase macro-
organizers, though differing dramatically in lexicon and syntax, are
built on the same pattern and have the same function.

6.2.2   The recognition problem

The occurrence of groups of phrases built on the same pattern, and
having the same function, is an aspect of discourse which has especially important implications for teaching comprehension, particularly
with respect to comprehension of academic lectures by non-native
speakers, though, of course, they are applicable to many other
troublesome problems of listening comprehension. While these lexical phrases pose no particular problem for native speakers, they do
indeed pose difficult problems for non-native speakers. The reason is
that, unlike the formal type of markers usually found in written
discourse (see Chapter 4), these formulaic phrases often cannot be
interpreted literally and, since they are not taught in any systematic

way in second language classes, non-native speakers often do not recognize, let alone comprehend these signals which are so crucial in indicating the direction of the lecture, the relationship of its parts, and the relative importance of its parts. That is, they fail to recognize or comprehend the signals which facilitate top-down processing.

Given the formulaic nature of lexical phrases, a simplified and systematic methodology can be devised for teaching those patterns and functions which are generally found in academic lectures, together with representative lexical items, phrases, or clauses which commonly occur in the slots allowing variations. Though functions and other details differ somewhat, this methodology is similar in its essentials to that discussed in Chapter 5 for teaching conversation. In section 6.5, we will suggest specific applications of this methodology to the teaching of lexical phrase macro-organizers common to academic lectures. Before turning to the teaching of these phrases, however, we will examine more closely the types of phrases that need to be taught. Factors to be considered are various styles of lectures and the characteristic lexical phrases that occur in them, and the ways in which macro-organizers function in the comprehension of lecture discourse.

6.3   Styles of academic lectures

Styles of lectures can vary widely, depending on factors such as the personality, training, and experience of the lecturer. Some are close to the conversational style of other transactional spoken discourse, and they include pervasive use of more idiomatic, informal types of macro-organizers. Others are closer to the style of written transactional discourse, with the predominant use of more formal, usually more literal types of macro-organizers. Sometimes a lecture can be a curious combination of the two. A lecturer who favors a more formal style, and who begins and ends the lecture in this manner may nevertheless slip temporarily into a conversational tone in the middle of the lecture, particularly with the use of one or more idiomatic macro-organizers. For the most part, though, lectures can usually be easily identified as predominantly one style or another.

Dudley-Evans and Johns (1981), for example, distinguish three different styles of lecturing. One is 'reading style', where the lecturer either reads from prepared notes or speaks as if reading from notes, and where there is little interaction with students. The second is 'rhetorical style', where the lecturer is more like a performer, and the third is 'conversational style', characterized by informal speaking and more interaction with the students. In conversational style, idiomatic phrasal verbs are also especially frequent.[1]

All three lecture styles occurred in the recorded lectures we analyzed, although conversational style was by far the most common. Rhetorical style appeared only in the few video-taped lectures examined, and it seems likely that that is more often where it would occur. Class size and subject matter did not seem to be factors in determining styles, since conversational style was the one most commonly used in the majority of the lectures, even though the classes varied considerably in size, and the lectures were on a wide variety of topics including anthropology, applied linguistics, biology, ecology, ethnology, history, linguistics, literature, sociology, and speech communication.[2] Because it seems to be much more common, at least in US colleges and universities, we concentrate more on conversational style.

Dudley-Evans and Johns distinguish conversational style lecturing according to the characteristics of informal speech (use of contracted forms, slang phrases, etc.) and of more interaction with students. With respect to lexical phrases, those found in this style tended more often to be those with idiomatic meaning and/or greater variability of the lexical phrase frame, as compared with those found in reading style. They also tended to have more contracted forms. In other words, they are macro-organizers that are similar to those commonly found in other types of spoken transactional discourse, as discussed in Chapter 3.

The sharpest contrast to conversational style lecturing is reading style lecturing, which is characterized as reading from prepared notes, or speaking as if such notes were committed to memory. The lexical phrases found in this style tended to be more literal in meaning rather than idiomatic, with less syntactic variability than those in conversational style. Contracted forms are much less frequent. In other words, while the lexical phrases found in conversational style lectures are, in this sense, more like those in the spoken transactional discourse examined in Chapters 3 and 4, the discourse of meetings, conferences, political discussions, giving directions, and so on, reading style lectures are more like the ones found in written transactional discourse.

6.3.1   Lecture styles and macro-organizer characteristics

Even in brief fragments taken from these two styles of lectures, the contrast in the types of macro-organizers is quite clear. Two such fragments are given below. The first, from a lecture on linguistics, is conversational style, and the macro-organizers that occur are predominantly more informal ones characterized by idiomatic features and contracted forms; the second, from a lecture on literature, is reading style, and the macro-organizers are more formal, with a more literal meaning, and with less tendency towards contractions.

Conversational style

. . . Now, what I'd like to do today is (TOPIC MARKER) talk about black speech. If you're a reading teacher . . . how can you judge how well a person understands reading? OK, now, . . . (falling intonation + pause, TOPIC SHIFTER) let's look at pronunciation. Here are some differences . . . in any spoken dialect there's going to be a loss of consonants . . . Black dialect has a lot more silent letters, a lot more consonants dropped . . . You'd say something like this one (EXEMPLIFIER) Forward. Would you say this one? [Background: forward]. Forward, oh yeah, you say it right now. But if I'm screaming at somebody in a car and I say [Background: forward—laughter]. OK so (level intonation, no pause, SUMMARIZER) sometimes it's there, sometimes it's not . . . Lot more to talk about, but on to (TOPIC SHIFTER) grammar . . . [sentence written on board] That seems to be grammar only of White standard English . . . Black English would put that together differently. Ask Albert do he have any pencils, something like that (EXEMPLIFIER) . . . OK, (pause)[3] functional differences. This is how people use language . . . it has to do with (RELATOR) verbal skills . . . the community warmly accepts and rewards people who are verbally skillful. The catch here is (QUALIFIER) that the verbal skills these black kids consider are certainly not the skills that a white teacher in a classroom will consider . . . I think the most interesting one is (EVALUATOR) a kind of phenomenon called playing the dozens. But this is highly ritualized for a lot of these black children. And they're very, very good . . . A sounding contest takes place. Two people square off verbally. The object of the game is to make the insult somebody throws at you, make it more complex, syntactically, semantically, and throw it back. A sounding contest can take, you know, by somebody pointing out the window at a fire hydrant or anything and say, 'That yo mama' . . . Here's one. (EXEMPLIFIER) 'There go your mother right there, look like a fish' . . . Money says 'Yo mama look like Flipper'. Flipper's not a fish, but who cares? He swims. So that's a successful sound . . . Why not have Black speech texts that are much closer to the Black dialect? And here're (EXEMPLIFIER) some of the attempts at doing that. (Examples follow.) It's simply closer to what those Black kids are going to say. The theory goes, then, (SUMMARIZER) if it's closer to what they say, they will learn how to correlate sound and symbol more quickly . . . And here's speech and when you learn how to read, what you're doing is you're learning to match symbols of writing with symbols of sounds that you've got, that what you're doing in the beginning is learning a matching operation, as in mathematics . . . All this says is (SUMMARIZER) beginning to learn how to read is a very different thing from learning to read other kinds of scripts and dialects.

Reading style

. . . Now I would like to give you (TOPIC SHIFTER) a few quotations that might interest you, having to do with (RELATOR) the attitudes of Hemingway and Faulkner toward each other. We will see from these quotations that Hemingway had the highest admiration for Faulkner, but misunderstood a few statements Faulkner made quoted in the press . . . In 1947—this passage I am quoting (EXEMPLIFIER) [is from] Carlos Baker's biography of Hemingway (quotation follows) . . . Faulkner did, late in his career after he had won the Nobel prize, visit various universities in response to invitations. I would imagine (EVALUATOR) he was near drunk on every occasion because he was so shy. He had to drink to get himself up there. On one occasion, (EXEMPLIFIER) near the end of his life, at the University of Virginia there was some kind of reception, and he vomited right there. A thing like that made him physically ill . . . Alcohol is a kind of occupational hazard among writers. I think that this is due to the fact that (EVALUATOR) writing is such a cruel, self-punishing activity. Faulkner did it rhythmically and it had, it had a kind of sacramental and even religious function for him too, that is, (RELATOR) it gave him feelings that he would not have otherwise . . . Now I'd like to give you (TOPIC SHIFTER) a biographical sketch with some comments on the most interesting and pertinent features of his life . . . Mississippi was the most backward state in the Union. And relations between the sexes, for instance, (EXEMPLIFIER) were polarized in the manner of American society in the Nineteenth Century . . . his mother Maude Faulkner was a domineering woman, but Faulkner was devoted to his mother nevertheless . . . During World War II he tried to enlist in the US Air Force, but he was rejected for being too short. So he went to Canada and joined the Canadian Royal Air Force. According to the legend he was wounded in action as a pilot in France . . . and he allowed that legend to get around. As a matter of fact, (EVALU-ATOR) Faulkner did not even seem to care to correct falsehoods about his life . . . And he said 'The writer's only responsibility is to his art. He will be completely ruthless if he is a good one . . . if the writer has to rob his mother, he will not hesitate.' Now of course he really acted contrary to that you know. My point is that (SUM-MARIZER) he said things like that, in part, (QUALIFIER) because he was so sacrificial, he was conscientious, he gave up so much to support all these people who relied upon him.

These excerpts include a sampling of the macro-organizers typical of the ones occurring throughout each of the entire lectures. The ones illustrated include topic markers and shifters, exemplifiers, summarizers, relators, qualifiers, and evaluators. When these are grouped according to category, the differences in style are especially obvious:

Topic markers and shifters:

Conversational style: *OK, now,* . . . (falling intonation + pause)
                        what I'd like to do today is X
                        lot more to talk about, but on to _____

Reading style: *now I would like to give you X*
                        now I'd like to give you X

Exemplifiers:

Conversational style: *something like this one*
                        _____, *something like that*
                        here's one
                        and here're Xs

Reading style: *this passage I am quoting is from X*
                        on one occasion
                        for instance

Summarizers:

Conversational style: *OK so* (level intonation, no pause)
                        the theory goes, then
                        all this says is X

Reading style: *my point is that X*

Relators:

Conversational style: *X has to do with Y*

Reading style: *X, having to do with Y*
                            that is

Qualifiers:

Conversational style: *the catch here is X*

Reading style: *in part*

Evaluators:
Conversational style: *I think the most interesting one is X*

Reading style: *I would imagine*
                            I think that this is due to the fact that X

Most of the macro-organizers found in the reading style are the more literal, formal type and most of those in the conversational style ones are the more idiomatic, informal type. There is, of course, some overlapping, at least partially, in the case of the literal phrases. In the conversational style fragment, the topic marker *what I'd like to do today*, for instance, is not so different from the one in reading style, *now I'd like to give you*, but the topic markers *OK, now, . . .* (with falling intonation + pause), and *lot more to talk about, but on to ____* are more idiomatic, and informal in style. Likewise, distinct differences are apparent between the more informal type of exemplifiers in the conversational style, *something like that, ____, something like that, here's one*, etc., and the more formal ones in the reading style, *the passage I am quoting is from X* and *for instance*; between the idiomatic summarizers in conversational style, *OK so* (with level intonation, no pause), *the theory goes then, all this says is X*, as opposed to the more literal summarizer *my point is that X*; and between the idiomatic qualifier *the catch here is X* and the more literal qualifier *in part*.

In the case of evaluators, there is more overlapping in the use of literal lexical phrases. The only one that appears in the conversational style fragment is *I think the most interesting one is X*, which is not very different from the reading style, *I would imagine*, or *I think that this is due to the fact that X*, although the lexical material *due to the fact that* tends to lend a somewhat more formal tone to the latter.

For the most part, however, evaluators in conversational style lectures are more often informal, idiomatic ones like *no problem with that, X is fine/OK with me, look what's going on here*, and so on.

In sum, in reading style lectures instructors mainly read from detailed notes or speak as if such notes were committed to memory, and there is little interaction with the students. With respect to lexical phrases, we find a predominance of formal, more literal macro-organizers like *the/my point is that X, that is, in fact, in summary, in conclusion*. Conversational style involves considerably more interaction with the students, and it is not surprising that the result is a more relaxed atmosphere in which informal, idiomatic macro-organizers like *OK, now, . . ., OK so, so there you've got X, same way here, on/back to* ____, tend to predominate.

Compared to those in conversational style and reading style, the macro-organizers in rhetorical style are somewhat more difficult to characterize. It was easy enough to identify the style itself on the tapes we examined, since, like the conversational and reading styles, it conformed closely to the criteria given in Dudley-Evans and Johns. That is, in rhetorical style the lecture was more like a performance being given for an audience as if by cue, with a wide intonational range, often exploiting high key. But of the two types of macro-organizers discussed above, the more literal formal ones and the more idiomatic informal ones, neither seemed to be especially predominant overall.

Lexical phrases found in rhetorical style are sometimes informal macro-organizers, such as *OK, now, . . ., so this seems to be X, the other thing X is Y*, like conversational style lectures; but a large number of more formal markers also occur, such as *let me suggest some ways, I suggest to you, you should be able to see that X, recognize that X, although Y, are also Z*. At least for video-taped lectures, because the camera seems to promote a stage-like atmosphere in which the lecturer 'performs' for the camera, this performance factor may well be related to the use of some of these markers, chosen perhaps for their 'rhetorical' effect.

6.3.2   Style switching

Generally speaking, the style in a given lecture tends to be consistent. In rhetorical and conversational styles, switching from one style to another does not usually occur. The only style in which it is fairly common is reading style. In this style, where most of the text is quite formal and contains formal macro-organizers, especially the beginning and ending portions, the middle portion is sometimes marked by informal phrases such as *all right, OK so those are X, where was I?* This temporary lapse illustrates the sociolinguistic fact that lecture discourse, in reading style at least, tends to begin and end in a more formal register, with less formal in the middle (Labov 1966, 1972).

This switch seems to occur either when the lecturer momentarily loses the train of thought because of a question or other interruption by a student, or when some portion of the lecture is humorous or has some other particular emotional impact. An example is an excerpt from the mid-portion of the reading style lecture from which the fragment given in the previous section was taken.

(1) There are sixteen characters in *As I Lay Dying*, all
(2) rendered from the inside. But he wasn't making any
(3) money, and nobody was buying his stories. So he sat
(4) down and deliberately wrote a potboiler, a shocker,
(5) and he wrote *Sanctuary*, the story of a Southern belle
(6) named Temple Drake ... She's superficial, shallow ...
(7) she is ironically the temple of Southern womanhood,
(8) Temple Drake. She is ironically kidnapped by a gangster
(9) from the North named Popeye. [Laughter] Popeye is
(10) impotent and mechanical ... he carries her off and since
(11) he's impotent ... watches her in bed with a gangster
(12) named Red. How does that sound? Do you think that'll
(13) interest the editors in New York? [Laughter] Of course
(14) it will! They, they grabbed it right away. But Faulkner
(15) was so embarrassed by it [Laughter] that he wrote the
(16) editor and asked for it back. So then, they sent it back
(17) to him and he rewrote it, and he turned it into an
(18) allegory of the North and the South. And Temple Drake
(19) is the ah, superficial, ah, ah, modern South. Well,
(20) *Sanctuary* was published in 1931.

Although the less formal portions of this excerpt do not represent a clearly informal, conversational style, it is, nevertheless, a departure from the highly formal, reading style typical of the rest of the lecture. In line (9), following the first instance of laughter by the students, the lecturer becomes somewhat more animated, speaking faster and with more emphasis up to line (13). And following the second instance of laughter, in line (13), informal lexical items and lexical phrases begin to appear, i.e. the item *grabbed* in line (14), the relator *so then* in line (16), and *well* in line (19).

6.4   The function of macro-organizers in comprehending lectures

Lexical phrase macro-organizers play a more prominent role in lecture discourse than in other types of spoken transactional discourse. They occur more frequently and usually provide more listening cues that help to frame the discourse in terms of a general outline of the lecture material. They are especially frequent in conversational style, perhaps because in a more relaxed atmosphere in which students often ask questions or enter into the discussion, the task of steering the discussion becomes more difficult, and the lecturer must provide more cues, and more reminders of previous cues, in order to continue to guide the direction of the discourse.

With respect to categories, macro-organizers found in lecture discourse represent the same functions found in the transactional discourse discussed in Chapter 4, such as organizational meetings, departmental meetings, conferences, study groups, and so on. The global macro-organizers are topic markers, topic shifters, and summarizers, and the local macro-organizers are exemplifiers, relators, evaluators, qualifiers, and aside markers. As in our previous classification, we justify including aside markers as macro-organizers because, especially in lecture discourse, it is essential to know which material *is not* important to pay attention to, just as it is essential to know which material *is* important to pay attention to. A listing of a wider range of examples in these categories, taken from a variety of lectures, is given in the next section.

Although in lecture discourse the category types themselves are basically the same as those for other transactional discourse, there are other kinds of important differences between the two. In addition to the difference that lexical phrase macro-organizers occur more frequently and provide more listening cues in lecture discourse than in non-lecture discourse, many of the ones found in lecture discourse seldom occur at all in non-lecture discourse. For example, common in (conversational style) lecture discourse but not in non-lecture discourse are macro-organizers like *if you've seen X then you've seen/you know Y, if you/we look at/see/go to X, you'll/we'll find/see Y, (now) look what's going on here/what X says*, which occur fairly often as exemplifiers, especially in science or social science lectures. Other examples are lexical phrases such as *so let's turn to X, that brings us to X, lot more to talk about, but on to ____* (topic shifters); *X, so you would expect to find Y, if you look at X, here's Y* (relators); *look how important, X is worth noting/mentioning* (evaluators); *to tie this up, so the theory goes (then), that's about it* (summarizers).

Of course, there is also a good deal of overlapping with macro-organizers used in other transactional spoken discourse, at least in conversational style. Examples of those common to both include exemplifiers like ____, *something like that,   to give (you) an example,   not only X, but also Y,* a number of relators and evaluators like *it has to do with X, this ties in with X, X is fine/OK with me, no problem with that,* and many of the qualifiers.

Concerning interactional, social discourse, it cannot be emphasized too strongly that a great many of these lexical phrases that occur in transactional discourse, whether lecture or non-lecture, do not occur at all in interactional discourse. Second language learners need to know, for instance, that phrases like *OK, now, . . ., all right, . . .* used as topic shifters, with pronounced falling intonation and pause, would be too abrupt and authoritarian for discourse that has as its purpose social interaction. Likewise, summarizers like *so there you've got X* or *to tie this up* are inappropriate in social discourse because they seem to indicate that the speaker is taking too much control of the conversation, and perhaps even that the hearer's 'turn' on a given topic is being usurped.

Many of these lexical phrases, then, generally serve only macro-organizer functions in transactional discourse, either in lecture or in non-lecture discourse, or in both. Native speakers have no difficulty in distinguishing these pragmatic functions as appropriate to a given type of discourse, but non-native speakers would not necessarily be able to make this distinction unless it is pointed out. Hence, students should be aware that these macro-organizer forms and functions are extremely important for the purpose of comprehending academic lectures and other transactional discourse, and that they need to learn them for this purpose mainly as recognition vocabulary; but they should also be aware that, in general, it cannot be assumed that these particular phrases are appropriate for them to produce in social conversation, unless they have been so instructed in the language classroom.

6.4.1   Range of functions in lecture discourse: a comprehension problem

If students have already learnt to recognize, and to analyze, lexical phrases for social conversation, and have learnt to segment and construct new phrases based on this knowledge, then learning to recognize and to comprehend the macro-organizers found in lecture discourse should not present any special problems; if not, however, then they do present special problems, as will be illustrated shortly. A listing of some of the most typical and most frequent macro-organizers occurring in academic lectures is given in Figure 12, on pages 145–7. Although we have concentrated more on conversational style, as the one most common in current use, for comparison Figure 12 includes examples of lexical phrases from all three lecture styles: conversational, rhetorical, and reading.

The term 'macro-organizer' rather than 'macro-marker' seems especially apt here, since we want to stress the angle of the listener's perception of lecture organization, and to stress the importance of these cues in helping students mentally organize the lecture as it goes along.

Figure 12 illustrates in more detail some of the differences examined in previous sections. In the discussion of these differences in this section, the focus will be more on why they are ones that students need to know about. Just as in the lecture fragments in section 6.3.1, one of the most obvious differences shown in Figure 12 is that reading style has predominantly literal, formal type lexical phrases. In reading style lectures in general, topic markers, for instance, tend most often to be phrases like *let me/us begin with X, today/now I would like to (talk about/give you) X, you (may) recall (from last time)*, and topic shifters phrases like *let me go from there to X, the next point is X, and finally we have X* (columns 1 and 2 in Figure 12).

In conversational style, on the other hand, more idiomatic and more informal type phrases predominate, phrases like *we'll be taking a look at X, the first thing is X, maybe we should start with X,* as topic markers, and *OK, now, . . ., all right, . . .,* (both with falling intonation + pause), *lot more to talk about, but on to ____,   on to ____, back to ____,* as topic shifters.

The question is whether non-native speakers would be expected to recognize, for example, idiomatic phrases like *OK, now, . . ., all right, . . ., on to ____,* or *back to ____* as signals of topic shift. Undoubtedly they would not, and especially so in the case of the frequently used phrases *OK, now, . . .,* with falling intonation plus pause, and *OK so,* with level intonation and no pause, since the first signals topic shift, whereas the second signals summary. Further, we have found that *now (of course)* with level intonation can function as a qualifier, and though less frequently, even as a relator. These differences would be especially difficult for non-native speakers to distinguish, and yet, as emphasized earlier, these phrases are ones that

Lexical phrase discourse organizers

A. Global macro-organizers

	1. Topic markers	2. Topic shifters	3. Summarizers
'Conversational style'	we'll be taking a look at X maybe we should start with X what I'd like to do is X we'll be looking at X I'd like to talk about X let me start with X let me talk about X, then we'll go to Y first of all the first thing is X	OK, now. . . . (falling intonation + pause) all right . . . (falling intonation + pause) on/back to _____ lot more to talk about, but on to _____ so let's turn to X the other thing X is Y that brings us to X let's look at X we hafta get/move on to X more to the point enough on that	OK so (level intonation) so then (level intonation) so the theory goes (then) (so) (there) what we've got is X so there you've/we've got X _____, so much for that _____, that's about it in short to tie this up what I'm saying is (that) X in other words all this says is X
'Rhetorical style'	I'll be talking to you about X let's first deal with X let me suggest some ways (that) X what I'd like to do (today) is X	the other thing X is Y let me talk a little bit about X this leads to X let me go to X another thing (about all of this)	so this seems to be X you should be able to see that X (remember that) this means X in short
'Reading style'	now I would like to give you X let us begin with X today I would like to (talk about) X today we're going to hear X first and foremost you recall (from last time)	the next point is X the second X is Y let me go from X to Y now I'd like to give you X as to what is _____ end of quote any other comments before I turn to X? (and) finally we have X	in summary/conclusion to sum up my point is that X the main point is (that) X that points the way to X and that's the X this means that X in other words

(Figure 12—continued overleaf)

B. Local macro-organizers

	4. Exemplifiers	5. Relators	6. Evaluators
'Conversational style'	see if X clears this up maybe if I show you X, that'll/ this'll clear it up if you/we look at/see/go to X, you'll/we'll see Y if you've seen X then you've seen/known Y ———, something/things like that take (something like) (say) X (here) (for example/instance) one way is X same way here here's one to give (you) an example for example	now (of course) (level intonation) same way here you might say that X this ties in with X it/this has to do with X (but) how about ———? that would go/goes not only for X but (also) for Y any time X, there's Y X, so you would expect to find Y if you look at X, here's Y not only X, but also Y along the same lines	as X would have us believe X is fine/OK with me no problem with that but it ———, let me tell you look what's going on here (look how) X is (very) important X might not (always) work (that way) which seems (rather) odd/curious (to me) I'm a great believer in X X is worth noting/mentioning I think the best/most interesting (one) is X
'Rhetorical style'	one of the ways this can be seen/takes form is X take X, for instance/example we can see this if we look at X and that is X the easiest way to think about X is Y one of the most common ——— is X	keep in mind that X ———, like we just talked about along the same lines recognize that X, although Y, are also Z we should think of this not so much as X but as X we would think that X, but in fact Y we should be careful not to think of X as Y	I guarantee (you) that X ——— is worth noting and this is really the key to X I (would like to) suggest to you (that) X we should be careful not to assume that X
'Reading style'	for example/instance one of them was X as we'll see (that) X X is what I meant by Y we should see this in X on one occasion	that is in fact we will see from X that Y the next X also comes from Y in connection with X, Y first look at X, then look at Y	the X I would (like to) offer is Y but as a matter of fact it seems (to me) that X I prefer the explanation that X the critical thing is X I would (like to) suggest that X

7. Qualifiers	8. Aside markers
'Conversational style'	
now (of course) (level intonation)	(I) guess I got off the track here
the catch here is X	where was I?
it turns out that X	(well) forget about X
in the sense that/of _____	X doesn't (really) concern us here
there's more here than meets	(at the moment)
the eye	I've thrown X in (simply) to let you
whether you want to say X is	see (that) Y
another Y	I'm gonna stop writing on the board
but X does not mean that Y,	I'm gonna turn the overhead off now
(by any means)	(well) don't worry about X (right now)
(well) X is not even/really Y	
it's sort of like X, but not really	
it's only in X that Y	
actually the X is Y	
that's true but X	
we don't want to just accept X	
at face value	
'Rhetorical style'	
that's not really what we mean by X	(none found)
it doesn't mean that X	
well of course	
I should say/add that X	
at least (after) _____	
you would think that X is Y,	
but in fact it's (really) Z	
what I mean by X is Y	
it depends on how you define X	I'd like to pass over X
as far as I know/can tell	I won't trouble you with X
it turns out that X	but I'm getting a little ahead of myself
in the sense that/of _____	let me just make a parenthesis
do not assume, however, that X	
be careful not to X	
at least in _____	

Figure 12

are particularly common in conversational style lectures. What we are suggesting is that, while learning these lexical phrases as macro-organizers should not create any special problems for students, neglecting to teach them to students does create a special problem— namely, the problem of not being able to comprehend the direction of the discourse, nor the relationship among the parts within it.

With respect to rhetorical style, the macro-organizers seem to fall somewhere between those found in reading and conversational styles, though usually with a somewhat larger number of more literal type phrases. Topic shifters found in rhetorical style, for instance, include ones like *let me talk a little bit about X, this leads to X*, which are similar to those in the reading style such as *let me go from there to X, now I'd like to give you X*. However, rhetorical style includes frequent occurrences of the informal topic shifter *the other thing (that) X is Y*, which is also frequent in conversational style. It also includes phrases beginning with *so*, such as the summarizer (column 3 in Figure 12) *so this seems to be X*. Again, summarizers beginning with *so* are common in conversational style, as in *so there you/we have/you've/we've got X, so the theory goes, so much for that*.

Overlapping of the more literal, formal phrases and the more idiomatic, informal ones does, of course, occur also in the other two styles. The main difference is one of degree, for as Figure 12 illustrates, the idiomatic, informal lexical phrases predominate in conversational style, whereas the literal, formal ones predominate in reading style. In rhetorical style, however, neither type seems more prominent than the other. This mixing does not occur so commonly in conversational and reading styles. If somewhat more formal phrases appear in conversational style lectures at all, they more often tend to be topic markers at the beginning of a lecture. If a lecturer does begin with a lexical phrase such as *let me start with X* or *we'll be looking at X* he or she tends very quickly to shift to the typical informal phrases like *OK, now, . . ., on to ____, all this says is X*, and so on. Of course, there are other types of overlapping, as with the qualifiers *it turns out that X, in the sense that/of ____*, and exempli-fiers such as *to give you an example, for example*, which are often found in both styles. In general, though, the lexical phrases in the two styles are quite distinct.

Further differences between lexical phrases found in conversa-tional and reading styles are illustrated in summarizers (column 3). These differences, again similar to those found in the fragments in section 6.3.1, are consistent across lectures given on various topics by different lecturers. Reading style often includes *in summary/*

conclusion, the point is that X, whereas conversational style has *so then, all this says is* X, *so much for that.* Likewise, in column 5, relators, for instance, reading style has phrases like *that is, in fact,* phrases and functions students are likely to know already from their reading or writing classes. But in conversational style, we more often find discourse organizers like *now of course, so again, same way here, any time* X *there's* Y, phrasal forms and lecture discourse functions students are *not* likely to know unless they are taught in their language classes.

Evaluators (column 6) include *as* X *would have us believe,* which, according to reports from ESL teachers, non-native speakers invariably fail to understand. Other conversational style evaluators that students should be aware of are ones like X *is fine with me* or *no problem with that.* These are just as important as signals of a shift in topic, of a summary, or of relations among topics, because they signal the lecturer's evaluation or opinion of the material being presented—evaluations that the student needs to be aware of.

Again, under qualifiers (column 7) we find *the catch here is* X, a lexical phrase which non-natives would probably miss entirely. Others that non-natives would very likely fail to interpret correctly are those such as *whether you want to say* X *is another* Y, *that's true, but* X, *it turns out that* X, and so on. Students need to know that lexical phrases like these signal that previous information is being qualified in some way.

Finally, students need to be aware that aside markers like *(I) guess I got off the track here* mean that the immediately preceding material is not important, and need not be included in the lecture notes.

In short, conversational style lectures, and to some extent rhetorical style lectures, contain many crucial macro-organizers that cannot be interpreted literally. We have illustrated that these include not only organizers like *OK, now,* . . . and *OK so,* with different intonational patterns, but others like *on to* ____, *back to* ____, *so the theory goes, in short, take something like* X, *you might say that* X, *as* X *would have us believe, the catch here is* X, and so on. Students not only frequently misinterpret such lexical phrases, they also fail to understand that they are macro-organizers signaling important functions in the lecture discourse. And, although we have indicated that in reading style lectures the macro-organizers are more likely to be understood because they are usually literal, unfortunately for non-native learners reading style is not very common, at least in US schools, whereas conversational style is.

Thus, in teaching lexical phrase macro-organizers to high school or to college-bound non-native students, emphasis should also be placed on teaching ones like those found in conversational style in Figure 12, which commonly occur in lecture discourse, and not just those found in ordinary discourse.

6.4.2   Patterns of frequency in lecture discourse

We stated earlier that certain types of these macro-organizers are much more common and tend to recur quite often in lecture discourse. For example, in conversational style, among the most frequently used lexical phrases are *OK, now, ...*, *all right, ...*, and *OK so*, functioning as topic shifters or summarizers, respectively. In addition to those already mentioned, other examples of frequently occurring phrases are those like *so (there) you've/we've got X, so (there) you/we have X, so much for that, what I'm saying is X* as summarizers; *the other thing X is Y, this/it has to do with X, along the same line(s), same way here* as relators; *take (something like) (say) X (here) (for instance/example), if you/we look at/see/go to X, you'll/we'll find/see Y, here's one* as exemplifiers; or *it turns out that X, in the sense that/of _____*, as qualifiers.

The frequency of occurrence of a relatively small set of lexical phrase macro-organizers has obvious implications for teaching. Non-native learners, whether they understand the literal meaning of some of these phrases or not, are nevertheless unlikely to recognize their function as major signals of the direction of discourse and the relations within it. Very likely, this problem is one of the main reasons non-native speakers claim to understand the lectures but still fail the course. But if these lexical phrases and their lecture discourse functions are taught systematically to second language learners, and the high frequency ones especially, then non-native students in high school or college can improve their listening comprehension strategies considerably.[4]

6.5   Teaching lexical phrases for the comprehension of lectures

If students have already become familiar with lexical phrases as taught in conversation, discussed in Chapter 5, then teaching them as macro-organizers in lecture discourse would be a logical second phase for more advanced students. Instead of learning to produce them, however, they would learn to recognize them and their corresponding functions. One way would be to integrate them into reading and vocabulary classes. More ideally, though, they could also be integrated into courses in listening comprehension.

6.5.1   Reading and vocabulary class

To provide appropriate context for integrating the teaching of macro-organizers into reading and vocabulary classes, it might be helpful to adapt or supplement some of the techniques in Lebauer (1984), who offers some excellent suggestions for using lecture transcripts, including pseudo-cloze procedures.

Lebauer demonstrates, in detail, how transcripts of academic lectures and pseudo-cloze exercises, developed from these transcripts, can be used to help second language learners become aware of the skills involved in the process of listening to lectures. Samples of analyzed lecture discourse are given, together with suggested exercises. Through the analysis of complete and pseudo-cloze lecture transcripts, students are introduced to the concept of 'cues' (discourse devices), organizational patterns, redundancy, and paraphrase.

If adapted to the Lebauer approach, the teaching of lexical phrase macro-organizers could be done in a systematic way. A word of caution is in order, however. In cultures like the US, where conversational style is much more common, the teacher should take care that conversational style transcripts are well represented. Further, transcripts taken from video-taped lectures should not be used exclusively because the ratio of formal lexical phrases is usually much higher, and a typical range of conversational lexical phrases will probably not appear.

In learning macro-organizers for conversational style, students could start with some of the most frequently used but simple ones found in the lecture transcripts they read and analyze, such as *OK, now, . . ., OK so,* and *now of course,* with the teacher illustrating the distinction between intonation patterns for the functions of topic shifters, summarizers, and relators. Next, they could look at a few basic fixed lexical phrases with slots, analyzing them as increasingly variable patterns as they are exposed to more varied phrases.

If, in a given reading and vocabulary class, it is not feasible to include enough transcripts for students to learn the basic range of commonly occurring macro-organizers, the transcript analyses would probably need to be supplemented with less time-consuming exercises illustrating a broader range. These should include for instance, any high-frequency phrases, particularly those with variable patterns, which did not happen to appear in the transcript analyses. Further, even if the number of transcripts studied does provide an adequate sampling of typical macro-organizers, it is unlikely that the range of variations that are common for a given basic frame would be adequately represented. Thus, supplemental exercises giving practice with the various substitutions for the slots within the frames, would still be necessary if students are to achieve adequate facility in recognizing the basic frames and their functions.

Some of the most useful of these varied phrases include those high-frequency phrases with lower variability, such as *on to* ____, *all this says is X, so there you've/we've got X,* ____, *something like that, it/this has to do with* X, and later, high-frequency phrases with higher variability like *the other thing X is Y*, which is often expanded from the minimal *the other thing is (the fact) (that) Y* to the greatly expanded *the other thing (that is a little less obvious) (but one (I think) I should mention) is (the idea/fact that) Y.*[5] Other very useful high-frequency phrases with high variability are those such as the basic frame *take X*, which is expanded in various ways from the choice of fillers in *take (something like) (say) X (here) (for example)*, the basic frame *X might not work*, which is expanded variously as *X might not/doesn't (always) work (that way)*.

As with teaching lexical phrases for social conversation, then, these macro-organizers can be taught by first illustrating a basic lexical phrase frame, then teaching some representative lexical material that appears in the slots within that basic frame, and finally, teaching some representative variations and expansions of the frame itself. Students should also be taught to recognize and analyze more and more on their own these lexical phrase frames as they occur in lecture discourse. That is, they should be encouraged to recognize and segment new phrases on their own, on analogy with the kind of analysis done in the classroom.

6.5.2 Listening comprehension class

The listening comprehension class is ideal for incorporating the lexical phrase approach. This class, because it focuses on listening rather than reading, provides a more natural setting for learning to recognize and comprehend macro-organizers in lecture discourse. In learning these lexical phrases, the emphasis should be on recognizing macro-organizers as they appear in recorded lectures.[6]

There are several current texts on the comprehension of academic lectures, with accompanying taped lectures, which could be adapted for this purpose. Young and Fitzgerald (1982), for instance, provide a beginning by distinguishing categories like addition, comparison, contrast, exemplification, explanation, result, sequence, transition, and so on. No distinction is made, though, between macro- and micro-organizers, and thus some of these categories, like addition, comparison, or contrast, could contain either or both. Nor is any distinction made between global and local levels of co-ordination and subordination, levels needed to help the student develop an outline form in the lecture notes.

The teacher could adapt this book by reorganizing the categories into micro-organizers and macro-organizers according to function, using perhaps Figure 12 as a guide. Tapes could also be supplemented by using lecture tapes recorded by the teacher, in order to ensure that typical lecture style, especially conversational style, is well represented.[7]

Mason (1983) is an example of a text that does list various macro-organizers, under headings such as generalization, illustration, return to an earlier point, introduction to a new series, summing up, moving on, etc. And although, again, global and local levels are not recognized, these headings could be reorganized along these lines. Further, the teacher could help the students to recognize other common lexical phrases that occur in these lectures, though without being mentioned in the text, such as *X is something like Y, all we are saying is X*, which can easily be categorized according to the macro-organizers functions as listed in Figure 12.

Ruetten (1986) is another text that could be adapted and supplemented. Ruetten also lists mainly macro-organizers as listening cues, and she does sometimes point out the distinction between global and local levels, as for instance, a phrase like *for example* is often used to 'connect a generalization and an example' (1986:10). Again, however, macro-organizers mentioned are for the most part only those that occur in the sample lectures accompanying the text, which tend to be mainly in reading or rhetorical style. Thus, they are not at all typical of those found in our corpus of lectures recorded in a natural setting (a setting in which at least some of the lecturers agreed to be taped randomly, when they were not aware that the taping was being done).

On those few occasions when *all right* or phrases beginning with *so* appear, they are not singled out as signals of particular functions in the direction of discourse. Nevertheless, this text and the others mentioned above, provide a good general format, including not only macro-organizers as listening cues but also other valuable information needed in any course on listening comprehension of lectures, such as the settings, expectations, main parts of academic lectures, vocabulary review, outlining, and so on. Therefore, as a starting point, these texts could be adapted and supplemented in such a way that global and local macro-organizers could be integrated and their functions taught in a systematic way.

Notes

1   We recognize that the distinctions for these three categories are not sharply drawn. It is a very difficult matter to identify precise and clear differences among the three, because there is a certain amount of overlapping with respect to the language used, and thus the boundaries are somewhat fuzzy. Nevertheless, we believe the distinctions drawn by Dudley-Evans and Johns are useful ones for teaching purposes, since they can be used to characterize, in at least some general way, the types of lectures that students may be expected to encounter.

2   The lectures were recorded in 1986 at Portland State University and at University of California at Irvine. The video lectures were pre-recorded for classroom use by the advanced ESL classes at Portland State. We are especially grateful to Roni Lebauer for providing us with the UC Irvine data.

3   *OK* here, spoken with falling intonation and pause, is used to signal topic shift. In Chapter 5 it was suggested that this *OK* is an ellipted form of *OK, now, . . .*, spoken with the same falling intonation and pause, and used to signal topic shift.

4   It should also be noted that in addition to idiomatic lexical phrases, there are a few single word items that are idiomatic and that also function as macro-organizers. Students also need to be aware of these because it is unlikely that they would understand them unless they are taught.

    Two in particular that we found to be frequent in academic lectures were *now* and *OK*, used with varying intonation patterns. While we suggested in Chapter 5 that *OK*, for instance, is an ellipted form of *OK, now, . . .*, with identical falling intonation and pause, we hesitate to classify these single-word items as lexical 'phrases'. Alternatively, they could be classified with single-word items such as *thus*, *further*, which also serve as discourse devices to signal the direction of the discourse. Whatever the classification of *OK* and *now*, we found that some lecturers tend to use them quite frequently. For instance, some lecturers (in conversational style) use the ellipted *now* as a topic shifter; others favor ellipted *OK* for the same function.

A further difficulty for students is that lecturers sometimes use one of these two to signal more than one function during the course of the lecture. It is particularly important for students to be made aware that, for example, a lecturer may use *OK* (ellipted form of *OK, now, . . .*) to signal topic shift, but also *OK*—with rising intonation—as a signal that clarification is being sought from the students. Likewise, *now* (the second possible ellipted form of *OK, now, . . .*) may be used as a macro-organizer to signal topic shift or qualification, depending on intonation.

Topic shifter
OK (falling intonation + pause)

Clarifier
OK? (rising intonation)

Topic shifter
now (falling intonation + pause)

Qualifier
now (level intonation, no pause)

Relator
now (level intonation, no pause)

An example of the use of *OK* is this excerpt taken from the first day in a social science course on human development:

Extra credit for this course will involve going to the library . . . into the current periodical room and pulling out some of the current journals . . . *OK so* (SUMMARIZER: not ellipted) restrict yourself like it says on here to current issues of the journals . . . *OK,* (TOPIC SHIFTER: ellipted) um, what I want to do in the time remaining . . . is to sort of give you an overview of what we're going to cover . . . *OK,* (TOPIC SHIF-TER: ellipted) . . . the other thing I should probably mention is this is . . . not what's known as a life span course . . . *OK, now,* . . . (TOPIC SHIFTER: not ellipted) what's going to happen is we're going to start next time in a prenatal stage . . . We'll also be talking about perception . . . um when does the kid hit the point when the kid knows that when a thing is out of sight it hasn't disappeared completely . . . but it continues to exist . . . *OK?* (CLARIFICATION)

As is common in conversational style lectures, this one also included many lexical phrase macro-organizers such as ＿＿, *something/things like that* (exemplifier), *it's sort of X but not really* (qualifier), *it turns out that X* (qualifier), *the other thing (that) X is Y* (topic shifter), *so we've got X* (summarizer), *so much for that* (summarizer), and so forth.

On the other hand, some lecturers favor *now*, while seldom using *OK*, as in the following excerpt taken from a lecture on the second day of a course in biology.

> *Now*, (TOPIC SHIFTER) I think it is much easier . . . to discuss the abiotic components of an ecosystem first . . . *Now*, (TOPIC SHIFTER) I'll spend quite a bit of time on the availability of water in the soil . . . One of the weaknesses of this first edition is that there is very little discussion of the ways in which light and temperature vary . . . *Now of course* (QUALIFIER) it's not really possible to separate light and temperature . . . This is the calorie . . . *Now* (RELATOR) don't confuse this with the calorie of the calorie counter . . . calorie of the calorie counter is a bigger unit.

Other frequent lexical phrases in this lecture were those like *so there you/we have/you've/we've got X* (summarizer) and *if you/we look at/see/go to X, you'll/we'll find/see Y* (exemplifier), each of which occurred a number of times. Others were *if you look at X you will find/see that X is (very) (much) like/unlike Y* (relator), *it isn't X (at all)*, *it's (that) Y* (evaluator), etc.

5   This latter expansion was taken verbatim from our lecture corpus. Many variations occurred in various of the lectures in conversational style, and to a lesser extent, in rhetorical style, but all were easily recognizable as the same basic lexical phrase frame. The same is true for all other macro-organizers discussed, whether relatively simple, or highly variable.

6   For an excellent discussion and general overview of approach, design, and procedures in the listening comprehension class, see Richards (1983). This paper also includes a section on practical applications of the methodology suggested, and illustrates useful techniques in developing materials for listening comprehension.

7   One good way to be sure that the natural style of the lecturer will appear on the tape is to obtain the permission of co-operative colleagues to allow the taping to be done randomly when the lecturer is not aware that the particular lecture is being recorded. There are various small and inconspicuous tape recorders on the market which can be used for this purpose.

7 Teaching written discourse: reading and writing

7.1 Introduction

In previous chapters, we have suggested that the principle aim of language teaching is to have students understand the communicative value of linguistic items in discourse, and that an effective way to do this is to have them learn the form/function composites we call lexical phrases. We have also suggested that communication itself is the result of a creative process involving both producers and receivers, which is essentially the same process for both. As Widdowson says:

> From the cognitive point of view both the initiation and the interpretation of discourse involves creative activity. Learning to comprehend efficiently involves the activation of interpretive techniques or procedures and the same procedures are brought into play in reverse when discourse is composed.
> (Widdowson 1979:156)

In other words, the productive process of writing and the receptive process of reading can be taught through similar sorts of techniques and procedures.

7.2 Theoretical stances

To choose the techniques that will most effectively do this, we need to consider current theoretical stances towards written discourse, and review the attitudes towards writers and readers that follow from these particular stances.

7.2.1 Written discourse as both process and product

These days, most researchers are likely to view written texts as the result of co-operative process rather than as structural products divorced from context. Most now assume that writers and readers discover meaning through a process, rather than simply finding appropriate structures to fit already developed ideas. Further, many researchers stress the symbiotic nature of the writer and reader. Phelps (1985), for example, argues for a unified theory in which the 'overarching process' is a co-operative enterprise whereby writers and readers construct meanings together, and offers an analysis of the dynamic interaction between them. These discourse-as-process approaches underscore the importance of the writer–reader interaction in discourse comprehension.

On the other hand, the discourse-as-product approach, though not as influential as it once was, still has its adherents. Although product research has been condemned by a few, several researchers feel that descriptions of writing processes have been largely achieved by analyzing sequences of different kinds of products. They believe, in fact, that text analysis of written products complements process-centered research and is needed for an integrated theory of writing.

Early discourse analysts worked with product-centered models almost exclusively, and were mainly interested in the cohesive devices that linked sentences together in a text. Lately, with the turn to models that emphasize discourse process rather than sentence form, analysts investigate those devices that create coherence among textual elements. Three of the most important of these process-centered models are: (a) predication, which views texts as predictable arrangements of elements serving particular rhetorical functions; (b) cognitive-based, in which the role of cognition in text processing assumes primary importance, and accounts for coherence as a function of the text and of the equipment the reader brings to its interpretation; and (c) the interactive-based, which stresses that to communicate successfully, writers need to be aware of their audience and either conform to expected patterns or purposely break from them for surprise effect. These last two overlap to some extent. The overriding theme of both the cognitive and interactive approaches is communicative intent, and the focus is on the function of linguistic elements and how these are processed by both the producer and by the receiver.

In sum, two major approaches—the product centered and the process centered—can be distinguished among empirical studies of written discourse, and both approaches are necessary for a comprehensive theory (Connor 1987). If written discourse is most accurately analyzed as simultaneously process and product, in teaching it, we must then concentrate on both the cognitive strategies that writers and readers employ to interpret texts and the structures with which they construct them. We need, in other words, to teach the communicative function of linguistic elements as well as their structure. And as we have suggested above, lexical phrases are ideal units for this since they are composites of function and form, and thereby synthesize process and product.

7.2.2   Writers and readers as active participants

These particular stances towards written discourse have each characterized the participants of that discourse also, and it would be well here to summarize the attitudes towards writers and readers that follow from each.

Following a sentence-based approach, many teachers view writing and reading as essentially mechanical enterprises, consisting of mapping written symbols on to spoken language in a rigorous one-to-one fashion. These teachers are primarily concerned with cohesive surface features in the written text. Apparently, many ESL writing teachers view themselves as this sort of teacher, in that they attend to surface-level features of writing, some going so far as to read and react to a text as a series of separate pieces at the sentence or clause level, rather than as a whole unit of discourse (Zamel 1987). In these classrooms, students learn to compose and read at only the local, structural level.

There is no doubt that surface, cohesive elements are important markers of meaning; but if considered as ends in themselves and not in relation to more global markers of organization in the discourse, they will not lead to efficient production and interpretation of text. For example, there is good evidence that L2 readers tend to be more linguistically bound to the text than are L1 readers. That is, they follow local strategies and are most attentive to the surface structure of the language. L2 readers often process texts in a bottom-up manner, focusing on surface structure features and building comprehension through analysis and synthesis of this visual input. Because many of the words that L2 readers perceive may be relatively or even completely unfamiliar, however, the 'chunking' or word-combining strategies that they use automatically in the native language may be rendered inoperable in an L2 context. When chunking is impeded, less information can be stored at one time in short-term memory. Such a reduction in storage capacity means that less linguistic data can be analyzed simultaneously, which results in inefficient use of redundancy and contextual cues. Because of limitations in human attention and memory processing capacity, these additional cognitive demands may account for the observation that good L1 readers are often not able to apply their reading skills to L2 texts (Kern 1989).

With the recent popularity of process-oriented models, some teachers have come to see writers and readers as actively involved in the process of creating and interpreting texts, and have adapted their teaching materials accordingly.

When writers are viewed as creators, it follows that learners of the composing process must be given optimum opportunities to develop ideas and engage in interaction with potential readers. What is needed is training, to enhance strategies of interaction and interpretation. The same is true of readers. A small but increasing number of researchers, curriculum designers, and teachers are now thinking of ways in which to help L2 readers develop such skills as making and confirming prediction, creating pre-reading expectations, identifying a text's macro-structure, and using textual redundancy, context signaling cues, and background knowledge to enhance comprehension. What is needed, in other words, is explicit instruction in reading comprehension strategies.

Successful readers tend to skip words they view as unimportant to total phrase meaning, while unsuccessful readers seldom skip any, viewing all words as equally important in their contribution to the total meaning. Less proficient readers, such as the L2 readers described above, tend to focus on reading as a decoding process rather than as a meaning–getting process, and depend almost entirely on local strategies, having to do with sound-letter, word-meaning, sentence syntax, and text details. Global strategies dealing with background knowledge, text gist, and textual organization are much more important for text understanding, but are hardly relied on by unsuccessful readers.

7.3   Teaching written discourse

Teachers need to provide strategies to assist both reading and writing students in synthesizing meaning in larger segments of text. These strategies must be based on elements that provide both cohesion and coherence in the discourse, and must divert students' attention, whether on the local or global level, from individual lexical items to larger lexical phrase form/function composites. If their cognitive resources can be released from such time-consuming surface-level processes as individual word recognition, students would have more time for processing meaning and would find the organization of information in the discourse more obvious. Training would, therefore, essentially involve bringing these already-possessed strategies into conscious awareness. Such strategies are of interest in themselves for what they reveal about the way readers and writers manage their interaction with written text, and how these strategies are related to text comprehension in general (Carrell 1989).

At the same time, writers and readers must be provided with a certain number of structural forms, because these interlock with the strategies for comprehending them. The provision of explicit knowledge about target-language discourse forms is a necessary component of classroom support for the writer and reader, for these forms are the structures that trigger specific strategies. Many of these forms will become apparent as students practice the particular strategies discussed above.

7.3.1 Knowledge of discourse forms

Empirical studies in both first and second language comprehension of written texts, have found that rhetorical organization influences the comprehension as well as the recall of both narrative and expository text (Carrell 1984). These studies have provided evidence that formal schema—that is, the organizational structure of the passage—is an important factor in comprehension. Providing non-native readers with information regarding the structural organization of a text seems to be an effective technique for enhancing their recall of that text (Lee and Riley 1990). Teachers can present this structural organization from both a sentence-based and process-centered discourse perspective.

7.3.2 Sentence-based perspective

In functional sentence analysis, Lautamatti (1987) looks at sequences from a sentence-based perspective and examines how the topics in sentences work through the text to build meaning progressively. Lautamatti identifies three possible progressions that result in cohesive discourse: parallel, in which topics are semantically identical; sequential, in which topics are always different (i.e. the comment of the previous sentence often becomes the topic of the current sentence); and extended parallel, in which the sequence of parallel topics is temporarily interrupted. Students must follow three procedures in performing a topical structural analysis: they must identify sentence topics, then determine sentence progression, and finally chart the progress of sentence topics. The idea, of course, is that the more students become aware of the characteristic progression of topics in well-written essays, the better they will be able to interpret intersentential relationships and incorporate them into their own writing.

Problems have arisen in applying this procedure, however. One is that there are at present no generally accepted criteria for determining how similar two topics must be before they are considered 'parallel'. Another is that the analysis of topic progression alone says very little about coherence in the surrounding discourse. According to Schneider and Conner:

> As with previous studies, our research shows that simply counting occurrences of parallel, sequential, and extended parallel progressions can distinguish between groups of essays. But to understand how these types of topic progression relate to coherence through features such as elaboration, supporting details, and examples requires more subtle distinctions in topic progressions that have been made.
> (Schneider and Conner 1990:423)

We suggest that such subtle distinction can be made by identifying the lexical phrases that occur along with the particular topics.

For one thing, surrounding lexical phrases can signal cohesive patterns of co-ordination and subordination among sentences. One of the major problems in producing and interpreting written discourse is determining the cohesive linear relationships among sentences, that is, determining whether the relation of a sentence to the one that precedes it and the one that follows it is a co-ordinate relationship or a subordinate one. Students can examine topic progression with lists of lexical phrases that signal either co-ordination or subordination (of low-level information)—for example, micro-organizers, such as *however, on the other hand, because of ____,* etc.—thereby rendering the overall cohesive pattern more obvious (see Chapter 4).[1]

Once students become adept at identifying sentence level cohesion and signaling cues, they will apply the same principles across sentence boundaries and begin to focus on the global cues and questions that lend coherence to discourse, such as which sentences are more important than others, in what specific ways sentence X is related to previous material, in what ways idea X is related to idea Y, and which devices signal co-ordination or subordination of high-level information. The cues here could, of course, be macro-organizers—

for example, *the main point is that X, as a result, for example*, and so on (see Chapter 4).

To highlight these cues, teachers can employ exercises for isolating lexical phrases, similar to those we described in Chapter 6, for teaching lexical phrases in academic lectures. Reading activities are important for learning such lexical phrases, and serve both writing and reading pedagogy. Texts must be selected and modified to expose students to the most frequent of these phrases or to those that are the center of a particular lesson.

7.3.3   Process-centered discourse perspective

From a process-centered discourse perspective, Carrell believes that complementary findings from reading comprehension and from composition research suggest that 'teaching ESL writers about the top-level rhetorical structure of texts' and 'teaching them how to signal a text's organizational plan through linguistic devices' (Carrell 1987:55) will make their writing more effective and their reading more efficient. In other words, we can train students to identify and use top-level organizational structures along with appropriate signaling devices. Mapping and hierarchical outlining of high-level discourse movement in terms of interlacing lexical phrases would increase students awareness of information flow. In section 7.5 we show how this could be accomplished.

In a related procedure, sentences are typically reduced to propositions, which fulfill rhetorical functions in the text. Each proposition consists of a predicate (relator) and one or more arguments. These relators are rhetorical predicates which serve such functions as explanations, response, manner, and so on. Independent sentences serve as arguments and are linked by rhetorical predicates which come in many levels, creating a hierarchy of superordinate and subordinate ideas. For example, 'response' is a top-level rhetorical predicate which can have as its arguments 'problem' and 'solution'. This could be called a problem-solution, top-level structure. Other top-level structures include comparison, collection of descriptions, and causation. Each would display a characteristic network of lexical phrase discourse devices, combining particular patterns of macro- and micro-organizers. Many of the highest-level relationships in these patterns, those that guide the general type of discourse that follows from them, are similar to adjacency pairs mentioned in Chapter 5. High-level rhetorical organizers such as problem–solution and cause–effect, are similar to expected conversation pairs such as question–answer and assertion–response, and should be taught in similar ways that foster their paired nature.

Providing such an expanded rhetorical framework as a text adjunct would facilitate production and comprehension of written discourse for students. This expanded framework would provide relevant contextual information sufficient to improve recall of the overall content and top-level ideas of written texts.

7.4   The structure of three kinds of written discourse

For a more specific illustration of how all of this might work, we first need to examine the ways that lexical phrases are organized in different kinds of written discourse, and select three kinds of writing that most ESL students become familiar with during their college experience. First is the formal essay, which develops an argument or states the results of a scientific investigation. What we present here typifies the 'idealized' essay framework taught in most North American universities, and is usually the most transactional sort of writing that students learn. The second type of writing we examine is that of the informal letter, in which one writes to friends about personal matters. This is one of the most interactional kinds of writing students become acquainted with, for the main purpose of such letters is to maintain social relationships rather than impart factual information. It is included to illustrate the contrast between transactional and interactional written discourse. The third type is the business letter, which acts to maintain social relationships, but at the same time to transmit information. The audience of this letter is less familiar to the writer, so the style of the letter is more formal than that of a personal letter.

7.4.1   Structure of a formal essay

The typical essay a student writes in North American universities, either to express an opinion, develop an argument, or report on scientific investigation, adheres to the following structure:

1   Opening:

   (A) Topic priming: sets the scene and prepares the reader for what is to follow.

(B) Topic nomination:
  (a) statement of purpose: explains what the writer intends;
  (b) statement of topic: explains what the writer will talk about;

(C) Statement of organization: explains how the writer will talk about the topic.

2 Body: sets forth the argument, conveys the information.

3 Closing: brings the argument to a close.

Some representative lexical phrases for the above categories would be the following:

1 Opening: characterized by lexical phrases of discourse maintenance.

(A) Topic priming *for a long time X, it has been the case that X; it is/has been (often) asserted/believed/noted that X; most accounts of X state/claim/maintain that Y; according to ____, X is Y; one of the most controversial/ important Xs (in the recent literature) is Y.*

(B) Topic nomination:
  (a) statement of purpose *this paper intends/is designed to X; the (basic) emphasis/purpose/goal of the paper/article is to X; I/we intend to show/ demonstrate/illustrate that X; the purpose of this study/analysis/discussion is to X.*
  (b) statement of topic *this paper treats/discusses/claims that X; it is the case that X; my/our argument is essentially that X; I/we claim/maintain/contend that X.*

(C) Statement of organization: lexical phrases here signal the direction the discourse will take. They are rather like a road map in giving the reader an idea of what route the argument will take.
this paper will compare/contrast/describe/demonstrate that X (first) (by analyzing/comparing/demonstrating (that Y) (then by ____ing Z, and finally by ____ing A; in what follows, X will be examined in terms of Y (and Z).

2 Body: The body consists of a mosaic of phrases of discourse purpose, necessary topics, and discourse devices. Phrases from the latter two categories are similar to the ones described for conversation in Chapter 4. Phrases of purpose are somewhat different, however, as can be seen from the following categories of discourse purpose and representative phrases:

(a) assert: *it can be claimed/said/assumed that* X; *it seems certain/likely/doubtful that* X; *I/we maintain/claim that* X.

(b) agree: *as* X *perceptively states*; *I/we rather/somewhat/ strongly agree with/support (the idea that)* X; X *provides/lends support to* Y's *argument/claim/conclusion that* Z.

(c) disagree: *as* X *would have us believe*; *I/we rather/ somewhat/strongly disagree with* X; *as* X *states (somewhat) unclearly/erroneously*; X *does not support* Y's *argument/claim/conclusion that* Z; *although* X *contends that* Y, *I/we believe that* Z.

(d) compare: *both* X *and* Y *are (quite) similar in that* Z; X *is like/resembles* Y; *both* ____ *and* ____; X *and* Y *have/share some aspects of* Z; X *and* Y *have in common that* Z; X *is not unlike* Y *in that/with respect to* Z.

(e) contrast: X *is (quite) different from* Y *(in that* Z); X *is not the case that/the same as* Y; X *in no way resembles* Y; X *contrasts with* Y *(in that* Z); X *is unlike* Y *in that/ with respect to* Z.

(f) recommend: *let me recommend/suggest that* X *be/have/do* Y; *what I want to recommend/suggest is that* X; *one suggestion is that* X *(do* Y).

(g) substantiate: *as proof/evidence/an example (for this) (let me cite/quote)*; *according to* ____; *as* X *says/claims*; X *provides evidence/support that* Y.

(h) classify: X *can/may/might be divided/classified into* Y *(and* Z); X *and* Y *are categories/divisions of* Z; *there are* X *categories of* Y.

(i) demonstrate: X *demonstrates/shows that* Y; X *is an illustration of* Y.

(j) generalize: *generally speaking*; *in most cases*; *one can generalize that* X; *in general*; *for the most part*.

3 Closing: characterized by lexical phrases of discourse

maintenance: *in sum/conclusion; to sum up/conclude; to tie this (all) together.*

Just as in conversation, lexical phrases of maintenance and purpose provide the framework for the discourse, necessary topics the actual subject matter of the discourse, and discourse devices the cohesive force that binds the text together.

7.4.2   Structure of an informal letter

The sort of formal, transactional writing above is quite different from the more spontaneous, casual writing we use in quick letters. In this sort of writing, the audience is known and the message is personal, and in that respect it is much closer to speech than the formal language used for the transactional writing above. The general shape of such an informal letter is the following:

1 Opening
2 Body (Topic nomination)
3 Closing

Each of these sections is characterized by certain lexical phrases:

1 Opening: begins with a salutation, *Dear (NAME), hi/hello (NAME)*, often followed by an apology or excuse, *I'm (really) sorry for not writing/getting in touch sooner; I've been meaning to write for a long time, but X*, then continues much as a one-sided conversation, with many of the lexical phrases we described in Chapter 5.

2 Body: nominates topics which are often phatic (*how are you/have you been?; I'm good/fair/poor; there's really no news*), and when they do center on information, it is usually personal (*do you remember X?; how's X?; let me tell you about X*). Topic shifts can occur as abruptly as they do in conversation, and are often signaled by the same conversational lexical phrases, *(oh) by the way, (oh) and another thing*. Lexical phrases of discourse purpose are similar to those used in conversation; agreement can be expressed by *I'm sure that X*; recommendation by *why don't you X?, I think we should X*, and so on.

3 Closing: usually consists of signals to close (*well, that's about it*) and the actual closing (*see you later, so long (for*

now), with love/affection.) Many of these are the same ones used to close conversations.

7.4.3   Structure of a business letter

The categories of lexical phrases in business letters closely resemble those in informal letters, for the language is also highly interactive. However, the actual phrases are more formal, and they more explicitly signal their function than the ones in personal letters.

1   Opening: begins with a salutation, usually *dear [TITLE] + LAST NAME,* often followed by a phrase referring to what prompted the letter: *thank you for/we are in receipt of your letter (of DATE) (requesting X),* then moves quickly into the main purpose of the letter by nominating the topic.

2   Body: nominates topics with such lexical phrases as *this is/I am happy/regret to inform you that X; in reference to ____; re our meeting/your letter (of DATE) (in which X).* As mentioned above, phrases signaling discourse purpose are more formal and explicit than those used in informal letters. For example, agreement is likely to be expressed by a phrase such as *I/we are in (total) agreement with X;* recommendation by *let me advise/suggest/recommend that you X.*

3   Closing: frequently consists of extended formulas that signal imminent closing (*please let me know what you think (about all of this); I'll be happy to answer any questions you (might) have (about all of this/the above); I'd be pleased to discuss this with you at your convenience,* etc.), actually closing with such phrases as *with best regards/wishes, sincerely/respectfully/very truly (yours).*

Although some phrases remain the same in all three types of writing, most are specific to a particular type. Students must learn to recognize and use the appropriate variant, either formal or conversational, for the written discourse at hand. As mentioned in Chapter 4, fluency is not so much the ability to coin appropriate phrases for novel situations as it is the ability to retrieve from a wide assortment of lexical phrase variants for recurring situations. It is discouraging and tiresome for language learners (and their audience!) to have to use the same phrases repeatedly for the same functions.

Essay	Informal letter	Business letter
Opening:		
for a long time X	*hi/hello/dear* _____ *do you remember X?*	*dear* _____ *I am happy/regret to inform you that X*
it has been the case that X	*let me tell you about X*	
one of the most important/ controversial _____ *(in the recent literature) is X*		*in reference to* _____
Body:		
agreement:		
it is (undoubtedly) true that X	*I'm sure/certain that X*	*I/we are in (total) agreement with X*
it seems/is clear that X		
recommendation:		
X should/might/can be undertaken/ accomplished	*you should X why don't you X? I think we should X*	*let me advise/ suggest/ recommend that you X*
Closing:		
in sum/conclusion	*see you later*	*with best regards/wishes*
to summarize	*well, that's about it (for now)*	

7.5   Teaching written discourse with lexical phrases

The following exercises illustrate that, just as Widdowson (1979) suggests, writing and reading are similar but reverse processes, requiring similar strategies, and allowing a natural way of integrating reading and writing instruction.

At very early stages of language learning, the teacher may wish to start with a few useful, invariable phrases for the student to memorize, or with some phrases with variable slots which students can fill out in rather controlled sentence-completion exercises. Then, as in teaching conversation, teachers can introduce variations of these particular phrases as the student progresses. For topic priming, for example, students might practice writing the variants of the phrase *it is/has been (often) asserted/believed/noted that* X:

> *It is believed that* X
> *It is often asserted that* X
> *It has been noted that* X etc.

Soon afterwards, teachers could show students the basic outline of such written discourse, rather as we have done above, and then begin working through it section by section, introducing them to phrases that are commonly used to express the function of each section. Students will learn that sentence builder lexical phrases provide the framework for the body of a text, that polywords and phrasal constraints serve as transitions among these sentence builders and the arguments they contain, and that phrasal constraints occur most commonly in openings and closings. The most common lexical phrases are macro-organizers that signal the functions of the opening, of the body, and of the closing, and can in that way be systematically presented. Ideally, students will have already learnt many of these basic phrases in the early exercises of memorization and sentence-completion.

Students should then begin to practice piecing together phrases that are characteristic of particular sections, discovering effective ways of joining lexical phrases from the three categories of interaction, topic, and discourse devices. For this, it would be well to work with relationships among functions, just as in conversation. For example, if students are learning phrases for openings in a formal paper, it would be efficient to teach those in terms of the natural connection between topic priming (for example, *for a long time, many researchers have believed* X) and topic nomination (for example, *this paper will show that* Y). Students could then progress to a full introduction, taking these lexical phrases for topic priming and for topic nomination, and attaching them to a phrase that states the organization (for example, *this paper will compare/contrast/describe/demonstrate that* X *(first) (by analyzing/comparing/demonstrating (that* Y)) *(then by* ____*ing* Z, *and finally by* ____*ing* A). One result of amalgamating these particular phrases might be: *For a long time, many researchers have believed* X. *This paper will show that* Y, *by comparing and contrasting* Z, *and recommending that* A.

Progressing to a complete essay, students might work with the following structure of functions and phrases:

Opening

topic priming:	*it is/has been (often) asserted/believed/ noted that X*
topic nomination purpose:	*the (basic) emphasis/purpose/goal of this paper/article is to X*
topic:	*I/we claim/maintain/contend that X*
organization:	*this paper will show/compare/contrast/ describe/demonstrate that X (first) (by analyzing/comparing/demonstrating (that Y)) (then by ____ing Z, and finally by ____ing A).*

Body

assert:	*it can be claimed/said/assumed that X*
agree:	*X provides/lends support to Y's argument/claim/conclusion that Z*
disagree:	*X does not support Y's argument/claim/conclusion that Z*
compare:	*both X and Y are (quite) similar in Z*
contrast:	*X is unlike Y in that/with respect to Z*
generalize:	*one can generalize that X*
Closing:	*in conclusion/sum*

Students would practice combining many of the variations of these, creating a skeleton structure for the essay, later filling in the specific arguments for X, Y, and Z. One such structure for the preceding phrases might be the following:

Opening:	*It has been often asserted that . . . The purpose of this paper is to . . ., and to maintain that . . . The paper will show that . . . by comparing . . . and by contrasting . . .*
Body: first paragraph	*It can be said that . . . . . . lend support to the argument that . . .*
second paragraph	*. . . does not support the argument that . . .*

third paragraph   *Both . . . and . . . are similar in that . . .*
                     . . . is unlike . . . with respect to . . .
Closing: *In conclusion, one can generalize that . . .*

Teachers can also have students outline texts that have been written by others, essays from texts they are using in other university classes perhaps, using macro-organizers and other sorts of lexical phrases described above. This will not only help them become acquainted with various sorts of phrases used in different types of written discourse, but will also illustrate the co-ordinate and subordinate hierarchies in the text. As mentioned earlier, determining co-ordinate and subordinate relationships among individual sentences seems to be one of the hardest problems students face. Outlining typical patterns of co-ordination and subordination, and relating them to specific lexical phrases that trigger these relationships, will help make these patterns more obvious.

Students can also outline their own, draft copy of an essay, and then compare this outline with those of other students, or with earlier ones done for written essays from texts or other sources. This activity will lead them to analyze their own weaknesses in organization. Very likely, their writing will be deficient in subordinate-level information and accurate macro-organizers, which seems to us to be typical of ESL learners.

A further advantage is that such outlining will no doubt reveal cultural differences in writing styles. Arabic restatement, for example, occurs frequently through co-ordinately marked sequences rather than subordinate ones, as would be most common in English. Discourse outlines would provide for a quick look at such contrastive rhetorical styles, and would allow students to see what kinds of lexical phrase organizers are required in particular cultures.

A possible criticism teachers might have of the above technique is that it may seem to them to emphasize the written product over the writing and reading process. We do not believe this is so, at least to any detrimental effect. First of all, as mentioned at the beginning of this chapter, we feel that the distinction drawn between product and process in the literature is often overstated, since, after one jots down initial, indirectly connected thoughts, one revises principally by shaping structures to match the evolving coherence among these thoughts. Process and product are in this way inseparable. Secondly, as we have also claimed, lexical phrases are unitary structures, different from words only in being used for particular functions. Therefore, revising lexical phrases should be little different from revising single words, or selecting vocabulary. In fact, since lexical phrases are units of function as well as of form, revising in terms of them ought to lead more quickly to a satisfactory balance of overall form, function, and coherence.

Notes

1   When possible, cohesive elegance uses unstated structures of expectation to avoid those explicit ties that add words without adding new information. Ties of collocation associate propositions (words associated with particular themes, unstated logical progressions, other conventional orderings of ideas). This is one of the areas in which a wide window analysis in computational research would reveal interesting relationships (see also note 4, Chapter 1).

8 Conclusions and prospects

8.1 Introduction

Lexical phrases are basic, pervasive units in language production, which should thus prove to be empirical and intuitively significant guides for researching many problems in applied linguistics. In this chapter, we mention some areas that could be further explored using lexical phrases as a measure and, as we will see, many researchers have already begun such explorations, employing units of measure that closely resemble lexical phrases. Following in a general way the format of previous chapters, we will first discuss concerns of a theoretical and descriptive nature arising from Part One, and then turn to concerns of a pedagogical nature arising from Part Two.

8.2 The need for further empirical research

A general observation to be made about all of these areas is that they require additional empirical fieldwork. Because language is so complex and because our understanding of it is still so elementary, we need additional studies utilizing actual data of language use to investigate further the kinds of lexical phrases that occur and how they are used in particular situations.

Empirical research has shown that the structures many current texts teach for certain functions are either never used or used infrequently, while quite unexpected structures are the ones that actually occur. In a study of the language of business meetings, for example, Williams (1988), to cite one of many articles recently that document this disparity, finds that the many structures for functions taught by business English texts were almost never used in recorded transcripts of business meetings. The structures actually used resembled lexical phrases rather than traditional sentences: they were prefabricated chunks, seldom complete sentences, and were almost always sequenced as part of a discourse. The structures taught, however, were just the contrary: they *were* complete sentences, which were not sequenced or considered in combination with other utterances. In other words, the structures for the functions presented to the students took no account of these utterances as parts of ongoing discourse. For example, instead of the bald, textbook *I disagree with that*, actual transcripts show *well/yes, (I can see that) but X*, or *wouldn't it be better to X* to be the actual signals for disagreement. Likewise, for explaining, speakers used such phrases as *(because) you see X*, *the thing/argument is X* instead of the prescribed *let me explain what I mean*.

Another problem is that language forever varies, changing to be appropriate to the situation in which it is used, so there is no such thing as natural speech in any absolute sense. Lexical phrases, being an intersection of structure, function and use, ought to provide an effective unit for measuring linguistic variation. Such measurement will be difficult, however, because most lexical phrases are used so automatically that they are quite beyond conscious retrieval. We are also used to thinking that people speak more like us than they really do, so we may have such preconceived notions of what things ought to be that we are blinded from seeing what is really there. Simply asking informants to describe the phrases they use in particular circumstances will not be sufficient, a lesson the authors learnt when compiling the examples from Spanish, Chinese, and Russian in the Appendix, nor will it suffice to assume that all speakers of a certain group characteristically use certain lexical phrases.

The solution again appears to take the form of empirical investigation of actual language variation. In one such study, Holmes (1989) examines the differential use of formulas for compliments and for apologies by women and men, and demonstrates how social roles of participants play a major part in the particular formulas used. She concludes that textbooks that assume uniform phrases (generally those she finds in male-to-male interactions) as basic for language performance present an unrealistic picture of actual language behavior. Also needed are additional studies of cross-cultural variation, similar to those discussed in Chapter 5.

The range of lexical phrases for the different functions varies, but for each category they seem to range from the aggravated to the mitigated. Frequently, foreign students do learn the neutral forms, but they lack the softened or strengthened forms that smooth over difficult interactions. Probably it is the case that the conditions when one uses a softener, when one hedges, are different in different cultures, but this needs to be systematically investigated as well.

8.3   The theoretical nature of lexical phrases: further inquiry

One of the primary and perhaps most difficult tasks is to resolve further questions involving the nature of lexical phrases. Characteristics of lexical phrases must be more rigorously defined to permit reliability in further research with these units. In particular, we need better criteria for identifying exactly what counts as a formulaic phrase. Wong-Fillmore, for example, requires these phrases to: (1) have a single invariant form, or a frame that allows for a variety of forms in a grammatical slot within the formulaic construction, (2) be repeatedly used by the speaker, (3) be situationally dependent, (4) be grammatically advanced compared to similar constructions in the child's speech, or (5) be community-wide formulas (Wong-Fillmore 1976: 310). These criteria, though accurately describing characteristics of lexical phrases, have little diagnostic value for more rigorous work, and could easily become generalized to the point of vacuity. Bohn levels exactly this criticism:

> It seems that Wong-Fillmore extends the notion of frame structure so far that it becomes vacuous. If all utterances that have one lexical item in common in one position ... are considered instances of frame structure, then formulaicness is nothing short of a pervasive phenomenon in the speech of learners and of competent speakers.
> (Bohn 1986: 191)

In other words, there must be some kind of constraint on the number of variable slots in a phrase and the types of substitution allowed in the slots, for if there are too many, the notion of prefabrication disappears. Bohn suggests that one of the problems with Wong-Fillmore's work is that she describes too many dissimilar phrases as variations of the same unit. Obviously, definitions need to be tightened.

8.3.1   Criteria for defining language patterns

Previous work in collocation seems to offer the most direct path to such definition. While collocations are distinct from lexical phrases in that lexical phrases are form/function composites, research in collocations suggests a possible direction for more rigorous definitions of the distinctions among various lexical phrase categories (such as polywords, institutionalized expressions, phrasal constraints, and sentence builders, described in Chapter 2).

Instead of assuming a qualitative, either–or distinction between idiomatic language and regularly generated language, collocationists are more prone to see language on a cline, with completely invariant clusters at one end of the continuum, freely combining morphemes at the other, and all degrees of combinational flexibility in between. Wood (1981) perhaps offers the best model for what we describe in this book. As mentioned in Chapter 1, she makes a case that there is no qualitative break between prefabricated and creative syntax. She believes that these exist only at opposite ends of a continuum, separated by infinite shadings of syntactic and semantic variation. Her work goes further than most in proposing both syntactic and semantic criteria for judging frozenness of form. Whereas most collocationists use only a semantic criterion of whether a combination is fully 'compositional' or not, that is, whether the meaning of the collocation is fully predictable from the individual meanings of the words that compose it, she employs as well a syntactic criterion of whether the form of a combination is fully productive or not, that is, whether a form is structurally unique, whether it is fully canonical, or whether it is somewhere in between these two poles.

Using these parameters, she then is able to define the continuum more precisely. A fully non-compositional, non-productive collocation is a true idiom, a truly frozen piece of language. Phrases such as *hell for leather, by and large* qualify, for they make no compositional 'sense', nor do they have syntactic patterns that generate other such structures. At the other end of the continuum, a phrase like *see the river* is fully compositional and productive; its meaning is a combined meaning of the individual units, and its form is the basis for an unlimited number of phrases. In between these two extremes are phrases that are limited in compositionality and productivity in various degrees. For example, the oft-cited *kick the bucket* is not completely frozen, since the word *kick* in the sense of *die* exists in a few other phrases, such as *kick off* and *kick out*, and is therefore less an idiom than *hell for leather*. This meaning of *kick* is certainly restricted, however, and so the phrase is not as compositional as *drink milk/tea/coffee*, which demonstrates full compositionality. Likewise, the phrase *off with his head* permits only limited lexical variation, (*down with the king, away with all X*), always carrying the meaning of 'Directional Particle + *with* + NP', and therefore is more restricted in the combinations it can form than is a fully productive phrase like *see the river*.

Using these criteria, Wood suggests that language patterns itself along the continuum represented in Figure 13.

idioms — collocations — colligations — free combinations

Figure 13

Idioms are one of a kind, both compositionally and productively, and are completely unpredictable in their meaning and form. True idioms (*by and large, hell for leather, happy go lucky*) are thus completely frozen and relatively few in number, since most phrases permit some degree of compositionality or productivity. Collocations are roughly predictable yet are restricted to certain specified items and thus are nameable by words. *Take umbrage*, for example, is a highly restricted collocation that invites a compositional interpretation, but the unique noun and the empty verb baffle it. Substitution of synonyms is possible in many collocations, and where possible will produce what are called 'idiom families' (*pay heed/attention, open-and-shut case/issue/problem*). When substitution is bounded only by syntactic category and semantic features (and predictability of meaning is greater than ever), one arrives at what Mitchell calls 'colligations', a term coined by J. R. Firth. Colligations are generalizable classes of collocations, for which at least one construct is specified by category rather than as a distinct lexical item:

> As collocations are nameable by words, so colligations involve the use of word-classes to name the collocational class. Colligational labels underline the necessary admixture of 'formal' and 'functional' as in the case of ('motive' verb + 'directional' particle) [describing 'tear/lope/race etc. . . . up/along/across etc.].
> (Mitchell 1971:53)

As phrases are less restricted to specific lexical items and can be described in terms of more word classes, the more they approach the freely compositional and productive end of the continuum (see Figure 14).

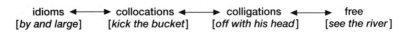

idioms ←——→ collocations ←——→ colligations ←——→ free
[*by and large*]   [*kick the bucket*]   [*off with his head*]   [*see the river*]

Figure 14

8.3.2   Criteria for defining categories of lexical phrases

Such a model might possibly be adapted for refining the categories of lexical phrases. We have, throughout, talked about degrees of frozenness, syntactic frames with lexical fillers, and so on, all of which are characteristic of this particular description of language. We have also characterized lexical phrases as occupying a 'pragmalinguistic', or interface position between syntax and general pragmatics. However, some types of lexical phrases condition, or constrain, the syntax more than others. For example, a phrasal constraint such as *a ____ ago* (*a month ago, a year ago*) allows only noun phrase substitution; a sentence builder such as *it's only in X that Y* restricts the Y slot to a full (finite) sentence, but allows either a noun phrase or a gerund phrase in the X slot (*it's only in Venice that you find gondolas, it's only in running uphill that I have trouble breathing*); a sentence builder such as *the other (thing) X is Y* allows a great deal more variation in the X and Y slots (*the other thing I think I should mention is that there will be a quiz tomorrow, the other thing bothering me is the missing documents, the other part of the puzzle is who shredded the documents?*).

An important difference is that lexical phrases, as form/function composites, are associated with particular pragmatic functions. Comparison is difficult, then, since our categories are descriptive of language functions and use, as well as of syntax and semantics. For example, the category 'institutionalized expressions' can include chunks of fully compositional, fully canonical language, yet it is language that a speaker has learnt to *use* in an unvarying, idiomatic way. Thus, while it may be analyzed as 'unrestricted' in terms of semantic and syntactic flexibility, it must be seen as idiomatic or collocational in terms of language use.

Interesting results await research that pursues three particular problems:

(1) The problem of specific tests for grouping lexical phrases in one category or another. Though Wood specifies the problem in ways that may make it more approachable, we still need more rigorous tests for determining degree of compositionality and productivity for form/function composites than she or other collocationalists offer. At present, commutation tests are the sole criterion: the amount of possible synonymic substitution to indicate degree of compositionality, and the amount of possible morphemic substitution to indicate productivity. As with all commutation tests, however, problems of use and interpretation intrude and make the procedure less than objective.

(2) The problem of the relationship between the semantic and syntactic characteristics of the construct, its particular pragmatic

function in the discourse, and the degree to which this construct is used as a frozen or as a freely generated chunk of language. Here the dimensions of form, function, and use converge in a broad and realistic portrait of language. We will return to this question briefly in our discussion of language acquisition below.

(3) The problem of the kinds of restrictions imposed on the syntax by particular lexical phrases; for example, how many substitutions are allowed within a particular slot, and what they are. As our examples at the beginning of this section show, there are different kinds of restrictions for different lexical phrase slots. The slot in *a _____ ago* is regularly restricted to noun phrases that refer to time, while the slots in *the other (thing) X is Y* are much more flexible in the kinds of structures that they accept. We need to explore the individual syntactic worlds of lexical phrases and map their particular grammars.

8.3.3   Discourse analysis

Another question for investigation has to do not only with the categories of lexical phrases, but also the relationship between these and the discourse categories to which they belong. The problems are numerous, and are well known to all discourse analysts. We not only need to assign the specific lexical phrases used in particular encounters to appropriate structural and functional categories, but we need to evaluate the categories themselves, not only pedagogically but also empirically and theoretically.

First, the number and kinds of functions in language use need to be described as explicitly as possible. Second, the organization of these functions in discourse need to be investigated. Are they generally arranged hierarchically, the pattern we found in our description of transactional discourse in previous chapters, or do they sometimes take a more co-ordinate, linearly-chained order? As indicated in Chapter 4, conversational language seems to rely more on the latter than the former.

Underlying these are concerns about the adequacy of discourse analysis in general. Sinclair and Coulthard (1975) sum up the problem concisely in four criteria of adequacy, which they feel any description of discourse should meet: (a) Descriptive categories should be finite, otherwise there is only the illusion of classification and the temptation of *ad hoc* addition. There is no obvious limit to the functions which language may serve. (b) Descriptive categories should be explicitly tied to the lexical and syntactic forms that realize them, otherwise they cannot be replicated. (c) Descriptive categories should give comprehensive coverage of data, otherwise they ignore inconvenient facts. Certainly we have at times been selective in earlier chapters by using parts of conversations, lectures, etc., which demonstrate more clearly particular points, but sometimes ignoring those aspects of texts which were not easily included in the categories we established. (d) Description should place constraints on possible combinations of symbols, otherwise no structural claims are being made. This criterion suggests that the study of lexical phrases be examined in connected discourse, not as a series of isolated units, for the pragmatics of sentences significantly depends on their place within the discourse sequence. This we have tried to do as much as possible.

These criteria outline the steps that need to be taken in further research so that, as the data accumulate, a more complete analysis of the role of lexical phrases within discourse can be achieved.

8.3.4   Lexicography

Further research of descriptive matters will also lead to more sophisticated characterizations in related areas of language study. For example, we believe that a lexical phrase approach has a great deal to offer the practice of lexicography. Dictionaries select lexemes along the paradigmatic, vertical axis, and treat them as individual items in a substitution relation, listing them singly and assigning them an exclusive reference. Apart from idioms, two-part verbs, and other such fixed collocations, however, these dictionaries have little to say about words along the corresponding syntagmatic axis, and present almost nothing about the collocational possibilities for individual entries. This exclusion is perhaps the result of the fact that the focus of collocational studies is on the co-occurrence of lexical items as items rather than on their referential function.

But the meaning relations of words that occur along the syntagmatic axis also contribute to description of the meaning of a lexeme. The collocations that a lexeme regularly enters into contribute to its sense, and is a factor that needs to be taken account of in a description of its meaning. Sinclair suggests that there is a surprising amount of semantic information to be derived from the collocations in which particular lexical items most frequently occur (Sinclair 1987b).

First of all, different collocations will almost certainly lend special senses to a lexeme, such as the different shades of meaning *strong* assumes in the collocations *strong personality*, *strong odor*, and *strong tea*. Secondly, the lexical items that regularly fill the same slot in a particular collocation exist in a 'collocational range', and usually share meaning to a great extent. Fillers for *a _____ ago*, for example, are usually words like *day, week, year*, etc., and share the meaning relation of 'measure of time', which perhaps adds to their individual meanings. When an unexpected lexical item fills this slot, that is, when the slot is filled by a word out of the usual collocational range, that word assumes a new meaning by doing so. When the poet creates the collocational variant *a grief ago*, *grief* now absorbs the general sense of the collocational range for this slot, and becomes, for the moment, a measure of time. This is, of course, one of the major mechanisms for creating and interpreting metaphor. Finally, the strength of the mutual expectancy of words in a collocation may not be equal in both directions. *Tooth* is more likely to occur in combination with *false* than *false* is likely to occur with *tooth*. That is, the range of possible items to fill the slot *false _____* is greater than those fillers for the slot *_____ tooth*. That means its likely combination with *false* is part of the meaning of *tooth*, but it is not clear at all whether the meaning of *false* is any way dependent on its combination with *tooth*. The smaller the collocation range, the more this is true. For example, *rancid*, co-occurring with an extremely few items like *fat* and *butter* derives a great deal of its meaning from this fact (Jackson 1988).

Such syntagmatic description is an area of lexicography that is yet to be developed to any great extent, and is only now beginning to appear possible with the power and storage capacity of modern computers (Jackson 1988). Lexicographers need to pick out significant patterns of words in vast amounts of text that the unaided human mind could not possibly find, let along grasp and rank in order of importance. The large machine-readable corpora and tools for exploring them, which were referred to in Chapter 1, are now generally available, and await lexicographical research along collocational lines (Church and Hanks 1989).

A thorough dictionary, of course, would not stop with collocations, but would select those that play particular functional roles in the language and further label them as lexical phrases. Such a dictionary would be a major resource for information about the language, for it would list not only the form and reference for particular collocations, it would also assign each its function, similar to the methods we have used in preceding chapters.

8.4 Language acquisition

While prefabricated language is a generally accepted element of learner language, its specific role in language acquisition is not clear. As mentioned in Chapter 1, there is no agreement as to how prefabricated language becomes part of rule-governed language behavior over time, only that much of it does so, and that prefabrication is important for the early-stage learner to gain access to conversation with other speakers of the language.

VanPatten, in searching for 'psychologically "real" production rules' (VanPatten 1988), offers a discussion of language acquisition and prefabrication that incorporates the dimension of language use over time. He has examined beginning language acquisition, from both classroom and natural contexts, and suggests that early utterances may arise from the following production rule (which he calls the X + Y Rule):

> Take any unit X and place it immediately before any unit Y. Y may be of any size (word, phrase, or an internally generated string), but X is limited to an unanalyzed unit or word. Y must fall under the semantic or pragmatic scope of X.
> (VanPatten 1988:3)

For example, the unanalyzed chunk *I wanna* seems to be one of the earliest such X units, which learners prefix to a number of verbal and nominal predicates such as *play, ball,* etc. This chunk introduces the second part, the Y, which itself can be either an unanalyzed unit or a syntactically generated string. When X units are used in the Y frame, they then become candidates for segmentation and analysis. The Y of the formula X + Y, for example, could itself be composed of a sequence X + Y, which presumably could also contain an X + Y, and so on:

$$X + Y$$
$$|$$
$$[X + Y]$$
$$|$$
$$[X + Y] \text{ etc.}$$

When, VanPatten thinks, *me gusta* is used by the learner not just as an X (*me gusta + los deportes*) but also as part of a Y (*no creo que + me gusta mucho*), it becomes a candidate for segmentation, since in effect it leaves the fixed X unit frame. If the learner used it only in the

X position, then it would not be subjected to analysis and may either 'freeze' as an unanalyzed unit or might drop out.

From a theoretical perspective, this proposal is interesting in that it suggests different distributional potential of units and characteristic patterns of fixed and variable patterns in discourse:

(1) Different distributional potential of units. An ESL learner's X, *I don't know*, such as in *I don't know where's the car*, is an example of a unit which is difficult to imagine occurring in a Y unit. As such, it is likely to remain as an unanalyzed X unit while *do* and negation develop independently. In such cases, *I don't know* would remain as a fixed unit, while the learner's use of *I do not (care to) know* and other variations of the string show that syntactic processing of the frame is developing. Learners may in this way move back and forth between a type of 'pragmatic-communicative processing mode' (e.g. X + Y) and a 'syntactic mode' (e.g. one with phrase structure and movement rules), and could then, simultaneously, be producing both *where are you going?* (X + Y) as well as *where are you going?* (phrase structure with movement).

(2) Characteristic patterns of fixed and variable patterns in discourse. Such rules as X + Y suggest that discourse may be seen as a sequence of slots that are filled by language chunks of differing yet predictable variation. For example, beginning and ending sequences of conversational discourse may be characterized by a high degree of invariant, idiomatic formulas, while intervening patterns of collocational, colligational, and creative chunks of language weave together in a somewhat predictable fashion.

VanPatten is concerned about order and hierarchy in determining the X chunks from the Ys. Considering the functional dimension of units is bound to enhance such an analysis, for certain categories are likely to be characterized by different potential variation. Fluency devices, for example, seem to be very fixed units, while sentence builders are typically quite free.

From a pedagogical perspective, the rule offers an explanation as to why error correction in early stages of language learning is often unsuccessful. If teachers correct learners' language based on syntactic rules, but learners are operating under different 'psychologically real' production rules, then there is a mismatch between cause of error and remediation. In such a case, error correction will obviously be of little value.

Another gain is in research on fossilization. If there is a gradual shift from 'mostly X + Y rule' to 'mostly syntactic-like rules', might not some fossilization arise from a learner's persistent use of X + Y in the formation of utterances? Perhaps the learner with 'fossilized' speech has not allowed syntactic analysis to take precedence over something like the X + Y rule. In other words, the learner has simply fixed a lexical phrase when futher analysis is required. Perhaps degrees of fossilization can be investigated via the relative contribution that X + Y rule usage and syntactic rule usage make to speech production. Further research along these lines should yield interesting results.

8.5   Teaching

Distinguishing lexical phrases as social interactions, necessary topics, and discourse devices seems to us the most effective distinction for pedagogical purposes, but that is not to say that a more effective way of grouping might be found necessary in the wake of further research. Many suggestions have been made for dividing up the world of discourse theoretically, and some of these may be categories that better suit the classroom. For example, van Ek (1976) divides discourse into a finite number of things that we do with language, and describes categories which are similar to Searle's five speech acts (directives, representatives, commissives, expressives, and declaratives). We (1) exchange factual information, (2) exchange intellectual attitudes, (3) exchange emotional attitudes, (4) exchange moral attitudes, (5) use suasion, and (6) socialize. (1) seems similar to Searle's 'representatives', (5) to 'directives', (2), (3), and (4) to 'expressives'. Each of these functions has a number of sub-categories, and contains both statements and questions. For example, (3) includes '(dis)likes', '(non)preference', '(dis)satisfaction', 'worry/confidence', 'fear/optimism', 'surprise/boredom', 'hope', 'sympathy', and so on.

This model also includes notions, the things we talk about, which are classed as either 'general' or 'specific'. General notions, often called 'concepts', consist of such categories as 'time', 'space', 'qualitative', 'evaluative', 'mental', 'relational', 'deixis' and 'existence', while specific notions seem somewhat similar to speech situations and identify 'people', 'objects', and 'places in the environment'.

Van Ek's categories may map discourse territory more realistically than our social interactions, necessary topics, and discourse devices, but it is a question whether such detailed mapping will be pedagogically effective. What is not in question is that whatever the categories ultimately selected, they will have to be rigorously evaluated for pedagogical effectiveness.

Also to be evaluated is the effectiveness of different phrases themselves and methods for teaching them. Chaudron and Richards (1986), in one of the earliest attempts at such evaluation, demonstrate that certain phrases lead to more satisfactory comprehension of academic lectures than do others. Throughout this book, we have suggested that the most effective lexical phrases to teach in beginning stages would be those with a number of variable slots, since these would lead students more quickly to syntactic analysis. But that notion itself needs to be put to an empirical test. All of these questions need to be investigated in terms of different student populations and teaching environments.

There also remain questions about the most effective methods for introducing these phrases to students. We have taken it as axiomatic throughout this book that language users take great care in selecting strategies and planning tactics to achieve their purpose in the most effective way; that is, that speakers and writers tend to manipulate language structures to express their views in appropriate and consistent ways by being aware of the needs of their audience, and selecting strategies accordingly. Bygate (1988) is one who calls for longitudinal studies to establish the connection between learners' communicative strategies, their language, and the learning process. Certainly this would provide for more effective teaching materials than would lists of formulas or sentence long exponents for various functions.

Throughout the book, we have proposed lexical phrases as the basic units in strategies of oral and written discourse. People do not produce language in finite clauses. Rather, to a significant degree clauses in language production emanate from 'lower-level' lexical phrases, which carry much of the load of communication and are the units of structural manipulations. Most standard linguistic and pedagogical approaches to grammar assume the reverse, however, that lower-level elements are called up by sentence frames.

Bygate describes some of the principal surface relationships in which language chunks, rather than complete sentences, are used to structure and elaborate discourse:

(a) repetition (or reduction): involves repetition (or reduction) of a lexical phrase:
    A: I hope it's at the corner.
    B: OK, at the corner.

(b) expansion: consists of repeating a unit and adding a lexical item to it:

   A: I think, I really think that X.

(c) substitution: occurs when a speaker simply substitutes items in the preceding frame:

   A: She's talking on the telephone.

   B: By the telephone, yes.

(d) framing or completion: consists of a speaker starting a phrase in one turn, and another speaker completing it:

   A: Let's meet at

   B: At the corner of Broadway and Fourth.

(e) marking: consists of directing attention of the audience and maintaining the flow of discourse:

   A: It faces eastward.

   B: Yes, I know.

Each of these has its own sub-categories, a few of which are listed below:

(a) repetition or reduction:

   (1) back-focusing: a phrase or entire utterance is picked out of a previous turn and used in one of several ways: to question, to agree, to confirm, or to check understanding;

   (2) holding device: involves a use similar to the preceding, but here the purpose is to signal that the speaker has heard the previous turn while giving time to formulate the reply:

   A: Did you buy a new car?

   B: A new car. I didn't buy a new car.

(b) expansion:

   (1) amplification: further specify a previously introduced unit by adding material:

   A: In front of the boy, the little boy who is outside.

   (2) sentence construction: a false start strategy for building up a sentence, a retreat to permit better advance:

   A: He isn't a man who is sitting on a chair, it's a woman.

   B: A woman we just have a woman sitting on a chair.

   (3) re-using: occurs when speakers use part of the preceding in the next contribution. This may either involve speakers in reusing a unit that they themselves have already uttered, or else be pieced up from other speakers. In the former case, this often occurs after a holding device. Speakers use the holding device as an element in their eventual main move, when they may take the form of an answer. If the speaker is using an element uttered by

an interlocutor this also often occurs in question and answer
sequences:
    A: It's big your country?
    B: Big, no it's not big.
(c) substitution:
    (1) semantic correction: speakers substitute one unit for another
for accuracy:
    A: Some of the girls, no, one girl was X.
    (2) paraphrase: a circumlocution strategy, when a word is
unknown:
    A: It's like X, similar to Y.
(d) framing or completion:
    (1) sympathetic: listeners complete speakers sentences, perhaps
to save them the trouble, more probably to show convergence;
    (2) competitive: listeners complete speakers' sentences as soon as
there is the slightest hesitation.
(e) markers:
    (1) focus of attention: left-dislocation, to preface sentence with
the topic:
    A: That new Volvo, he bought that new Volvo yesterday.
    (2) stage markers: indicates a new stage in the discourse, marking
the topic for several turns:
    A: As to Chapter Six . . .
    (3) achievement markers: similar to focusing attention, but
instead of signaling what is to come, focuses on the goals
achieved:
    A: They don't wear shoes; one difference.

All kinds of syntactic units occur as lexical phrases, and the more
experienced the speakers, the more they draw on different kinds of
units to maintain communication. Concentrating on these phrases,
rather than on complete sentences enables learners to manipulate the
direction of discourse effectively without imposing the additional
processing load implied by the requirements of having to produce
finite syntactic structures.

    Exercises need to be devised that incorporate group work, and
make use of other situations that require actual communicative practice, for these seem essential in learning language with these units.
For a detailed discussion of many such communicative activities, see
DiPietro (1987) and Widdowson (1990). Real interaction will allow
production and monitoring of language at the level of dependent

units, and with them learners can negotiate their own way to clauses. As listeners, they can intervene at those points where they need the incoming units to be broken down, working towards 'parsing' by interrupting and clarifying where it is necessary.

Further longitudinal studies such as these seem to be very promising for further research in language acquisition and language teaching.

Appendix

Lexical phrases in other languages

As was true in the text, the translations that follow the lexical phrases below indicate the pragmatic function of those phrases rather than their literal meaning.

Chinese:

Social interactions

A. *Conversational maintenance*

Summoning:	duibuqi, darao yixia, *pardon me*; qiao, ni kan, *lookit*; (ni) hao ma?, *how are you?*; (ni) qu nar le?, *where're you going?*
Responding to summons:	you shi ma?, *can I help you?*; hai hao ni na?, *fine thanks and you?*
Nominating a topic:	(zhe) jiao shenma?, *what's X?*; (ni) renshi/jide X ma?, *do you know/remember X?*; (ni) you X de xin/xiaoxi ma?, *have you heard from X?*
Clarifying: (1) audience:	(ni) (shuo) shenma le?, *(you) (said) what?*; (ni) (shuo) shi zhi shenma?, *what did you mean by X?*
(2) speaker:	(wo) shi zhi/yisi shi X, *what I'm trying to say is X*; (wo) zai shuo yibian, *let me repeat*
Checking comprehension:	you (shenma) wenti mei you?, *OK?/all right?*; (ni) dong le ma?, *do you understand?*

Shifting a topic:	shunbian ti yixia, *by the way*; (aiya) (wo) xiangqi/jiqi le, *oh, that reminds me of X*; jiu zhe yang, *so, OK*
Shifting turns:	wo xiang/zhe shi (rising tone), *well/I think*; duibuqi, (wo) da duan yixia?, *could I interrupt for a minute?*
Closing:	wo yao zou le, *I must be going*; hao, jiu zheyang, *well, that's about it*
Partings:	zaijian, *goodbye*; hui (tou) jian, *see you later/so long*; hao zou, *take care*

B. *Conversational purpose*

Expressing politeness:	xie xie/feichang ganxie *thanks very much*; (ni) ruguo buzai yi de hua, *if you don't mind*
Questioning:	(ni) + V?, *do you . . .?*; (zhe/na) you mei you?, *is/are there . . .?*
Answering:	dangran le, *of course*; you, *yes, there . . .*; meiyou, *no, there . . . no*
Requesting:	(wo) neng/keyi?, *may I . . .?*; (ni) meiyou yijian ba ruguo . . .?, *do you mind if I . . .?*
Complying:	dangran bu/mei + V (zai yi/you yijian), *of course*; mei (you) wenti, *sure thing*;
Refusing:	dangran buxing, *of course not*; juedui buxing/meimen, *no way*; (ni) zui hao + V, *I'd rather you + V*
Complimenting:	(ni) zhen/hen + Adj, *you're really very Adj*; (wo) (zhen/hen) xihuan X, *I really like X*

Asserting:

(wo) xiang/renwei/kan X, *I think/believe X*; ting shuo X, *word has it that X*; X zhe shi baizhi heizi Y, *it is written that X*; kanlai/haoxiang/sihu X, *it seems that X*

Responding:

o, a, *uh huh*; dui, (wo) zhidao le, *yeah, I know*; hao (de), *OK*; (wo) juedui/hen/wanquan/zancheng/tongyi, *I absolutely/completely agree*; (zhe) bucuo/tai hao le, *very good*; bu yiding ba, *not true, not necessarily*

Complaining:

hen yihan, you dian wenti, *sorry, but there's a problem*; (wo) (shizai) buxiang ti/shuo zhe shi, buguo X, *I hate to mention it, but X*

Excusing:

duibuqi, (wo) (zhen) bu zhidao/mei xiang dao X, *sorry, I didn't know/realize that X*; duibuqi, (wo) wangle, *sorry, it slipped my mind*

Denying:

zhe bushi wode cuo, *it isn't my fault*; zheshi (ke) bu neng guai wo, *I'm not to blame for X*

Apologizing:

(shizai) duibuqi/(hen) baoqian, X, *I'm (really) sorry about X*; (wo) baozheng/juedui buzai fasheng zhe shi, *I won't let it happen again*

Expressing gratitude:

xie xie (ni) (de) (X), *thanks (very) much (for X)*; (wo) (hen) ganxie ni wei wo xiang de zhouquan/nide haoye/ni wei wo, *I (really) appreciate your thoughtfulness/kindness/deed*

Expressing sympathy:

(wo) ye (hen) nanguo, *I'm (very) sorry*; tai kepa le, zhen mei xiang dao, *that's terrible*; zhen kelian, *what a shame*

Necessary topics

Autobiography: wo xing/jiao . . ., *my name is* . . .; wo cong/shi . . . lai/ren, *I'm from* . . .; wo shi . . ., *I'm a* . . . (occupation)

Language: ni jiang . . . yu/hua ma?, *do you speak* . . .? ; . . . yu/hua zenme shuo?, *How do you say ____ in ____* ?; wo (shuo/jiang) . . . shuo/jiang de bu/hen hao, *I don't/do speak* . . . *very well*

Quantity: you duo shao X?, *how much X is there?*; hen duo, hen duo, *a great deal*; hen/hao/xu duo X, *lots of X*

Time: shenme shihou/shihou?; *when is/what time is it/X?*; hen chang hen chang shijian/hen jiu, *for a long time*

Location: zai na/shenme difang?, *where is (place)?*; nabian/duimian, *across from*

Weather: yao + V le ma?, *is it going to + V?*; hen + Adj, *it is (hot, cold, etc.)*

Likes/dislikes: (wo) (bu) xihuan X, *I (don't) like X*; (wo) xiang/yuan yi . . ., *I'd like to* . . .; X hen you yisi/qu ji le, *X is lots of fun*

Shopping: X (zhe) yao duo shao qian?, *how much is X?*; (wo) xiang/yao mai X, *I want to buy X*; tai gui le, *too much*

Discourse devices

Logical connectors: yizhi/yinci, *as a result*; buguo/raner, *nevertheless*; buguan/bugu/bulun, *in spite of*

Temporal connectors: di er tian/na tian yihou X, *the day after X*; ranhou/jiezhe, *and then*;

Spatial connectors:	zhe yidai/zhongwei/fujin, *around here*; zai nabian, *over there*; zai jiao (luo) shang, *at the corner*
Fluency devices:	da jia/women zhidao, *you know*; wo juede X, *it seems to me that X*; wulun ruhe, *at any rate*; zong (er yan) zhi, *by and large*
Exemplifiers:	huan yan zhi, huan ju hua shuo, *in other words*; jiuxiang X, *it is like X*; juli/dabi shuo, *to give an example*; bifang, biru, *for example*
Relators:	zhe yu X you guan/lianxi, *it has to do with X*
Qualifiers:	zhe you lai/qujue yu X, *it depends on X*; zhi you zai X zhong Y cai, *it's only in X that Y*
Evaluators:	ju wo suo zhi er yan, *as far as I can tell*; kai men jian shan, zhijie liaodang, *frankly*; wu yi X, *there is no doubt that X*; wo renwei/kan, *I guess*; wo (guedui) kending X, *I'm (absolutely) positive that X*
Summarizers:	jian er yan zhi, chang hua duan shuo, *to make a long story short*; wo (zhe) de yisi shi X, *my point (here) is that X*; hao le, *OK*

Spanish:

Social interactions

A. *Conversational maintenance*

Summoning:	perdón(e) (me), (con) permiso, *pardon me*; buenos/as días/tardes, *good morning/afternoon*; ¿qué tal?, *what's up?*
Responding to summons:	diga(me)?, *yes?*; ¿Si señor(a/ita)?, *yes, sir/ma'am?*; ¿en qué puedo servirle?, *how can I help you?*

Nominating a topic:	recuerda(s) X?, *do you remember X?*; lo que quiero/tengo es X, *what I want/have is X*; (X) me llama la atención (que X), *X has/it's been brought to my attention (that X)*

Clarifying:

(1) audience:	¿qué dice(s)?; *what (did you say)?*; ¿qué quiere(s) decir (con X)?, *what do you mean (by X)?*
(2) speaker:	lo que quiero decir es X, *what I mean is X*; mejor dicho X, *X would be more like it*

Checking comprehension:	(no sé) si me explico bien, *I'm not sure if I'm explaining this well*; ¿(me) entiende(s)/comprende(s)?, *(do you) understand (me)?*
Shifting a topic:	a propósito, *by the way*; (esto) me hace recordar de X, *that reminds me of X*
Shifting turns:	bueno, pues (steady intonation), *well, so OK . . .*; si me permite(s), *(if you'll) let me say something*
Closing:	bueno pues (falling intonation), *well (that's about it)*; hay/tengo que X, *I've got to (go) (do) X*
Parting:	(a)diós, *goodbye*; (hasta) luego, *so long*; hasta _____, *until/see you* _____

B. *Conversational purpose*

Expressing politeness:	(muchas) gracias, *thanks (a lot)*; por favor, *please*; querría/quisiera X, *I would like to X*; de nada, no hay de qué, *you're welcome*
Questioning:	¿hay X? *is/are there X?*, ¿tiene(s) X?, *do you have X?*; ¿quiere(s) X?; *do you want X?*
Answering:	creo que sí/no, *I (don't) think so*;

	(no) (lo) sé, *I (don't) know (that)*; sí, (que) hay (X), *yes, there are (X)*; no, no (lo) hay (X), *no there are not (X)*; sí, señor(a/ita), *yes, sir/ma'am*
Requesting:	¿podría X?, *could I X?*; ¿me puede(s) X?, *would you do X for me?*
Complying:	*claro* (que sí), *of course*; me gusta/ gustaría (mucho) (hacerlo), *I'd like that/to do that (very much)*
Refusing:	claro que no, *of course not*; no tengo ganas (de X), *I don't want to do/feel like doing X*; prefiero X, *I'd prefer/rather do X*
Complimenting:	Qué + Adj + eres/es (X) (qué guapo eres), *you're very handsome*; qué linda es aquella niña, *that little girl is very pretty*
Asserting:	entiendo/creo que X, *I think that X*; se oye/dice que X, *I've heard (tell) that X*; (me) parece que X, *it seems (to me) that X*
Responding:	
(1) acknowledging:	bueno, sí (sustained intonation), *yeah, I see*
(2) accepting:	claro que sí (falling intonation), de acuerdo, *OK*
(3) endorsing:	tiene razón, *yes, that's right*; por supuesto, desde luego, *(I) certainly/absolutely (agree)*
(4) disagreeing:	bueno pues (protracted with s.i.), *well (I'm not at all sure)*; no, no estoy de acuerdo, *no, not at all*
Expressing gratitude:	(muchas) gracias (por ____), *thanks (very much/a lot) (for ____)*; le agradezco (mucho), *I appreciate it (very much)*

Expressing sympathy:	lo siento (mucho), *I'm (very) sorry*; qué lástima/pena (que X), *what a shame (that X)*; le/te tengo pena, *I feel sorry for you*

Necessary topics

Autobiography:	me llamo X, *my name is X*; soy de X, *I'm from X*; soy X, *I'm a(n) X*; tengo X años, *I'm X years old*
Language:	habla X?, *do you speak X?*; ¿cómo se dice/escribe X?, *how do you say/spell X?*; (no) puedo hablar X (muy bien), *I can (not) speak X (very well)*; hablo un poco de (X), *I speak X a little*
Quantity:	¿Cuánto mide X?, *how tall is X?*; mucho/poco (de ____), *a lot/little (of)* ____
Time:	¿a qué hora?, *when?*; hace mucho/poco tiempo (que X), *for a long/short time*; desde (hace) ____, *since* ____
Location:	¿dónde está X? *where is X?*; ¿está lejos/cerca (de X), *it's far (from) close (to) (X)*; al/a la derechá izquierda, *to the right/left*
Weather:	va a llover/nevar/hacer buen/mal tiempo, *it's going to rain/snow/be good/bad weather*; tengo calor/frío, *I'm hot/cold*; hace sol/calor/frío, *it's sunny/warm/cold*
Likes:	(no) me/le gusta(n)/apetece(n) (mucho) (nada) (X), *I/you (don't) like X (very much) (at all)*; me/le gustaría (X), *I/you would like to (X)*
Food:	me gustaría X/tener X/hacer una reserva, *I'd like X/to have X/to*

	make a reservation; (tráigame) la cuenta, (por favor), *(bring me) the check (please)*
Shopping:	cuánto (es/cuesta/vale X)?, *how much is X?*; querría (comprar) X, *I'd like (to buy) X*; (es) demasiado, *(it's) too much*

Discourse devices

Logical connectors:	por eso, *therefore*; a menos que, *unless*; no obstante, *nevertheless*; a pesar de (que), *in spite of*; porque, *because*
Temporal connectors:	al principio/final de ____, *towards/at the beginning/end of* ____; (en aquel) entonces, *at that time/then*; el ____ pasado, *last* ____
Spatial connectors:	(por) aquí/allí, *(around) here/(over) there*; al/a la centro/mercado escuela/esquina, *at the center/market school/corner*
Fluency devices:	me parece que X, *it seems to me that X*; creo que X, *I think that X*; si mal no recuerdo, *if I remember correctly*; más o menos, *more or less*; si me entiende(s), *if you get what I mean*; lo que quiero decir es X, *what I mean is X*
Exemplifiers:	o sea, es decir, *in other words*; por ejemplo, *for example*
Relators:	esto (no) tiene (nada) que ver (con X), *this has to do/doesn't have (anything) to do (with X)*; cuanto más/menos X más/menos Y, *the more/less one X the more/less one Y*
Qualifiers:	X depende de Y, *X depends on Y*;

por témino medio, *on the average*; con tal que, a/con la condición de que X, *provided that X*

Evaluators:
sin (ningún género de) duda, *without (any) doubt*; estoy seguro de X, *I'm sure that X*; apuesto (de) que X, *I'll bet that X*; de mala/buena gana, *(un)willingly*

Summarizers:
en suma/total/fin, en concreto/unas cuantas palabras, *in sum*

Russian:

Social interactions

A. *Conversational maintenance*

Summoning:
izvinite požalujsta, *excuse my calling your attention*; zdravstvujte, *hello*; dobrij den'/večer/utro, *good morning/afternoon*; v čem delo?, *what's up?*

Responding to summons:
čto vy xoteli? čem mogu pomoc?, *how can I help you?*

Nominating a topic:
pomnite?, *do you remember?*; mne nužno X, *what I want is X*; imenno X, *X itself*

Clarifying:
(1) audience:
čto vy skazali?, *what (did you say?)*; čto vy xotite ètim skazat'?, *what do you mean by saying it?*

(2) speaker:
ja imeju v vidu X, *what I mean is X*; (vot èto) skoree tak; poxože na èto, *it would be more like it*

Checking comprehension:
ne znaju jasno li èto, *I'm not sure if I'm explaining this well*; èto ponjatno?, *do you understand (me)?*

Shifting a topic:
meždu pročim, *by the way*; èto napominaet mne X, *that reminds me of X*

Shifting turns:

nu (čto že), *well, so OK*; esli pozvolite, *if you'll let me say something*; vot ešče čto, *listen, here is something else*

Closing:

nu čto že (steady intonation), *well, (that's about it)*; nu ladno ja dolžen idti delat' X, *I've got to go/do X*

Parting:

do svidanija, *goodbye*; do skorogo, *so long*; do vstreči, *until we meet again*

B. *Conversational purpose*

Expressing politeness:

bol'šoe spasibo, *thanks a lot*; mne by xotelos' X, *I would like X*

Questioning:

X tam?, *is/are there X?*; u vas/tebja est' X?, *do you have X?*; vy xotite/ty xočes' X?, *do you want X?*

Answering:

(ja tak) (ne) dumaju, *I (don't) think so*; ja (ne) znaju, *(I don't) know that*; da, tam est' X, *yes, there is X*; (net) tam net (X), *(no) there is/are not (X)*

Requesting:

mogu ja X?, *could I X?*; vy ne mogli by pomoč' mne X?, *would you do X for me?*

Complying:

konečno, razumeetsja, *of course/it goes without saying*; mne by (očen') xotelos' X, *I'd like X/to do X (very much)*

Refusing:

ni za čto, *of course not, never*; ja ne xoču, X, *I don't feel like having/ doing X*; mne xočetsja X *I'd prefer/rather do X*

Complimenting:

kak vy krasivij, *you're very beautiful*; kak ty prekrasna, *you're so beautiful*; kakaja xorošen'kaja devočka, *that little girl is very pretty*

Asserting: ja dumaju čto X, *I think that X*; govorjat čto X, *I've heard that X*; mne kažetsja čto X, *it seems (to me) that X*

Responding:
   (1) acknowledging: m-m-mdaa (sustained intonation), *uh-huh*

   (2) accepting: (da) xorošo, ladno (falling intonation), *yes/yeah*;

   (3) endorsing: (vot) imenno (tak), *yes, that's (just) right*; (ja) soveršenno/a absolutno soglasen/soglasna, *(I) certainly/ absolutely agree*

   (4) disagreeing: net (èto)/ne tak, *no, (it's) not at all (so)*

Expressing gratitude: (bol'šoe) spasibo (za X), *thanks (very much/a lot) (for X)*

Expressing sympathy: izvinite požalujsta (intense falling intonation), *I'm very sorry*; kak užasno, *what a shame*; ja vam tak sočuvstvuju, *I feel so sorry for you*

Necessary topics

Autobiography: menja zovut X, *my name is X*; ja iz X, *I'm from X*; ja X, *I'm a(n) X*; mne X (let), *I'm X (years old)*

Language: (vy) govorite po anglijski?, *do you speak English?*; kak skazat' X (po russki)?, *how do you say X in Russian?*; kak pišetsja X?, *how do you spell X?*; ja ne očen' xorošo govorju (po russki), *I cannot speak (Russian) very well*; ja nemnogo govorju (po russki), *I speak (Russian) a little*

Quantity: kakogo razmera X?, *how big/tall is X?*; nemnogo/mnogo X, *a little/a lot (of) X*

Time:

nedolgo/dolgo, *for a short/long time*; s tex por kak X, *since X*

Location:

gde X?, *where is X?*; èto (ne)daleko (ot X), *it's (not) far (from X)/close (to X)*; napravo/nalevo (ot X), *to the right/left (of X)*

Weather:

(skoro) pojdet dozd' sneg/budet xorošaja/ploxaja pogoda, *it's going to rain/snow/be good/bad weather*

Likes:

mne (ne) (očen') nravitsja X, *I (don't) like X (very) much*; mne sovsem ne nravitsja X, *I don't like X at all*; mne xotelos' by X, *I would like (to do) X*

Food:

ja xoču zakazat' stol/mesto, *I'd like to make a reservation*; sčet/ček, *the check/receipt*

Shopping:

skol'ko stoit X?, *how much is X?*; mne xotelos' by (kupit') X, *I'd like (to buy) X*; sliškom mnogo, *too much*

Discourse devices

Logical connectors:

poetomu, *therefore*; esli ne, *unless*; tem ne menee, *nevertheless*; nesmotrja na, *in spite of*; potomu čto, *because*

Temporal connectors:

v načale/konce X, *towards/at the beginning/end of X*; v to vremja/togda, *at that time/then*; prošloj zimoj/osen'ju/vesnoj, *last winter/autumn/spring*

Spatial connectors:

vot tam, *(around) here/over there*; v X, *at the X*

Fluency devices:

znaete, *you know*; mne kažetsja čto X, *it seems to me that X*; esli ja pravil'no govorju, *if I remember correctly*; bolee ili menee, *more or less*; esli vy menja ponimaete, *if you get what I mean*; ja imeju v vidu X, *what I mean is X*

Exemplifiers:
drugimi/inimi slovami, *in other words*; naprimer, *for example*

Relators:
èto (ne) imeet otnošenija k X, *this has nothing to do with X*

Qualifiers:
X zavisit ot Y, *X depends on Y*; v srednem, *on the average*; pri uslovii čto X, *provided that X*

Evaluators:
bez (vsjakogo) somnenija, *without any doubt*; ja uveren/uverena čto X, *I'm sure that X*; gotov prosporit' čto X, *I'll bet that X*; (ne) oxotno, *(un)willingly*

Summarizers:
v celom/obščem/v summe, *in sum*

Bibliography

Austin, J. L. 1962. *How to Do Things with Words.* Oxford: Clarendon Press.

Azar, B. S. 1989. *Fundamentals of English Grammar.* Englewood Cliffs, NJ: Prentice-Hall.

Bateson, M. 1975. 'Linguistic models in a study of joint performances' in M. Kinkade, K. Hale, and D. Werner (eds.) *Linguistics and Anthropology: in Honor of C. F. Voegelin.* Lisse: Peter de Ridder Press.

Becker, J. 1975. 'The phrasal lexicon' in B. Nash-Webber and R. Schank (eds.) *Theoretical Issues in Natural Language Processing* 1. Cambridge, Mass.: Bolt, Beranek, and Newman.

Bickerton, D. 1981. Roots of Language. Ann Arbor: Karoma Press.

Bohn, O. 1986. 'Formulas, frame structures, and stereotypes in early syntactic development: some new evidence from L2 acquisition'. *Linguistics* 24:185–202.

Blum-Kulka, S. 1989. 'Playing it safe: the role of conventionality in indirectness' in S. Blum-Kulka, J. House, and G. Kasper (eds.) *Cross-Cultural Pragmatics: Requests and Apologies.* Norwood, NJ: Ablex Publishing.

Blum-Kulka, S. and **E. Levenston.** 1987. 'Lexical-grammatical pragmatic indicators'. *Studies in Second Language Acquisition* 9:155–70.

Bolinger, D. 1975. *Aspects of Language.* Second edition. New York: Harcourt Brace Jovanovich.

Brown, G. and **G. Yule.** 1983. *Discourse Analysis.* Cambridge: Cambridge University Press.

Brown, P. and **S. C. Levinson.** 1978. 'Universals in language usage: politeness phenomena' in E. N. Goody (ed.) *Questions and Politeness: Strategies in Social Interaction.* Cambridge: Cambridge University Press. Reprinted (1989) as *Politeness: Some Universals in Language Usage.*

Brown, R. 1973. *A First Language: the Early Years.* Cambridge, Mass.: Harvard University Press.

Bygate, M. 1988. 'Units of oral expression and language learning in small group interaction'. *Applied Linguistics* 9:59–82.

Carrell, P. 1984. 'The effects of rhetorical organization on ESL readers'. *TESOL Quarterly* 18:441–69.

Carrell, P. 1987. 'Text as interaction: Some implications of text analysis and reading research for ESL composition' in U. Connor and R. Kaplan (eds.) *Writing Across Languages: Analysis of L2 Text*. Reading, Mass.: Addison-Wesley.

Carrell, P. 1989. 'Metacognitive awareness and second language reading'. *Modern Language Journal* 73:121–34.

Chafe, W. 1982. 'Integration and involvement in speaking, writing, and oral literature' in Tannen, D. (ed.) *Spoken and Written Language: Exploring Orality and Literacy*. Norwood, NJ: Ablex.

Chaudron, C. and **J. Richards.** 1986. 'The effect of discourse markers on the comprehension of lectures'. *Applied Linguistics* 7:113–27.

Church, K. and **P. Hanks.** 1989. 'Word association norms, mutual information, and lexicography'. *Proceedings of the 27th Annual Meeting of the Association for Computational Linguistics*. Association for Computational Linguistics: 76–83.

Clark, R. 1974. 'Performing without competence'. *Journal of Child Language* 1:1–10.

Connor, U. 1987. 'Research frontiers in writing analysis'. *TESOL Quarterly* 21:677–96.

Corder, S. 1973. *Introducing Applied Linguistics*. Baltimore: Penguin Books.

Cowie, A. P. 1988. 'Stable and creative aspects of vocabulary use' in R. Carter and M. McCarthy (eds.) *Vocabulary and Language Teaching*. London: Longman: 126–39.

Crick, F. 1979. 'Thinking about the brain'. *Scientific American* 9:218–32.

Cruttenden, A. 1981. 'Item-learning and system-learning'. *Journal of Psycholinguistic Research* 10:79–88.

Davison, A. 1975. 'Indirect speech acts and what to do with them' in P. Cole and J. Morgan (eds.) *Syntax and Semantics* Vol. 5. New York: Academic Press.

DeCarrico, J. 1986. 'Tense, aspect and time in the English modality system'. *TESOL Quarterly* 20:665–82.

DeCarrico, J. and **J. Nattinger.** 1988. 'Lexical phrases for the comprehension of academic lectures'. *English for Specific Purposes* 7:91–102.

DiPietro, R. 1982. 'The open-ended scenario: a new approach to conversation'. *TESOL Quarterly* 14:337–44.

DiPietro, R. 1987. *Strategic Interaction: Learning Languages Through Scenarios*. New York: Cambridge University Press.

Dudley-Evans, A. and **T. F. Johns.** 1981. 'A team teaching approach to lecture comprehension for overseas students' in *The Teaching of Listening Comprehension*. London: The British Council.

Dunkel, P. and **F. Pialorsi.** 1982. *Advanced Listening Comprehension*. Rowley, Mass.: Newbury House.

Ervin-Tripp, R. 1976. 'Is Sybil there? The structure of some American English directives'. *Language in Society* 5:25–66.

Faigley, L. 1985. 'Nonacademic writing: the social perspective' in L. Odell and D. Goswami (eds.) *Writing in Non-Academic Settings*. New York: Guilford Press.

Fingado, G., L. J. Freeman, and **C. V. Summers.** 1981. *The English Connection*. Cambridge, Mass.: Winthrop.

Firth, J. 1957. 'A synopsis of linguistic theory 1930–1955' in *Studies In Linguistic Analysis*. Oxford: Philological Society. Reprinted in F. Palmer (ed.) 1968, *Selected Papers of J. R. Firth*. Harlow: Longman.

Frank, M. 1972. *Modern English: A Practical Reference Guide*. Englewood Cliffs, NJ: Prentice-Hall.

Fraser, B. 1970. 'Idioms within transformational grammar'. *Foundations of Language* 6:22–42.

Fraser, B. 1983. 'The domain of pragmatics' in J. Richards and R. Schmidt (eds.) *Language and Communication*. London: Longman.

Garside, R., G. Leech, and **G. Sampson.** 1987. *The Computational Analysis of English*. London: Longman.

Gasser, M. 1990. 'Connectionism and universals of second language acquisition'. *Studies in Second Language Acquisition* 12:179–99.

Gazdar, G. 1979. *Pragmatics: Implicature, Presupposition and Logical Form*. New York: Academic Press.

Goffman, E. 1971. *Relations in Public: Microstudies of the Public Order*. New York: Harper and Row.

Green, G. 1989. *Pragmatics and Natural Language Understanding*. Hillsdale, NJ: Lawrence Erlbaum Associates.

Grice, H. P. 1975. 'Logic and conversation' in P. Cole and J. Morgan (eds.) *Syntax and Semantics* Vol. 3. New York: Academic Press.

Hakuta, K. 1974. 'Prefabricated patterns and the emergence of structure in second language acquisition'. *Language Learning* 24:287–97.

Hakuta, K. 1976. 'Becoming bilingual: a case study of a Japanese child learning English'. *Language Learning* 26:321–51.

Hakuta, K. 1986. *Mirror of Language: the Debate on Bilingualism*. New York: Basic Books, Inc.

Halliday, M. A. K. 1970. 'Language structure and language function' in J. Lyons (ed.) *New Horizons in Linguistics*. Harmondsworth: Penguin.

Halliday, M. A. K. and **R. Hasan.** 1976. *Cohesion in English*. London: Longman.

Hatch, E. 1978. *Second Language Acquisition*. Rowley, Mass.: Newbury House.

Heubner, T. 1983. *A Longitudinal Analysis of the Acquisition of English*. Ann Arbor: Karoma Publishers, Inc.

Hockey, S. 1980. *Computer Application in the Humanities*. London: Duckworth.

Holmes, J. 1988. 'Doubt and certainty in ESL textbooks'. *Applied Linguistics* 9:21–44.

Holmes, J. 1989. 'Sex differences and apologies: one aspect of communicative competence'. *Applied Linguistics* 10:194–213

Huang, J. 1971. *A Chinese Child's Acquisition of English Syntax*. Unpublished Master's thesis. University of California at Los Angeles.

Hymes, D. 1972. 'On communicative competence' in J. B. Pride and J. Holmes (eds.) *Sociolinguistics*. Harmondsworth: Penguin.

Jackson, H. 1988. *Words and Their Meaning*. Longman: London.

Jakobson, R. 1960. 'Closing statement: linguistics and poetics' in T. Sebeok (ed.) *Style in Language*. Cambridge, Mass.: MIT Press.

Katz, J. 1977. *Propositional Structure and Illocutionary Force*. New York: Crowell.

Keller, R. 1979. 'Gambits: conversational strategy signals'. *Journal of Pragmatics* 3:219–37.

Kempson, R. 1975. *Presupposition and the Delimitation of Semantics*. Cambridge: Cambridge University Press.

Kempson, R. 1977. *Semantic Theory*. Cambridge: Cambridge University Press.

Kennedy, G. 1987. 'Rules and routines in prepositional usage'. Paper presented at the AILA Convention, Sydney, Australia.

Kennedy, G. 1989. 'Collocations: where grammar and vocabulary teaching meet'. Paper presented at the RELC Seminar, Singapore.

Kern, R. 1989. 'Second language reading strategy instruction: its effect on comprehension and word inference ability'. *Modern Language Journal* 73:135–49.

Krashen, S. D. and **R. Scarcella.** 1978. 'On routines and patterns in language acquisition and performance'. *Language Learning* 28:283–300.

Labov, W. 1966. *The Social Stratification of English in New York City*. Arlington: Center for Applied Linguistics.

Labov, W. 1972. *Sociolinguistic Patterns*. Philadelphia: University of Pennsylvania Press.

Lautamatti, L. 1987. 'Observations on the development of the topic in simplified discourse' in U. Connor and R. Kaplan (eds.) *Writing across Languages: Analysis of L2 text*. Reading, Mass.: Addison-Wesley.

Lebauer, R. 1984. 'Using lecture transcripts in EAP lecture comprehension courses'. *TESOL Quarterly* 18:41–54.

Lee, J. and **G. Riley.** 1990. 'The effect of prereading, rhetorically-oriented frameworks on the recall of two structurally different expository texts'. *Studies in Second Language Acquisition* 12:25–41.

Leech, G. 1983. *Principles of Pragmatics*. London: Longman.

Levinson, S. 1983. *Pragmatics*. Cambridge: Cambridge University Press.
Lyons, J. 1977. *Semantics*. Cambridge: Cambridge University Press.

Manes, J. and **N. Wolfson.** 1981. 'The compliment formula' in F. Coulmas (ed.) *Conversational Routine*. The Hague: Mouton.
Mason, A. 1983. *Understanding Academic Lectures*. Englewood Cliffs, NJ: Prentice-Hall.
Meyer, B. J. F., D. M. Brandt, and **G. J. Bluth.** 1980. 'Use of the top-level structure in text: key to reading comprehension of ninth-grade students'. *Reading Research Quarterly* 16:72–103.
Miller, G. 1956. 'The magical number seven, plus or minus two: some limits on our capacity for processing information'. *Psychological Review* 63:81–97.
Mitchell, T. 1971. 'Linguistics 'goings on': collocations and other lexical matters arising on the syntactic record'. *Archivum Linguisticum* 2 (new series): 35–69.

Nattinger, J. 1980. 'A lexical phrase grammar for ESL'. *TESOL Quarterly* 14:337–44.
Nattinger, J. 1986. 'Lexical phrases, functions and vocabulary acquisition'. *The ORTESOL Journal* 7:1–14.
Nattinger, J. 1988. 'Some current trends in vocabulary teaching' in R. Carter and M. McCarthy (eds.) *Vocabulary and Language Teaching*. New York: Longman.
Nattinger, J. and **J. DeCarrico.** 1989. 'Lexical phrases, speech acts and teaching conversation'. *AILA Review 6: Vocabulary Acquisition*: 118–39.
Nelson, E. 1984. 'How to be more polite in Japanese'. *The ORTESOL Journal* 5:41–58.

Oller, J. and **V. Streiff.** 1975. 'Dictation: a test of grammar based expectancies' in R. Jones and B. Spolsky (eds.) *Testing Language Proficiency*. Arlington, Va.
Oller, J. and **J. Richards** (eds.) 1973. *Focus on the learner: Pragmatic Perspectives for the Language Teacher*. Rowley, Mass.: Newbury House.

Pawley, A. and **F. Syder.** 1983. 'Two puzzles for linguistic theory: nativelike selection and nativelike fluency' in J. Richards and R. Schmidt (eds.) *Language and Communication*. London: Longman.
Peters, A. 1983. *The Units of Language Acquisition*. Cambridge: Cambridge University Press.
Phelps, L. 1985. 'Dialects of coherence: Toward an integrative theory'. *College English* 47:12–29.

Qin, X.-B. 1983. 'Cross-cultural differences and the teaching of English as a foreign language'. *The ORTESOL Journal* 4:54–60.

Richards, J. 1980. 'Conversation'. *TESOL Quarterly* 14:413–32.
Richards, J. 1983. 'Listening comprehension: approach, design, procedure'. *TESOL Quarterly*: 219–40.
Ruetten, M. K. 1986. *Comprehending Academic Lectures.* New York: Macmillan.

Sacks, H., E. Schegloff, and G. Jefferson. 1974. 'A simplest systematics for the organization of turn-taking for conversation'. *Language* 50:696–735.
Schmidt, R. and J. Richards. 1980. 'Speech acts and second language learning'. *Applied Linguistics* 1:129–57.
Schneider M. and U. Conner. 1990. 'Analyzing topical structure in ESL essays: not all topics are equal'. *Studies in Second Language Acquisition* 12:411–26.
Scollon, R. 1979. 'A real early stage: an unzipped condensation of a dissertation on child language' in E. Ochs and B. Schiefflin (eds.) *Developmental Pragmatics.* New York: Academic Press.
Searle, J. 1969. *Speech Acts.* Cambridge: Cambridge University Press.
Searle, J. 1975. 'Indirect speech acts' in P. Cole and J. Morgan (eds.) *Syntax and Semantics, Vol. 3: Speech Acts.* New York: Academic Press.
Searle, J. 1976. 'The classification of illocutionary acts'. *Language in Society* 5:1–24.
Searle, J. 1979. *Expression and Meaning.* Cambridge: Cambridge University Press.
Searle, J. and D. Vanderveken. 1985. *Foundations of Illocutionary Logic.* Cambridge: Cambridge University Press.
Simon, H. 1974. 'How big is a chunk?' *Science* 183:482–8.
Sinclair, J. 1987a. *Looking Up: An Account of the COBUILD Project in Lexical Computing.* London: Collins.
Sinclair, J. 1987b. 'The nature of evidence' in J. Sinclair (ed.) *Looking Up: An Account of the COBUILD Project in Lexical Computing.* London: Collins.
Sinclair, J. and R. Coulthard. 1975. *Towards an Analysis of Discourse: the English Used by Teachers and Pupils.* London: Oxford University Press.
Smith, N. V. and D. Wilson. 1979. *Modern Linguistics: the Results of Chomsky's Revolution.* Harmondsworth: Penguin.
Sperber, D. and D. Wilson. 1988. *Relevance: Communication and Cognition.* Cambridge, Mass.: Harvard University Press.
Stalker, J. C. 1989. 'Communicative competence, pragmatic functions, and accommodation'. *Applied Linguistics* 10:182–93.

Tannen, D. 1986. *That's Not What I Meant!* New York: William Morrow and Company.
Thomas, J. 1983. 'Cross-cultural pragmatic failure'. *Applied Linguistics* 4:91–112.

van Ek, J. 1976. *The Threshold Level for Modern Language Teaching in Schools.* London: Longman.
VanPatten, B. 1988. 'X + Y = utterance' in M. Pieneman and H. Nicholas (eds.) *Explaining Interlanguage Development.* Multilingual Matters, Ltd.

Wardhaugh, R. 1985. *How Conversation Works.* Oxford: Basil Blackwell.
Widdowson, H. G. 1979. *Explorations in Applied Linguistics.* Oxford: Oxford University Press.
Widdowson, H. G. 1989. 'Knowledge of language and ability for use'. *Applied Linguistics* 10:128–37.
Widdowson, H. G. 1990. *Aspects of Language Teaching.* Oxford: Oxford University Press.
Wilensky, R., Y. Arens, and **D. Chin.** 1984. 'Talking to UNIX in English: an overview of UC'. *Communications of the ACM* 27:574–93.
Wilkins, D. 1976. *Notional Syllabuses.* London: Oxford University Press.
Williams, M. 1988. 'Language taught for meetings and language used for meetings: is there anything in common?' *Applied Linguistics* 9:45–58.
Wilson, D. 1975. *Presuppositions and Non-Truth Conditional Semantics.* New York: Academic Press.
Wilson, D. and **D. Sperber.** 1986. 'Pragmatics and modularity'. *Papers from the Parasession on Pragmatics and Grammatical Theory at the Twenty-Second Regional Meeting.* Chicago Linguistic Society 22:67–84.
Wong-Fillmore, L. 1976. *The Second Time Around: Cognitive and Social Strategies in Second Language Acquisition.* Unpublished doctoral dissertation, Stanford University.
Wood, M. 1981. *A Definition of Idiom.* Manchester, England: Centre for Computational Linguistics, University of Manchester. Reprinted by the Indiana University Linguistics Club, 1986.

Young, L. and **B. Fitzgerald.** 1982. *Listening and Learning Lectures.* Rowley, Mass.: Newbury House.
Yorio, C. 1980. 'Conventionalized language forms and the development of communicative competence'. *TESOL Quarterly* 14:433–42.

Zamel, V. 1987. 'Recent research on writing pedagogy'. *TESOL Quarterly* 21:697–715.
Zernick, U. and **M. Dyer.** 1987. 'The self-extending phrasal lexicon'. *Computational Linguistics* 13:308–27.

Index

The Index covers the Preface, Chapters 1 to 8, and the Appendix. References to chapter notes are indicated by page and note number, e.g. 'adjacency pairs 130n2'.

academic lectures,
 comprehension and styles 131–41
 transactional discourse 76–7
accepting 62
 see also asserting–accepting exchange;
  invitation–acceptance exchange;
  offer–acceptance exchange
achievement markers 188
acknowledging 62
acquisition, language xiv–xv, 24–9,
 115–6, 183–5
adjacency pairs 130n2
amplification 187
analytic one-word-at-a-time approach 26
answering 62
 Chinese 191
 Russian 200
 Spanish 195–6
 see also question–answer exchange
aphasic speech 30n6
apologizing, Chinese 192
appropriateness 3
aside markers 80, 96, 147, 149
asserting 62, 87n11
 Chinese 192
 Russian 201
 Spanish 196
asserting–accepting exchange 120
asserting–disagreeing exchange 121
asserting–endorsing exchange 121
association ratio 21
authenticity 130n3
automatic speech 29n6

back-focusing 187
bad news 58n3
body,
 business letters 168

essays 165, 166, 171
 informal letters 167
bottom-up processing 103
brevity, maxim 19
business letters, structure 168, 169
business meetings, language 174–5

canonical sentence builders 43–4
category divisions,
 macro-organizers 102–3
Chaudron, C. 105–6
children's language 24–7
Chinese,
 discourse devices 68, 193–4
 necessary topics 67–8, 193
 social interactions 67, 125, 126–7,
  190–2
Chomsky, N. 2, 7
chunking 31–2, 159
clarifying 61, 83–4, 86n3, 154n4
 Chinese 190
 Russian 199
 Spanish 195
 see also topic nominating–clarifying
  exchange
clause-chaining 84–5
clichés 32–3
closing–parting exchange 120
closings 61, 86n6
 business letters 168
 Chinese 191
 essays 165, 166–7, 171
 informal letters 167–8
 Russian 200
 Spanish 195
cognitive-based model 158
cohesive patterns 162
colligations 178

collocations 36, 176–8
  computer analysis 20–2
  natural language processing 22–3
communicative competence xiv, 2–3
communicative grammar 9
competence 2–19
  communicative xiv, 2–3
competitive framing 188
complaining, Chinese 192
completion 187, 188
complimenting 62, 87n9
  Chinese 191
  Russian 200
  Spanish 196
complying 62
  Chinese 191
  Russian 200
  Spanish 196
  see also request–comply exchange
composites 29n5
comprehension 103
  checking 61
    Chinese 190
    Russian 199
    Spanish 195
    see also topic nominating–
    comprehension checking exchange
  effect of discourse markers 105–6
  listening 131–56
computer analysis of text 19–23
concepts 185
conjunctions 104–5
connectionist models of knowledge 23
connectors 102
  Chinese 193–4
  Russian 202–3
  Spanish 198
conventional indirect speech acts 49
conventionalized forms 29n5
conventionalized sets 49–54
conversation 71–80, 113–30
conversational implicatures 6
conversational maintenance 60–1, 83–4
  Chinese 190–1
  Russian 199–200
  Spanish 194–5
conversational purpose 62–3
  Chinese 191–2
  Russian 200–1
  Spanish 195–7
conversational style, academic
    lectures 134–50
co-occurrence 19–20

co-ordinate (global)
    macro-organizers 94–104, 145
corpora 20–2
cultural differences, writing styles 172

denying, Chinese 192
detachment 85
dictionaries 181–2
directions, understanding 104
directives, non-literal 87n8
disagreeing 63, 88n11, 121
discourse,
    spoken 71–80, 113–56
    written 157–73
discourse analysis 180–1
discourse-as-process vs.
    discourse-as-product 157–9
discourse community 82
discourse devices 60, 64–5, 66, 75–80,
    82–4, 98–9
  Chinese 68, 193–4
  Russian 70, 202–3
  Spanish 69, 198–9
double markers 93–4
drills 116–17
dual functions 108–10

emotive/referential 88n17
endorsing 62, 120–1
error correction 184
essays, structure 164–7, 169, 170–2
evaluators 65, 88n15, 96, 101, 139, 146,
    149
  Chinese 194
  Russian 203
  Spanish 199
  see also discourse devices
exchange 130n2
exchange structures 119–21, 127–30,
    130n2
excusing, Chinese 192
exemplifiers 79, 95, 101, 136–40, 146
  Chinese 194
  Russian 202
  Spanish 198
expansion 187
expectancy, grammar of 34
extended parallel progression 161, 162

false starts 78
fluency devices 64, 80
  Chinese 194
  Russian 203

Spanish 198
see also discourse devices
focus of attention 188
foreign-language lexical phrases 66–70,
    190–203
formal aspects 31–58
formal essays, structure 164–7
form/function relations 11–17
formulaic chunks 29n2
formulaic nature of phrases 132–4, 176
fossilization 184–5
framing 187, 188
frequency,
    macro-organizers 150
    words 19
functional aspects 59–89, 108–10
function/form relations 11–17
functions, universal 124–7

gambits 29n5, 119
general pragmatics 9
gestalt approach 26
global (co-ordinate)
    macro-organizers 94–104, 145
grammar 4, 9
    of expectancy 34
    rules 22–3
gratitude, expressing 63
gratitude, expressing Chinese 192
gratitude, expressing Russian 201
gratitude, expressing Spanish 196
gratitude–response exchange 129–30
Grice, H. P. 3, 6, 19

Hakuta, K. 24–5, 28
hearer-based forms 52, 122
holding devices 187
holophrases 29n5
Hymes, D. xiv

idioms 29n5, 32–3, 178
illocutionary force 48
imperatives 87n8
implicature 6
indirect speech acts 47–9, 121–30
informal letters, structure 167–8, 169
informal speech, academic lectures
    134–50
information, mutual 21
institutionalized expressions 39–40,
    44–7, 56
integration 84–5

interactional discourse markers vs.
    macro-organizers 97–101
interactional vs. transactional
    discourse 75, 88n17
interactive-based model 158
interchange 130n2
interconnected functions 72–5
interpersonal/ideational 88n17
interruptions 86n5, 119
invitation–acceptance exchange 128
invitation–refusal exchange 128
item-learning 26, 27

Japanese, requests 125–6

knowledge, connectionist models 23
knowledge vs. ability 7
Krashen, S. D. 25–6

language acquisition xiv–xv, 24–9,
    115–16, 183–5
language learning 116–18
language patterns, definition
    criteria 176–8
language-specific forms 124–7
language variation 175
Lebauer, R. 151
lectures, academic,
    comprehension and styles 131–41
    transactional discourse 76–7
Leech, G. 9–10, 56, 122
letters, structure,
    business 168, 169
    informal 167–8, 169
levels 97–101
Levinson, S. 4–6
lexemes 181–2
lexical co-occurrence 20
lexical items 22–3
lexicalized sentence stems 15, 29n3
lexicography 181–2
lexicons, computational 22–3
listening comprehension 131–56
    classes 152–4
local subordinate macro-organizers
    94–104, 146
logical connectors 78, 102
    Chinese 193
    Russian 202
    Spanish 198

macro-organizers 90–108, 154n4
    academic lectures 132–3, 135–50

marking 187, 188
maxims 6, 19
meetings (business), language 174–5
memory 31–2
micro-organizers 104–10
multiple functions 73, 88n16, 108–10
mutual information 21

natural language processing,
    collocations 22–3
necessary topics 59–60, 63–4, 65
    Chinese 67, 193
    Russian 70, 201–2
    Spanish 69, 197–8
nodes, collocations 20–1
nominating a topic *see* topic nomination
non-canonical phrases 33
non-conventional indirect speech acts 48
non-literal directives 87n8
notional–functional syllabuses 117
notions 185

offer–acceptance exchange 128
offering 52, 62
offer–refusal exchange 128
openings,
    essays 164–5, 171
    letters,
        business 168
        informal 167
organizational structure of texts *see*
    structure of texts
organizing function 90–110

parallel progression 161–2
paraphrase 188
partings 61
    Chinese 191
    Russian 200
    Spanish 195
    see also closing–parting exchange
patterns 24–5, 71–2, 82, 97–101, 150
pause fillers 104
performance 2–19
phrasal approach 23
phrasal constraints 41–2, 44–7, 54–7
    discourse devices 66
        Chinese 68
        Russian 70
        Spanish 69
    necessary topics 65
        Chinese 67
        Russian 70

Spanish 69
social interactions 65
    Chinese 67
    Russian 70
    Spanish 68–9
phrase length 107–8
poetic effects 29n1
politeness 50–3, 56–7, 57n2, 58n3, 62,
    122–6, 129
    Chinese 125, 126, 191
    Japanese 125–6
    Russian 200
    Spanish 125, 195
polywords 38–9, 44–7, 56, 109
    discourse devices 66
        Chinese 68
        Spanish 69
    necessary topics 65
        Chinese 67
        Russian 70
        Spanish 69
    social interactions 65
        Chinese 67
        Russian 70
        Spanish 68–9
pragmalinguistic competence 7
pragmalinguistics 9–11
pragmatic competence 6–17
pragmatics 2–19
praxons 29n5
preassembled speech 29n5
predication model 158
prefabricated language,
    language acquisition xv, 24–9
    psychological processing 31–5
prefabricated speech 30n6
probabilities, word 21–2
process-centered discourse
    perspective 163–4
processing effort 19
processing strategies 103
process and product, written
    discourse 157–9
pseudo-apologies 85n1
pseudo-cloze procedures 151
psychological processing, and
    prefabricated language 31–5

qualifiers 96, 101, 136, 138–9, 147, 149
    Chinese 194
    Russian 203
    Spanish 198–9
question–answer exchange 120

questioning 62, 87n8
  Chinese 191
  Russian 200
  Spanish 195

readers, active participants 159–60
reading 157–73
  classes 151–2
  style, academic lectures 134–50
recognition, academic lectures 133–4
reduction 186, 187
refusing 62
  Chinese 191
  Russian 200
  Spanish 196
  see also invitation–refusal exchange;
    offer–refusal exchange
relators 93, 95, 101, 139, 146, 149,
  154n4
  Chinese 194
  Russian 203
  Spanish 198
reluctance markers 123, 129
repetition 186, 187
request–comply exchange 128–9
requesting 49–3, 62, 87n8, 125–6
  Chinese 191
  Russian 200
  Spanish 196
responding 61, 62
  Chinese 190, 192
  Russian 199, 201
  Spanish 194, 196
  see also gratitude–response exchange;
    suggestion–response exchange;
    summons–response exchange
re-using 187
rhetorical structure 163–4
rhetorical style, academic lectures
  134–50
Richards, J. 105–6
ritualization 1, 27, 30n7
routines 24–5
rules 3–4, 6, 22–3, 29n1
Russian,
  discourse devices 70, 202–3
  necessary topics 70, 201–2
  social interactions 70, 199–201

Scarcella, R. 25–6
schema 161
Searle, J. 48–9, 50–3
selection 17–18

semantic correction 188
sentence-based perspective 161–3
sentence builders 42–8, 53–4
  discourse devices 66
    Chinese 68
    Russian 70
    Spanish 69
  necessary topics 65
    Chinese 67
    Russian 70
    Spanish 69
  social interactions 65
    Chinese 67
    Russian 70
    Spanish 69
sentence construction 187
sentence progressions 161–2
sentence stems 29n3,n5
sequential progression 161–2
shifting *see* topic shifting; turn shifting
signaling function, macro-organizers
  91–3
social–expressive/descriptive 88n17
social interactional markers 91–2, 98–9
social interactions 60–3, 65
  Chinese 67, 190–2
  Russian 70, 199–201
  Spanish 68–9, 194–7
socio-pragmatics 9
Spanish,
  discourse devices 69, 198–9
  necessary topics 69, 197–8
  social interactions 68–9, 125, 194–7
spans (windows), collocations 20–2,
  29n4
spatial connectors,
  Chinese 194
  Russian 202
  Spanish 198
speaker-based forms 52, 122
speech acts 47–9, 62–3, 87n7, 121–30
spoken discourse 71–80, 113–56
stacking 120, 123–4, 129
stage markers 188
statement of organization, essays 165
statements 87n8
statistical techniques, collocations 21–2
structure of texts 161, 164–9
styles, academic lectures 134–41
subordinate (local) macro-organizers
  94–104, 146
substitution 187, 188
suggestion–response exchange 128

summarizers 65, 79, 95, 101, 138, 145,
   148–9
   Chinese 194
   Russian 203
   Spanish 199
summoning 61, 85n1
   Chinese 190
   Russian 199
   Spanish 194
summons–response exchange 119–20,
   129
sympathetic framing 188
sympathy, expressing 63
   Chinese 192
   Russian 201
   Spanish 197
syntactic strings (definition) 36
system-learning 26, 27

tapes (teaching materials) 152, 156n7
teaching activities 118–21
temporal connectors 78
   Chinese 193
   Russian 202
   Spanish 198
textbook models 104
top-down processing 103, 104
topic markers 95, 101, 138, 139, 145
topic nominating–clarifying
   exchange 120
topic nominating–comprehension
   checking exchange 120
topic nomination 61
   essays 165, 171

letters 167, 168
   Russian 199
   Spanish 195
topic priming 85n2
   essays 164, 171
topic progressions 161–2
topic shifting 61, 86n4, 95, 101, 138,
   145, 148
   Chinese 191
   Russian 199
   Spanish 195
transactional discourse 74–85, 97–100
transactional macro-organizers 98–9
turn shifting 61
   Chinese 191
   Russian 200
   Spanish 195

universal functions 124–7

vocabulary classes 151–2

Widdowson, H. G. xiv, 3–4, 7–8,
   13–14, 121, 130n3
windows (spans) 20–2, 29n4
Wong-Fillmore, L. 25, 176
Wood, M. 177
word frequency 19
word probabilities 21–2
writers, active participants 159–60
written discourse 157–73
written discourse devices vs. spoken
   discourse devices 78–80